# Mozart's *Così fan tutte*

## A Compositional History

This study proposes a hypothesis to account for some of *Così fan tutte*'s long-standing 'problems'. It suggests that Mozart considered the idea that the pairings in Act II should not be crossed: that each of the two disguised officers should seek to seduce his own woman. Although this alternative plot structure was rejected, signs of it may remain in the final score, in the uneasy coexistence of dramatic duplicity and musical sincerity, and in the ending, in which the easy restitution of the original couples seems not to take account of the new passions that have been aroused. Evidence that several of the singers were re-cast is also presented.

In addition to these radically new ideas about the conceptual genesis of *Così*, the book also provides a full account of the work's compositional history, based on early Viennese and Bohemian copies. Four different versions are identified, including a significant revision in which Mozart removed the Act II finale canon. The composer's probable involvement in the 1791 Prague production is also discussed.

IAN WOODFIELD is Professor of Historical Musicology, School of Music and Sonic Arts, Queen's University Belfast.

# Mozart's *Così fan tutte*

## A Compositional History

Ian Woodfield

THE BOYDELL PRESS

First published 2008
The Boydell Press, Woodbridge

ISBN 978-1-84383-406-9

The Boydell Press is an imprint of Boydell & Brewer Ltd
PO Box 9, Woodbridge, Suffolk IP12 3DF, UK
and of Boydell & Brewer Inc.
668 Mt Hope Avenue, Rochester, NY 14620, USA
website: www.boydellandbrewer.com

A CIP record for this book is available
from the British Library

This publication is printed on acid-free paper

Typeset in Garamond Premier Pro by
David Roberts, Pershore, Worcestershire

Printed in Great Britain by
CPI Antony Rowe, Chippenham, Wiltshire

# Contents

# List of Illustrations

## Figures

## Musical Examples

# List of Tables

*For Thérèse*

# Preface

THIS STUDY OF *Così fan tutte* is based on a detailed examination of the original manuscripts in Kraków, Berlin, Frankfurt and Vienna. The long discredited idea that Mozart composed in his head before committing the ensuing masterpieces to paper in flawlessly written full scores has received new currency, at least in the popular imagination, thanks to the memorable portrayal of Salieri in a scene in *Amadeus* where he is given sight of a pile of his rival's unblemished autographs. The manuscript of *Così fan tutte* is elegantly written, especially in the early stages of Act I, and superficially it does seem relatively free from correction, but upon closer inspection abundant signs of the composer at work soon catch the eye. As Tyson demonstrated in his seminal study of this opera, palaeographic features such as ink colours, copying sequences, the foliation system, numbering sequences and continuity directions, all have much to contribute to an understanding of the compositional process.[1] In Part I of this study, these features will be examined in detail for the purpose of illuminating Mozart's working methods, and also, insofar as this is possible, in order to establish a chronology of how *Così fan tutte* was put together.

The composition of any opera in the late eighteenth century was the product of an active collaboration between the composer and his performers.[2] It has long been accepted that when writing an aria, Mozart would first consult its singer, listening carefully to any views expressed, but the nature of these essentially creative interventions from performers, especially during the critical phase when ideas and drafts were being brought to fruition, is difficult now to ascertain. In the autograph of *Così fan tutte*, however, there are fascinating hints of the collaborative nature of the dealings between composer and performer. This relationship will be considered through a detailed analysis of the process of revision in three arias. Other aspects of the compositional process also left clear traces in the autograph. Mozart's concern for the effective musical representation of drama on stage, his care in the choice of wind instrumentation, and his ceaseless quest to improve matters of fine detail are evident throughout.

The use of an autograph to shed light on its author's working practices is hardly controversial, but palaeographic evidence can also be deployed in support of theories of a more speculative character. Indeed, given the virtual silence of the documentary record concerning the birth of this opera, the original manuscripts may in fact provide our only chance of unearthing clues about the aesthetic decisions that resulted in the work as we have it today. Of course it is one thing to identify a series of revisions but quite another to infer a composer's motives for having made them, and to do so requires an imaginative engagement with the 'neutral' palaeographic facts. The dangers inherent in any attempt to fathom a creative artist's intentions are only too obvious, yet the potential benefits of so doing should not be underestimated.

In Part II two new theories are presented. First, consideration is given to the idea that difficulties in casting some of the roles influenced the development of this opera. It will be suggested that Francesco Benucci and Louise Villeneuve were originally cast as the philosopher and the maid, and that the Bussani couple were their replacements in these roles. This speculative mode of inquiry continues with a new conjecture to explain the enigma of the plot. There are certainly grounds for suspecting that the composer himself was worried by aspects of the basic drama, as demonstrated by the late and major changes made to its structure. My idea is that Mozart was unable to resolve to his satisfaction flaws in the plot in which each officer tests his friend's lover in disguise, and that together with Da Ponte (or possibly in opposition to him) he considered instead a structure with *unswitched* lovers, abandoning this when it proved unworkable. This radical theory was first made public at my Inaugural Lecture at Queen's University Belfast under the title 'Lovers Crossed or Uncrossed?' Readers will have to judge for themselves whether or not it provides a convincing explanation for the numerous puzzles that still surround the plot of this opera.

The idea that an eighteenth-century opera had a truly definitive form has long been discredited. A work given in one city would rarely be acceptable exactly as it stood in another, and even in the same theatre, a new production would usually be accompanied by significant revisions, if only to take account of the requirements of a new cast. This concept of the operatic work as an entity that never existed in a permanently fixed state, does not sit easily with the traditional view of the great master composer in sole control of his 'text'. Underlying this nineteenth-century attitude were two pervasive but often unspoken assumptions about the process of composition. The first of these was always a mirage: the idea that Mozart, having dotted the final 'i' and crossed the final 't' in his manuscript, laid aside his quill and delivered the completed masterwork to the theatre that had commissioned it. That simply bears no relationship at all to the realities of opera production in the late eighteenth century, when numerous individuals both before and long after the composer's direct involvement had the right to put their imprint on the work as performed in the theatre. The second of these conceptual moments has proved more influential. This is the idea that the night of the première was the critical juncture between the process of composition and the subsequent reception of the work. Yet the idea that the version of *Così fan tutte* performed on 26 January 1790 must, merely by virtue of having been the first official performance, constitute the text of the opera in its most authentic form, is also suspect. The performers on this undeniably historic occasion were no less subject to the vagaries of ill-health, fatigue and error than at any other time. Nor can we take refuge in the idea that what the composer would have wanted to hear on this particular night represents the 'true' text of the opera, even if that could be recovered, because there was the general expectation that the work would continue to evolve in the light of audience reactions. Indeed some operatic cultures placed great emphasis on the public dress rehearsal, precisely in order that the views of the patrons on the voices of the stars could be heard. And only in live theatrical performance was it possible to gauge accurately the effectiveness of comedy. There is thus no good reason to downplay any changes a composer might have made after the première, whether on his own behalf or at the behest of the other important players in this most intensively collaborative of art forms; these were all an accepted part of the ongoing life of any stage work.

There is, of course, a certain irony in the fact that our best hope of elucidating the various stages an opera went through, from its conceptual genesis to the death of its creator and beyond, lies in accurate source study, since this kind of detailed engagement with the original manuscripts traditionally took place in the context of the authoritative complete edition, itself just one manifestation of the powerful but dangerous concept of the master composer and his authentic text. Those engaged in the production of a score for a complete edition were usually well aware of the complexities of the situation, but, by its very nature, the enterprise on which they were engaged, obliged them to select and thus privilege certain moments. The impracticality of representing a constantly changing work of art in an unchanging edition is obvious, yet Mozart scholars, if anything, have had it rather easy. We have a Munich *Idomeneo* and one from Vienna, a Prague *Don Giovanni* and one from Vienna, a *Figaro* from 1786 and one from 1789; in each case, there is a pair of authentic versions both of which stem from the composer himself. Much more daunting challenges face the editors of some nineteenth-century operatic canons, who have to grapple with multiple versions. Away from the discipline of making choices about matters that are anything but clear cut – the lot of an editor – the processes through which Mozart went as he created, refined and then changed his operas, may of course be studied in their own right. Projects of this kind are becoming steadily easier to undertake, now that information about secondary sources has improved through *RISM* A II. My intention in Part III of this study is to present a detailed account of what can be learnt of the early history of *Così fan tutte* from these sources, distinguishing, where possible, revisions made during the initial period of composition and rehearsal, from those adopted after the première, and identifying any subsequent 'versions' with which the composer was associated.

A wealth of material is available, but two crucial sources have yet to be located. The autograph, now split between Kraków (Act I), Berlin (Act II) and Frankfurt (one bifolium of Act II), itself contains a few clues relating to the processes of revision, but a much more significant source in this respect is the Vienna Court Theatre copy **V1**, in which cuts were entered both before and immediately after the première and for a long time afterwards as well. An accurate chronological analysis of this manuscript is vital, but that depends on information contained in the copies made from it. In this respect we are fortunate that over twenty early scores of *Così* have survived, and there are also at least seven collections of parts – 'sets' seems too strong a term. These copies demonstrate that there were two main lines of transmission, which I have designated A and B. What is missing is a second score **V2** known to have been made in Vienna; from this originated a separate transmission line. Also yet to come to light are the all-important parts that were used at the première in 1790. The loss of this latter resource means that the precise dating of several aspects of the early chronology of this opera is likely to remain unclear. It is worth reiterating though, that the question of exactly when revisions were made in relation to the first perform-ance is only significant to the extent that this is regarded as a key conceptual moment. If instead we accept the idea of an ongoing process, then any changes Mozart (and indeed others) made after hearing the opera in the theatre and observing audience reactions to it are just as interesting.

Any scholar who engages with the sources and the early reception history of one of Mozart's major operatic works will rapidly amass an incredible mound of detailed facts, most of which are of at least some use in the task of constructing a compositional history. In this study I have tried to take a pragmatic attitude: giving full accounts of significant matters; summarizing or exemplifying the less critical details. A concentrated engagement with the text (or rather texts) of the opera, however, is unavoidable, and a few minutes spent looking at the defini-tions of terminology given in the glossary should assist the reader.

It may be helpful to present in summary form the main findings to have emerged from this detailed examination of the sources.

1  During the later stages of his work on the opera Mozart made a series of what I term 'agreed' cuts, first in some of the arias and ensembles and then in some of the recitatives. There is every indication that these formed part of what, even in the traditional sense, we would have understood as the compositional process, and it is very likely that they would have

been entered in the parts before the première. What Mozart's intentions were for the first performance and whether he was satisfied with what he heard are beyond the reach of historical investigation, but if we wish to perform the opera now as it was actually given on 26 January 1790, these cuts should be made. They were widely accepted and appear routinely in both lines of transmission. The opera would rarely, if ever, have been heard without them in the eighteenth century. Fortunately for anyone minded to reconstruct this 'version' in a modern performance, nothing of great consequence would be lost. The singer of the demanding role of Ferrando would obtain some relief, and some of the saucier elements of Despina's repartee in the recitatives would disappear.

2  At some point, Mozart made a more significant series of revisions with several further (and larger) cuts and one substitution: a replacement passage for the Act II finale canon. All of these changes he apparently entered in the lost Vienna score **V2**. In attempting to date them, several possibilities must be considered. Were they too made before the première as part of the ongoing process of revision? Were they made after the première in response to the way in which the work had been received? Or were they made for Domenico Guardasoni's Prague production of 1791? On balance it seems likely that they were made in Vienna, because although the Prague version was based on the revised score, it restores two of the cut passages. An important question arising from this will need to be considered: why was this revised version not then disseminated in the main line of the Vienna transmission? Was this simply an accident of fate, or was a deliberate decision taken to revert to the work in its earlier state, and if so by whom and why?

3  In the summer of 1791, the impresario Domenico Guardasoni decided to stage *Così fan tutte* in Prague. There are strong indications that Mozart was consulted, even if only briefly. The Prague libretto embodied a careful reading of Da Ponte's final text, in which most of its remaining errors were identified and corrected.

The composer's personal involvement with his last *opera buffa* may have come to an end in the summer of 1791, but his influence over the way it was received did not necessarily stop there. An intriguing aspect of reception history is its potential to provide retrospective evidence. A striking case in *Così fan tutte* is that of what I term the 'Two Sisters Problem'. Mozart's decision to change the characters of Fiordiligi and Dorabella part of the way through the composition of the opera was not fully worked out in the first part of Act I. Many early translators and editors were well aware of this difficulty, and their attempts to provide a remedy provide telling evidence, both of the perceived significance of the original problem, and of the extent to which people knew about it.

# *Acknowledgements*

T HE WORK on which this study is based was started during a period of study leave granted by Queen's University Belfast. Since then I have been fortunate to receive grants, from the Arts and Humanities Research Board and from the British Academy. I am very grateful to John Irving, Cliff Eisen and Neal Zaslaw for their support in obtaining these. It is a pleasure also to acknowledge the assistance of my colleague Jan Smaczny with Czech sources and literature, that of Kathryn Libin, who sent me details of scores and parts in the Lobkowicz Library at Nelahozeves Castle, and Claudia Zenck, who supplied me with a copy of her article on *Così*. Sona Cernocká facilitated my visit to Nelahozeves Castle to study the Lobkowicz sources and was very generous in offering assistance. A particular debt is owed to Agneza Mitelska-Cipierska at the Biblioteka Jagiellońska in Kraków and to Helmut Hell at Musikabteilung of the Staatsbibliothek zu Berlin, Preussischer Kulturbesitz for allowing me extended periods of access to their precious autographs, and to the staff at the Musiksammlung of the Österreichische Nationalbibliothek for their help during numerous visits to examine the Vienna materials. I was made very welcome during visits to the Bibliothek der Internationale Stiftung Mozarteum (Salzburg), the Moravské Zemské Museum (Brno), the Conservatory of Music and the National Library's Music Department (Prague), the Stadt- und Universitätsbibliothek (Frankfurt), the Stadtgeschichtliches Museum (Leipzig) and the Badische Landesbibliothek (Karlsruhe). Other institutions that have provided me with information or microfilms include: the Sächsische Landesbibliothek (Dresden), the Gesellschaft der Musikfreunde (Vienna), the Stadt- und Landesbibliothek (Vienna), the Universitätsbibliothek (Vienna), the Fürstlich Fürstenbergischen Hofbibliothek (Donaueschingen), the Bayerische Staatsbibliothek (Munich), the Herzogin Anna Amalia Bibliothek (Weimar), the Staats- und Universitätsbibliothek Carl von Ossietsky (Hamburg), and Det Kongelige Bibliotek (Copenhagen). I am very grateful indeed to David Buch and Dexter Edge who gave generously of their palaeographical expertise, and I am also indebted to Anne Oerbaek Jenson for supplying me with details of watermarks in an important manuscript in Copenhagen.

For permission to reproduce Figs. 3, 4, 5, 6, 7, 10, 11 and 12 from Mus. ms autogr. W. A. Mozart 588, vol.2, I am grateful to the Staatsbibliothek zu Berlin,

Preußischer Kulturbesitz, Musikabteilung mit Mendelssohn-Archiv. For permission to reproduce Figs. 1, 2, 8 and 9, I am grateful to the Biblioteka Jagiellońska, Kraków.

I should like to acknowledge with admiration and gratitude the three major pillars of scholarship that at various stages informed the writing of this book. Alan Tyson's classic article 'On the Composition of Mozart's *Così fan tutte*', republished in *Mozart: Studies of the Autograph Scores* (Harvard University Press, 1987) presented landmark discoveries concerning the watermarks and staff-ruling techniques seen in Mozart's autographs. Dexter Edge's erudite and monumental thesis 'Mozart's Viennese Copyists' appeared in 2001, but I delayed ordering it for a year, largely to give myself time to complete an independent analysis of the Vienna Court Theatre score. In 2003 the long-awaited critical commentary of the *Neue Mozart Ausgabe* appeared, edited by Henning Bey and Faye Ferguson. I hope I have done full justice to these three works of scholarship throughout this study, by identifying the main contributions of each, commenting on areas of agreement or disagreement, and noting differences of interpretation in significant details, but I have not been pedantic in recording all the minor discrepancies.

Finally, it is gratifying to be able to report a happy coincidence: as this study goes to press, a full-colour facsimile of *Così fan tutte* has just been published, part of a series that will make high-quality reproductions of Mozart's seven major operas widely available for the first time. Having a copy of this to hand during the reading of this monograph will enable the reader to place many of my paleographical interpretations under direct scrutiny.

# Glossary

| | |
|---|---|
| bifolium | a folded sheet containing two leaves (four sides) |
| bifoliation numbers | numbers applied to each bifolium, that is one number every fourth side |
| nested bifolia | a series of sheets folded inside each other, so that, for example, the following leaves are joined: 1-8, 2-7, 3-6, 4-5 |
| gathering | a consignment of paper, usually in the form of a number of nested bifolia, the basic copying unit of an opera |
| gathering numbers | numbers applied by copyists to successive gatherings: 1/1, 2/1, 3/1 ... for Act I and 1/2, 2/2, 3/2 ... for Act II |
| 'extra Blatt' | a term used by Mozart to indicate the existence of an additional leaf, usually containing the wind scores of finales or large ensembles |
| 'agreed' cut | a term used in this study to denote one of a series of cuts almost certainly approved by the composer although not entered in the autograph |
| particella | a continuity draft (often excluding the ending) containing, in the case of opera, the vocal line(s) and the bass, but only fragments of the upper strings or wind parts |
| red crayon | used by copyists and occasionally Mozart himself to correct, annotate or otherwise edit a score copied in ink |
| page- and line-break analysis | a method of recording the physical layout of a score by means of noting the number of bars copied per staff |
| reference score | one of (at least) two full scores produced for the Vienna Court Theatre from the composer's autograph and retained after the first performance run as an exemplar for commercial copies |
| conducting score | a second full score produced for the Vienna Court Theatre from the composer's autograph or from the reference score, for use in rehearsing and conducting the opera |
| **V1** | the version of *Così fan tutte* found in the reference score |
| **V2** | the version of *Così fan tutte* found in the (mostly lost) conducting score |
| O.A.146 | the extant Vienna Court Theatre score consisting of version **V1** up to the canon in the Act II finale, and **V2** thereafter |

# Abbreviations

## Editions

| | |
|---|---|
| *Briefe* | *Mozart: Briefe und Aufzeichnungen: Gesamtausgabe*, ed. Wilhelm Bauer, Otto Deutsch and Joseph Eibl (Kassel, 1962–75) |
| *Letters* | *The Letters of Mozart & his Family*, ed. Emily Anderson, 3rd edn (London, 1985) |
| *NMA* | *Neue Mozart Ausgabe* |
| *NMA: Così* | *Neue Mozart Ausgabe*, Serie II, Werkgruppe 5, Band 18: *Così fan tutte*, ed. Faye Ferguson and Wolfgang Rehm (Kassel, 1991) |
| *NMA: Dokumente* | *Neue Mozart Ausgabe*, Serie X, Supplement: *Mozart: Die Dokumente seines Lebens*, Otto Deutsch (Kassel, 1961) |
| *NMA: KB* | *Neue Mozart Ausgabe*, Serie II, *Kritische Berichte*, Werkgruppe 5, Band 18: *Così fan tutte*, Henning Bey and Faye Ferguson (Kassel, 2003) |
| *NMA: Skizzen* | *Neue Mozart Ausgabe*, Serie X, Supplement, Werkgruppe 30, Band 3: *Skizzen*, Ulrich Konrad (Kassel, 1998) |
| *NMA: Verzeichnüss* | *Neue Mozart Ausgabe*, Serie X, 33, Band 1: *Mozart's Eigenhändiges Verzeichnüss*, ed. Alan Tyson and Albi Rosenthal (Kassel, 1991) |
| *NMA: Wasserzeichen* | *Neue Mozart Ausgabe*, Serie X, 33, Band 2: *Wasserzeichen-Katalog*, Alan Tyson (Kassel, 1992) |

## Journals

| | |
|---|---|
| *AmZ* | *Allgemeine musikalische Zeitung* |
| *COJ* | *Cambridge Opera Journal* |
| *MJ* | *Mozart Jahrbuch* |
| *M&L* | *Music & Letters* |
| *MQ* | *Musical Quarterly* |
| *ZfM* | *Zeitschrift für Musikwissenschaft* |

## Early Manuscript Scores of Così fan tutte

| | | |
|---|---|---|
| B | Brno, Moravské Zemské Museum | A17.031 |
| Be1 | Berlin, Staatsbibliothek zu Berlin, Preussicher Kulturbesitz | Mus ms 15 153 |
| Be2 | Berlin, Staatsbibliothek zu Berlin, Preussicher Kulturbesitz | Mus ms 15 153/1 |
| C1 | Copenhagen, Det Kongelige Bibliotek | KBS/MA Weyses Samling, Acc. Nr. Mu 7502.0336 |
| C2 | Copenhagen, Det Kongelige Bibliotek | KBS/MA C I, 280, Acc. Nr. Mu 7502.0337 |
| Ca | Cambridge, Mass., Harvard University, Eda Kuhn Loeb Music Library | Merritt Room Mus 745.1.661.9 |
| D1 | Dresden, Sächsische Landesbibliothek | Mus 3972-F-518 |
| D2 | Dresden, Sächsische Landesbibliothek | Mus 3972-F-99 |
| F1 | Frankfurt, Stadt- und Universitätsbibliothek | Mus ms 380 (1) |
| F2 | Frankfurt, Stadt- und Universitätsbibliothek | Mus ms 380 (2) |
| Fl | Florence, Biblioteca del Conservatorio di Musica 'Luigi Cherubini' | F.P.T.260 |
| H | Hamburg, Staats- und Universitätsbibliothek Carl von Ossietzky | ND VII 250 |
| K | Karlsruhe, Badische Landesbibliothek | Mus.Ms.1389a–d |
| L | London, British Library | R.M.22.h.10-11 |
| Lo | Lobkowicz Roudnice Library, Nelahozeves Castle | X.De.10 k.588 |
| S | Salzburg, Internationale Stiftung Mozarteum | Rara 588/14 (M.N.9b I & II) |
| T | London, British Library | Tyson 16-17 |
| V1 | Vienna, Österreichische Nationalbibliothek | O.A.146 |
| V3 | Vienna, Österreichische Nationalbibliothek | O.A.328 |
| V4 | Vienna, Österreichische Nationalbibliothek | Mus. Hs. 39.321 |

# Plot Summary

## Act I

TWO OFFICERS, Ferrando and Guglielmo, engage in coffee-house banter with an older philosopher, Don Alfonso, on the question of fidelity. He claims that all women, even their lovers Dorabella and Fiordiligi, are fickle, and in order to prove his point, he makes a wager: provided the two men place themselves at his disposal, he will demonstrate that their lovers are no different from others of their sex. The two sisters, meanwhile, are seated in a garden, each gazing fondly upon a miniature portrait of her man, when Don Alfonso bursts in with terrible news: Ferrando and Guglielmo have been summoned to fight in a war. The two officers, acting convincingly (as agreed) in the deception, take their leave and embark to the sound of military music. For the moment all is tranquil.

The maid Despina is preparing a drink for the sisters when they burst in, unexpectedly distraught after the calm farewell. Dorabella seems beside herself. The maid responds by advocating her own light-hearted view of love: if these two officers have gone, there will soon be others. Don Alfonso recruits Despina to assist in his deception without, however, revealing that the new suitors will be none other than Ferrando and Guglielmo, disguised as Albanian noblemen. The 'Albanians' enter but their attempts to address the two sisters are rebuffed. Fiordiligi maintains a pose of rock-like constancy. Guglielmo again attempts to win them over, but they walk out, leaving both officers jubilant. Don Alfonso, however, insists on further tests, while Ferrando dreams of his true love. In a set-piece comic finale, the 'Albanians' pretend to drink poison so that they can be cured by the magnetic device of a quack doctor, in fact Despina in disguise. Coming to their senses, they continue to express their love for the two sisters, whose sympathy at least has by now been awakened.

## Act II

D ESPINA tries to win over the two sisters to her flirtatious view of love. Dorabella and Fiordiligi see no harm in considering which of the two suitors they prefer. Ferrando and Guglielmo return to the strains of a serenade, and Don Alfonso and Despina deftly arrange the quartet into couples. Each officer has now to seduce his friend's lover. Once alone, Guglielmo soon wins Dorabella's heart, but Fiordiligi rejects Ferrando's advances, though in private she effectively concedes that her emotions are beginning to change. Comparing notes, Guglielmo has every reason to be smug, while Ferrando has to cope with the bombshell of Dorabella's easy capitulation. Guglielmo reflects on the general shortcomings of women, yet for all his fury, Ferrando still recognises the voices of love in his head.

The maid, now with the active support of Dorabella, renews the attempt to persuade Fiordiligi to give in to her desires, but she continues to resist, making plans to flee to her real lover on the battlefield. Ferrando accosts her and his passionate declarations eventually have their effect. Guglielmo who has watched all this, expresses his impotent fury. Don Alfonso, his point made and the money secure, asks if the men still want to marry their original lovers.

Despina arranges a double wedding, still not knowing that she is dealing with Ferrando and Guglielmo in disguise. The newly formed couples toast each other, and marriage contracts are drawn up under the supervision of a notary, once again Despina in disguise. The military music that had signalled the original departure of the officers now heralds their return, and the entire deception quickly unravels. Despina is unmasked. The two officers put back on part of the recently discarded attire of their assumed identities, and with ironic gestures make it clear to the sisters and the maid that they have been deceived. Mutual forgiveness ensues, and it is to be supposed that the 'bella calma' with which the opera ends includes the restitution of the original couples, though this is not made clear.

# Introduction

Mozart's last Da Ponte opera was given its première on 26 January 1790. Written during the final months of the reign of Joseph II, *Così fan tutte* has come to symbolise the end of the brilliant era of the Enlightenment in Vienna. Rosselli described it as 'the fine flower of the old regime at its point of dissolution'.[1] Considering the opera's significance, the documentary legacy of its commission, composition, rehearsal and first performance is a meagre one. Legends that grew up subsequently, such as the idea that Joseph II himself suggested the libretto to Mozart, or that the story was based on an incident that actually occurred in Vienna, are now largely discredited.[2] In the absence of firm evidence to the contrary, it is usually assumed that the award of a commission for a new opera was a direct result of the successful revival of *Figaro* in the summer of 1789.

An improved understanding of the context in which Mozart came to work on *Così fan tutte* has been made possible by Rice's discovery of a short-lived attempt by Salieri to set this libretto.[3] The little that he managed to complete is in an autograph manuscript in the Österreichische Nationalbibliothek in Vienna (S.m.4531). It consists of the two opening trios 'La mia Dorabella' and 'È la fede delle fem[m]ine', separated by the first recitative on a text substantially different from the one set by Mozart. Literary and allusive in character, the libretto was well suited to Salieri's tastes, and it might well have been written for him specifically as a follow-up to his earlier success *La scuola de' gelosi*. It is not at all clear why he abandoned work on it so soon.

One reference to Salieri's interest in this libretto has long been known. In interviews given to the Novellos in 1829, Constanze confirmed that her husband's rival had attempted to set *Così*. She stated: 'Salieri's enmity arose from Mozart's setting the *Così fan tutte* which he had originally commenced and given up as unworthy [of] musical invention.' She amplified this statement as follows: 'Salieri first tried to set this opera but failed, and the great success of Mozart in accomplishing what he [Salieri] could make nothing of is supposed to have been the first origin of his enmity and malice towards Mozart.'[4] It is not known when Salieri began work on *La scuola degli amanti*, but it could have been as early as the end of 1788, presumably after 13 October, when Adriana Ferrarese del Bene (for whom Da Ponte later claimed to have written the libretto) made her début in Vienna.

Whatever his reasons for putting the libretto to one side, Salieri's decision coincided with a marked deterioration in his relationship with Da Ponte.

According to the (far from reliable) memoirs of the librettist, a dispute arose over the casting of *L'ape musicale*. Da Ponte, working on this project without the assistance of a composer, was very undiplomatic in his choice of singers, a matter of some significance since the performances were for the benefit of its cast. There was a place for his own mistress Ferrarese, but Salieri's *amour* Cavalieri was left out.[5] The composer was apparently angered by this, and his attitude towards Da Ponte cooled, although the two men continued to work together professionally.

This dispute did not fully surface until Da Ponte's dismissal in 1791, when he evidently felt able to give expression to his resentment. In a series of memoranda aimed at discrediting his enemies and perhaps retaining his position, he began by naming Salieri as his 'principal enemy'.[6] A series of wild accusations follow: that Salieri habitually ruined the operas of other masters; that he allocated operas, performances and roles to suit his own ends; and that he allowed Cavalieri to take leading roles ('per far cantare La Cavalieri la prima donna'), even though Da Ponte himself wished to have her pensioned off. The veracity of all these charges is open to doubt, but it is an intriguing thought that Salieri might have attempted to intervene in the casting of *Così fan tutte*, the opera that he had been unable or unwilling to complete himself.

Opposition to Da Ponte and his recent role in the company found expression in the satire *Anti-da Ponte*, published around the time of his dismissal in 1791, in which both Salieri and Mozart are called to the witness stand to register a complaint about the 'tasteless, clumsy and incoherent texts' that Da Ponte had provided for them.[7] Both composers had resolved 'not to set another note of a text by Da Ponte'.[8] In the fanciful context of this satirical skit, Mozart is shown standing side by side with Salieri in his condemnation of Da Ponte and all his works, but it is possible that back in late 1789, as a direct result of his new operatic collaboration, Mozart could have been seen as taking the librettist's side.

Until evidence of Salieri's attempt to set the libretto was discovered, there was no reason to doubt that *Così fan tutte* had been commissioned by the Vienna Court Theatre in the autumn of 1789. But since the libretto was available to other composers earlier than this, it is reasonable to consider an alternative possibility: that Mozart was initially attracted to it in the context of an attempt to win a contract to compose an Italian opera for a foreign theatre. There is only one hint in his correspondence during the first half of 1789 as to where his future operatic plans might lie. It comes in a letter to Constanze, reporting on the progress of his journey to Berlin. Within hours of his arrival in Prague on 10 April, he wrote to inform her that he had had been to see the manager of the National Theatre, Guardasoni, who had virtually reached agreement to give him '200 # [ducats] next autumn for the opera and 50 # [ducats] for travelling expenses'.[9] It seems that Mozart was actively exploring the possibility of a successor to *Don Giovanni* in Prague.[10] Solomon has argued that this reference to the fee was part of an elaborate deception on Mozart's part to conceal from Constanze the real purpose of his visit to Berlin, but if the more straightforward interpretation of the letter is correct, then Mozart had at least got as far as discussing potential payment for an opera with the Prague impresario.[11] His reference to 'the' opera – as though Constanze would know which one he meant – is consistent with his having already considered and accepted Da Ponte's latest drama.

The only other hint that Guardasoni had been interested in a successor to *Don Giovanni* comes in the much later memoirs of Da Ponte himself, which say little on the subject of *Così fan tutte* itself. In the English language version, published in New York in 1819, he wrote as follows:

> 'Our opera of Don Giovanni,' said he [Mozart] in a letter written to me from Prague, 'was represented last night to a most brilliant audience ... The success of our piece was as complete as we could desire. Guardassoni came this morning almost enraptured with joy, into my room. 'Long live Mozart, long live Da Ponte,' said he: 'as long as they shall exist, no manager shall know distress. Adieu! my dear friend. Prepare another opera for your friend Mozart.' I was so happy of the opportunity, that although I had on hand at that time two other dramas, nevertheless I did not neglect my favourite Mozart, and in less than three months I gave a tragicomic drama, entitled Assur, king of Ormus, to Salieri, ... an heroi-comic to Martini, called L'Arbore di Diana, and a comic opera to Mozart, with the title of La scola degli Amanti, which was represented in Vienna, in Prague, in Dresden, and for several years in Paris, with unbounded applause.[12]

The sequence of events as recalled here is impossible, because the première of *L'arbore di Diana* preceded that of *Don Giovanni*. On chronological grounds alone, there are excellent reasons for suspecting the reliability of this statement and indeed the authenticity of the letter itself. Da Ponte's claim to have received a request from Mozart for another libretto is either a complete fabrication, or else, since this part of the story is not inherently implausible, his memory of the chronology had become seriously muddled.

By the time that Da Ponte published the full Italian text of his *Memorie* in 1823, his account had changed somewhat. It is noticeable that the three librettos that he was claiming to have worked on simultaneously were now *Axur*, *L'arbore di Diana* and *Don Giovanni*.[13] The report of Mozart's letter from Prague now appears in a slightly more plausible chronology:

> I had not seen the *première* of *Don Giovanni* at Prague, but Mozart
> wrote me at once of its marvelous reception, and Guardassoni, for his
> part, these words: 'Long live Da Ponte! Long live Mozart! All impre-
> sarios, all *virtuosi* should bless their names. So long as they live we shall
> never know what theatrical poverty means!' [14]

Da Ponte continues by describing the preparations for the Vienna version of
*Don Giovanni* and its poor reception. As for *Così*, he now alludes to its composition in the context of his affair with Ferrarese:

> To my misfortune, there arrived [in Vienna] a singer, who without having
> any great claims to beauty, delighted me first of all by her voice; later, as
> she showed great propensity towards me, I ended by falling in love with
> her ... For her I wrote *Il pastor fido* and *La cifra* with music by Salieri, two
> operas that marked no epoch in the annals of his musical glory, though
> they were in many parts very beautiful; and *La scola degli amanti*, with
> music by Mozart, a drama which holds third place among the sisters born
> of that most celebrated father of harmony. [15]

Salieri's brief attempt to set the libretto had been forgotten.

Da Ponte's virtual silence about his role in *Così fan tutte* is puzzling. Although
his remarks on *Figaro* and *Don Giovanni* are disappointing, they at least have
some substance. The most likely explanation for his reticence about the third
opera is that by the time he was writing his memoirs in New York, attitudes to
the plot had become so unfavourable that there was little credit to be gained
from the claim of authorship. Also worthy of note is his insistence on referring
to the opera as *La scola degli amanti*. There is at least a hint here that he had
been at odds with his composer over the issue, but it would also be true to say
that the indelicate connotations of 'fan' in the title could by then have provided
sufficient grounds for a reluctance to use it.

In the light of his earlier triumph in Prague, Mozart would have had good
reason to welcome a chance to stage another opera there, but there were other
possibilities. In early 1787 he had actively considered a plan to travel to England,
although he had been persuaded by his father not to risk the journey. One factor
in his decision to remain was that Stephen Storace had already been engaged to
compose Italian opera during the forthcoming season at the King's Theatre. [16]
There is, of course, no direct evidence that a journey to England was once again
in Mozart's mind in the spring of 1789, yet the idea that he now saw his best hope
for a new opera commission outside his home city is by no means an implausible one. The prevailing circumstances in Vienna, which included the relatively
cool reaction to *Don Giovanni*, Joseph II's decision to end his support for the

Italian opera company, uncertainty as to whether the rescue package promoted by Da Ponte would work, the imminent departure of Benucci for London, and a general decline in new opera commissions at the Court Theatre, can hardly have encouraged Mozart in the belief that a new opportunity in Vienna was imminent.

If Mozart was entertaining hopes of a new opera commission elsewhere, he would have known that agreement on a contract could not have been delayed much beyond early autumn. In July he reached one of the lowest points of his entire career, and it is possible that his mood of despair was aggravated by the rejection of one or more of his operatic plans. The famous letter of 12–14 July speaks eloquently of his distress, but the underlying reasons for his anguish are not at all clear.[17] The list of misfortunes seems endless: his wife is ill; he too has been unwell and has been unable to work; instead of repaying past debts, he now has to seek further loans; and his attempt to raise money from a small-scale subscription series in his own home has flopped, the list returning with but one name on it. Referring to this particularly humiliating failure, Mozart concedes that the fates are against him, '*but only in Vienna*', a possible hint that he was looking elsewhere. Now that his wife is improving, he ought to be able to start work again, but he has apparently been unable to do so because of what he describes as 'this blow, this heavy blow'. The letter continues by contrasting the difficulty of his present circumstances with the brightness of his immediate prospects, a favourite ploy. He promises to work on quartets and easy piano sonatas, for which he claims to have agreement for royal dedications, but he then continues: 'In a month or two my fate must be decided *in every detail*.'[18] He seems to be alluding to something of potential importance to his career. He asks for a loan of 500 gulden, of which he promises to repay 10 gulden a month until his affairs are settled, 'which is bound to happen in a few months', when he will repay the whole sum with whatever interest Puchberg sees fit to charge. Although it does seem likely that these guarded remarks relate in some way to the future direction of Mozart's composing activities, there is no firm indication that a new opera was his preferred option. Yet if there had ever been a proposal to stage a successor to *Don Giovanni* at Prague, the idea came to nothing, while any thoughts of an English operatic appointment would have been terminated abruptly by reports of the complete destruction of the King's Theatre on 17 June, which probably started to circulate in Vienna during the first week of July.

If Mozart did make a start on a new operatic project in the spring of 1789, then *Così fan tutte* could have had a two-stage genesis: an early and very limited phase of work followed, after a gap of some months, by an intense period of completion, once a firm commission had been received from the Vienna Court

Theatre. Earlier in his career, Mozart had shown that he was quite prepared to make a speculative start on an opera. Before receiving a contract for *Figaro*, he worked for a while on two operas, *L'oca del Cairo* and *Lo sposo deluso*, in the case of the latter going so far as to cast roles for current members of the Italian troupe in Vienna, and even starting work on arias for Storace and Francesco Bussani.[19] Edge has demonstrated that work on *Figaro* itself also followed a two-stage pattern.[20] There were in fact significant benefits in a pre-contractual period of work on an opera: a project with some material already available for inspection might well be easier to sell to an opera house management; and the intense pressure to produce a work on time would be significantly alleviated if at least some of the ensembles were already in draft form.

There are a number of features in the autograph of *Così fan tutte* which do indeed point to a break in composition. These include: the use of two distinct paper types; a change in the spelling of the name 'Guglielmo'; the reversal of the parts of the two sisters in the first part of Act I; and uncertainty as to whether the line of Don Alfonso or Guglielmo should come lowest in the score. Yet any attempt to ascertain precisely how these two phases might have fitted into Mozart's overall plan of work in 1789 seems destined to fail. In the absence of specific clues in the letters, the only sources of evidence from this rather sparsely documented period of his life are entries in his own catalogue of works and the autograph scores. The evidence of the paper types he used during 1789 provides at best a broad framework for the discussion of these issues.

After so many months in the shadows, *Così fan tutte* finally emerges into the historical record in December 1789. Writing to Puchberg with a further request for a loan, Mozart offered as security his anticipated fee for the new opera: 'Next month I should receive two hundred ducats from the theatre management for my opera (according to the present agreement).'[21] By now he was working flat out and had to cancel a meeting with his creditor, whom he invited instead to a rehearsal: 'On Thursday I am inviting you (and you alone) to a small opera rehearsal at my house at 10 o'clock in the morning; – only you and *Haydn* are invited – I will tell you then about Salieri's intrigues, which, however, have already run into the sands'.[22] With this last comment, Mozart appears to confirm that his relationship Salieri was indeed an uneasy one in late 1789, yet it would be wrong to take this as clear evidence that the older composer was actively involved in 'cabals' against his younger rival. A period of heightened tension between the two men was perhaps only to be expected. The revised version of Salieri's opera *La cifra* had just been given its première, and with the first performance of *Così fan tutte* imminent, both composers would very naturally have had concerns about their respective reputations.

The veracity of Mozart's statement that a fee of 200 ducats for his new opera had been agreed has also recently come into question. The standard payment was 100 ducats (450 gulden), though twice or even three times this sum was sometimes awarded. In the relevant ledgers cited by Edge, only the basic fee is recorded in an entry for the week 20–6 February 1790: 'dem Mozart Wolfgang, für Componirung der Musi[que] zur Opera / Così fan Tutte: 450'.[23] In the absence of further information, it is impossible to know for certain whether Mozart was attempting to improve his chances of obtaining further credit from Puchberg by overstating his fee, or whether he had been promised the larger fee verbally, only to have it reduced following the death of Joseph II. Edge does not altogether rule out the possibility that the 100 ducats Salieri received in May 1790 for 'revising' various operas somehow found its way to him out of the larger fee that Mozart had been due to receive.

Of the rehearsal period for the opera almost nothing is known. Many years later, Mozart's pupil Joseph Eybler recalled that he had been asked to assist in rehearsing the singers Ferrarese and Villeneuve, so that his teacher could complete the instrumentation of the opera. This experience, he claimed, had acquainted him with the 'disorders, cabals and so forth' of theatrical life.[24] Once again there is a hint that *Così* had come to fruition against a background of intrigue, but there is nothing to suggest that this was felt to have been anything out of the ordinary. As for the two singers, Ferrarese was closely associated with Da Ponte, but Villeneuve belonged to the group angered by its exclusion from a benefit opera. In his memoranda, Da Ponte calls 'La Willeneuve' the third agent of his destruction: 'She forgot all my friendly favours and courtesies because I did not include her in *L'ape Musicale*.'[25] So there were at least some grounds for rivalry between the first Fiordiligi and Dorabella. It is interesting to note that a rehearsal score of their duet 'Ah guarda sorella' is extant, on which Mozart himself wrote: 'N.B. one part each must be written out separately.'[26] It seems that Ferrarese and Villeneuve wished to rehearse on their own.

Only days before the first performance, Mozart invited Puchberg to a full orchestral rehearsal scheduled for 21 January.[27] He requested a further loan of 100 gulden, probably a follow-up to his earlier plea for 400 gulden in response to which Puchberg had sent only 300.

Some time shortly after the première, as was his custom, Mozart entered his new opera in his catalogue of works. In fact there are two entries, one referring to an aria for Benucci, which he cut from the opera at a late stage:

im December

*seine arie* welche in die oper Così fan tutte bestimmt war für Benucci.
*Rivolgete à me lo sguardo* etc: –
2 violini, viola, 2 oboe, 2 fagotti, 2 clarini e Timpany e Baßi =

im Jenner 1790:

> *Così fan tutte; osia la scuola degli amanti. Opera Buffa in 2 Atti.*
> pezzi di Musica. – Attori. *Signore.* Ferraresi del Bene, Villeneuve et
> Bußani. *Signori* Calvesi, Benucci e Bußani.[28]

The first line of Benucci's rejected aria is given as 'Rivolgete à me lo sguardo', rather than 'Rivolgete à lui lo sguardo' as (eventually) in the autograph score. Mozart's final brief reference to *Così fan tutte* comes in another letter to Puchberg, written on or before 12 June 1790. He begins: 'I am here to conduct my opera.'[29]

The few comments following the première of *Così fan tutte* were bland but mainly positive. Count Zinzendorf found Mozart's music 'charmante' and the subject of the opera 'amusant'.[30] A report in the Weimar *Journal des Luxus und der Moden* (March 1790) felt it sufficient to say: 'That the music is by Mozart, I believe, says it all.'[31] As yet, there was no sign of the controversy that was to accompany the opera throughout its history.

# PART I

## Mozart's Compositional Methods:
## A Study of the Autograph Score

# The Autograph

AT THE END of World War II the autograph of *Così fan tutte* was split up. Act I disappeared for several decades and re-emerged only in the 1970s. It is now kept in the Biblioteka Jagiellońska in Kraków. Act II is in the Musikabteilung of the Staatsbibliothek zu Berlin, Preußischer Kulturbesitz. One bifolium containing 'Tutti accusan le donne' became separated from the main part of the autograph apparently at quite an early date, since it appears never to have been bound. It was discovered by Plath in the Frankfurt Stadt- und Universitätsbibliothek.[1] Its bifoliation number, 18 (the correct number in the original sequence), suggests that it was once with the main autograph. Missing from the autograph of Act II and not so far located is the chorus 'Secondate' and the *accompagnato* 'Ei parte'. Two linked recitatives ('Come tutto congiura' / 'L'abito di Ferrando') are now bound in with the autograph on two unnumbered bifolia, but they are in a copyist's hand. Mozart's originals apparently do not survive. Another significant element that exists only in a copyist's hand is the five-bar repeat of the 'magnetic' music for wind instruments in the Act I finale. This appears on a separate leaf, albeit in conjunction with a continuity indication from Mozart in the main score. Finally, the wind parts that Mozart copied on separate leaves in the larger ensembles are no longer extant in his hand.

There are two fragments of versions of 'Donne mie': the first resembles very closely the opening of the final version; the second is quite different, apparently combining some words from the text of 'Donne mie' with a musical figure used in Guglielmo's discarded Act I aria 'Rivolgete'.[2] A replacement for the canon quartet in the Act II finale in Mozart's hand is also extant.[3] There are only two sketches. Various drafts for the canon quartet itself appear on a leaf in the Internationale Stiftung Mozarteum in Salzburg.[4] A photograph of a further leaf containing some brief sketches for bars 545–74 of the Act II finale is in the Österreichische Nationalbibliothek in Vienna.[5] One further fragment of relevance is in Salzburg: the beginning of a clarinet quintet (in A) which uses the same melodic material as Ferrando's aria 'Ah lo veggio' (in B♭).[6]

## Paper Types

By the time that Mozart composed *Così fan tutte* in 1789, his scribal habits were
well established. The autograph of K588 thus appears as a normal score for its
period. It was copied in the usual oblong format on good-quality papers of Italian manufacture ruled with twelve-stave rastra. The individual unit of paper
consisted of a bifolium with two leaves conjoined horizontally. Earlier in his
life Mozart had worked with nested bifolia, but in the later 1780s he started
to adopt the practice of separating these pairs before use.[7] His own numbering
system was based on the unit of the bifolium, and so he put on one number
for every two leaves or four sides. The solid appearance of the autograph in its
nineteenth-century bindings is deceptive, as Mozart himself would have kept
his opera in piles of unbound sheets, presumably organised into folders for ease
of access. A coherent system of numbering and the provision of detailed continuity directions were therefore very important aids for the copyists. The single
bifolium in Frankfurt appears never to have been bound, and it thus gives a
good impression of how such a sheet would have looked on the composer's desk.
The harmonious balance of its layout as a piece of calligraphy catches the eye.

The study of paper types was Tyson's central contribution to Mozart scholarship. In addition to his superb catalogue of watermarks, he published his findings on *Così* in a substantial article.[8] The catalogue itself has recently been subjected to a valuable critique by Edge, who defines a paper type as 'a paper with
a particular watermark that has been ruled with a particular rastrum'.[9] Tyson
identified the watermarks and he also measured the total span of the various
rastra used, which he defined as the distance between the highest line of the top
staff and the lowest line of the bottom staff. Edge suggests a number of possible
refinements, taking into account the gradual deformation of watermarks over
time and the slight changes to rastra caused by repeated usage. Tyson did not
present his findings in a systematic time-frame, but Edge reconstructed a provisional chronology of Mozart's acquisition of paper types.[10] He identifies not
only the watermark and the rastrum of each paper type, but sometimes also the
composer's purchase of different batches of the same paper.

In any attempt to date a work through the study of its paper types, the physical evidence provides only part of the picture. Just as important is the human
element: the ways in which the composer acquired his stocks of paper. Tyson,
who himself made major contributions to questions of dating across Mozart's
entire œuvre, based his approach on one important underlying assumption: that
it was the composer's normal practice to purchase a relatively modest batch of
manuscript paper, to use it up, and then to obtain a new supply.[11] From this
developed his view that as a general rule compositions on the same paper-type

are likely to have been written – or at any rate to have been begun – within a limited period of time. Edge agreed that this was Mozart's 'normal operating procedure' when purchasing and using paper.[12] Indeed, by counting precisely the numbers of extant leaves of each paper type, he was able to suggest that Mozart's usual purchase consisted of a quire of around twenty-four or twenty-five bifolia. At the start of a major project like an opera, he would very likely purchase several quires at once. Tyson's assumption that Mozart used up virtually all of each batch of paper before moving on to the next one seems true only up to a point. Edge's chronology appears to demonstrate that leaves were often left over, and that these were then retained by Mozart for use in the future. The dating of single leaves is therefore much more problematic.

Tyson's main conclusions concerning the compositional chronology of the opera were based on the evidence of its two main paper types. He suggested that most of the ensembles in Act I and two arias ('Rivolgete' and 'Smanie') were composed first (on type 66 paper) and that the remaining Act I arias, the overture, both finales, and all of Act II were done subsequently (on type 100 paper).[13] The use of a few sheets of type 66 paper at the start of pieces completed on type 100 paper (and once during the Act I finale) were thus assumed to represent the transition between the two stocks of paper. As usual, there are a few isolated sheets of different papers, which represent moments when Mozart had recourse to his stock of left-over sheets. The one real surprise, described by Edge as a 'significant unexplained chronological anomaly', is the appearance of a single bifolium of type 96 paper in the middle of 'Alla bella Despinetta'.[14] Mozart's known use of this paper otherwise dates from the summer of 1791 when he was working on *Die Zauberflöte*, but the continuity of the ink colours in this section of the sestetto suggests that this sheet had somehow found its way into Mozart's pile of the main paper type. In broad outline, this represents a typical sequence of composition, with Mozart postponing work on the arias until he could take full account of the requirements of his singers.

In my examination of the autograph, I did not re-examine the paper types, but other palaeographical aspects of the score began to suggest a refinement of Tyson's analysis. This is the idea that when working on a major project such as an opera, Mozart adopted a system of paper *allocation*. Before starting to copy a particular piece, it seems to have been his practice to estimate its probable paper requirement and to set aside an appropriate quantity of blank sheets. It is not likely that he would have made such an allocation without marking the paper in some way, but it is certainly possible that on occasion he went no further than to put in the opening theme. It is demonstrable, for example, that he started to draft an aria for Don Alfonso ('La mano a me date') and that he left off work after eight bars, returning only later to refashion the opening into the quartet we now know. If this was his usual habit, then it is not necessary to assume that pieces in Act I copied wholly on type 66 paper were completed at an early stage, only that they were started early.

## Ink Colours and Copying Practices

While the study of watermarks and rastrology is well established, the serious study of ink types is of more recent date. Throughout this book, ink evidence will be used in the discussion of specific questions relating to the chronology of particular pieces or of longer sequences of pieces. Some preliminary observations about the potential value and limitations of this type of evidence are therefore essential. A pioneering discussion of the use of ink evidence to study the chronology of an opera was undertaken by Köhler, although his findings were necessarily limited by the unavailability at that time of Acts III and IV of his chosen opera, *Figaro*.[15] The best and by far the most comprehensive discussion of the inks used in late eighteenth-century Viennese manuscripts is to be found in Edge's thesis.[16] In the light of his critique of previous work in this area, it should be pointed out that in the following discussion I describe how the inks look on the page now, irrespective of whether or not they have faded (i.e. oxidised from black colour to a reddish or golden brown colour) in the decades and centuries after the music was written. However uniform the ink colours might have appeared when Mozart first copied his scores and in the days and weeks afterwards, it is quite clear that over time the different inks used began to discolour at different rates and in different ways, and it is the identification of these contrasts that enables ink colours to be used for chronological purposes.

Unlike watermarks which can be precisely identified or staves which can be accurately measured, inks are likely to remain a difficult area of study until such time as forensic equipment is more widely available for scientific analysis. Perception of ink colour is highly subjective, as was brought home to me during my first period of work in Kraków. On the occasion of this visit, the old reading room in the Jagellonian Library was often bathed in warm September sunlight as it streamed across the Vistula, but at other times it was darkened by late afternoon thunderclouds. The desk was provided with a lamp with a yellowish type of light. These various lighting conditions greatly influenced the look of the ink colours. Yet the variety of background lighting, atmospheric or manmade, far from posing an obstacle, proved very useful. In warm light, one of the brown inks used in *Così* appeared to the eye to glow with an almost golden colour. Under the same conditions, other very similar brown inks seemed to have less of the component that produces this effect. The well-lit room in the Musikabteilung of the Staatsbibliothek zu Berlin was not subject to direct sunlight, and the effect was altogether more neutral. This apparent uniformity is also actual uniformity, since there is little doubt that fewer inks were used to copy Act II. Comparing a passage copied in one medium-dark brown ink with another passage copied in an ostensibly similar ink later in the same Act is hard enough; making comparisons from memory between the two Acts in Kraków and Berlin is a near impossibility. Prudence dictates that only very striking and distinctive features should form the basis of any comparative discussion of inks used in Act I and Act II.

The colour of the ink itself (in its modern appearance) is of basic importance, but it is by no means the only factor to be considered; intensity is another significant and often very visible aspect, as is the fading characteristic of an ink. Some appear uniform in colour, retaining their initial look (both colour and intensity) until the composer next dipped his pen into the ink-well; others fade quite rapidly as the supply of ink on the quill dwindled. Sometimes inks of similar colour and intensity can be distinguished by other characteristics. Some of the black-looking inks used in *Così* are dull and soot-like in their appearance. Edge notes that different ingredients were often added to the basic mixture to enhance the black colour.[17] One blackish ink glistens as one alters the angle of vision, as though not yet completely dry. This crystalline element probably comes from the material used to blot the page, as it is particularly evident in the ink blobs that the composer sometimes inadvertently scattered around, all of which needed to be blotted immediately.[18] On occasion the composer's use of the ink-well could be a factor. As the pigment was not fully soluble in water, it could settle, and a shake of the container could therefore produce an intensification of the colour.[19] If the supply ran very low, some components of an ink might start to collect near the bottom in the dregs. The appearance of ink is also affected by the paper; some papers appear to absorb ink, others to repel it, leaving it sitting on the surface, with its curve apparently almost intact. Edge notes that paper intended for manuscript copies was sized in order to prevent the ink from running.[20] Variations in this process seem to be able to affect the look of a whole page. The paper of the last bifolium of the opera appears to have (or to have acquired) a slightly waxy feel to it. The ink looks exceedingly faint, so that the 'bella calma' unconvincingly encountered on fol. 310v appears by fol. 311 to be fading fast! On a few occasions, Mozart used an ink that spread slightly as on blotting paper, leaving a fuzzy impression. A delay in blotting is the probable explanation, as quite often it is small-scale corrections or revisions that appear thus.

The character of the pen obviously influences the look of an ink. Edge believes that Mozart cut his own quills.[21] The pens used by Mozart whilst copying *Così fan tutte* ranged from one with a very fine tip, which produced a spidery effect, to others capable of making quite broad strokes. There is also the question of the delivery of the ink to the page; a scratchy effect is produced by a tip which delivers insufficient ink to make smooth strokes. One pen used by Mozart produced what now appears as a blobby effect, delivering the ink inconsistently, for example with highly intense note-heads but very faint stems.

At the start of the twenty-first century, a range of different ink colours characterise the autograph manuscripts of *Così fan tutte*. It will be helpful to identify the main groups. Blackish-looking inks, dark and quite intense, which do not lighten much during the course of a passage copied after a single dip into the ink-well, are seen periodically throughout the autograph. Sometimes a black-looking ink is associated with a quill with a fine, perhaps newly sharpened tip. The overall effect of the penmanship is slightly spidery. It is possible that the use of a fine tip itself acted to concentrate ink flow, thereby contributing to the black colour. With a finely cut quill, the ink sometimes appears not to flow sufficiently, the result being a slightly scratchy look. This effect predominates in several of the early ensembles in Act I. Under magnification, 'black' ink often appears to be a deep brown, but this may not be particularly evident to the unassisted eye.

A characteristic ink in this autograph is one which lightens quickly to a medium brown. The look of the page can be extraordinarily dramatic, as at the start of 'Come scoglio'. The quill, after being dipped in the ink-well, at first delivered the ink to the page in an intense-looking black colour. With the excess gone, the remaining ink appears medium to light brown in colour. Striking though this looks, the effect is merely an exaggeration of the normal process whereby an ink appears to thin out, as subsequent strokes were made before the quill was dipped into the ink-well again. Occasionally there are indications that, in an attempt to overcome the shortcomings of this type of ink or quill, Mozart adapted his penmanship, by writing down note-heads and stems separately, in order to avoid blobs resulting from the attempt to draw note-stems directly from note-heads too liberally supplied with ink. The end result is a blackish colour which alternates dramatically with a light brown. Often the one appears to turn into the other with no gradation of tone. The first impression, indeed, can be of two inks, with Mozart having filled in the page impressionistically with dots and stems of one colour and then dots and stems of the other. Another characteristic of this ink or quill is a tendency, as in 'Smanie implacabili', to produce a spray of unintended blots on the page. In this case the location of these blots matches those places in the score where there are ugly splurges of ink, for example, the words 'implacabili' and 'sospir'. It tells us something about Mozart's personality, or the intensity with which he wrote, that he continued to work with the defective equipment for the rest of the aria.

Other inks look medium brown. The basic colour is a chocolate brown, occasionally with a slight hint of purple or plum coloration. In their darker forms, these inks have quite an intense look. The fading characteristics are usually less exaggerated than with the black-looking inks.

In some ways the most distinctive and varied inks in this autograph are the light brown ones. One has a very light brown-greyish appearance. It appears faint, even faded in character, distinctive by being nondescript. In sharp contrast is an ink with a warm, almost yellow-gold tinge, which comes out strongly under yellow light, an effect best seen when a whole page written in it glows. In between these two extremes is a light brown ink, warm in character, but lacking the yellow-gold tinge. Under magnification, reddish, russet coloured tones are apparent.

Mistakes made while copying with a quill and ink could be corrected in several ways.[22] The simplest technique was the finger-smudge, done while the ink was still wet. A small sponge could also have been used. This leaves what is usually a rather faint patch of light ink on the page, as even dark inks smudge to a lighter colour. What was written first is almost always visible. If a small correction had to be made once the ink had dried, Mozart would often cross out the offending note(s) with a series of crisp diagonal pen strokes from lower left to upper right. If a bar-line running across an entire brace had to be deleted, a wavy line would be drawn throughout its length. A redundant passage of several bars would be deleted using diagonal hatching, and additional bar-lines might be drawn at the start and the end of the passage to be eliminated. Text to be replaced would have a firm line drawn though it. If it could be done neatly, a musical revision would often be done as an adaptation of the original, with the existing symbols altered or deleted as appropriate, but often it was as easy to make use of a vacant staff above or below the brace. An alternative to crossing out was scraping the page with a knife. This could be effective, but there was always the risk that the operation might go wrong and leave an ugly blotch.

It is quite clear that as a rule Mozart copied his opera scores in several stages. Most frequently encountered is a three-stage process in the pattern noted by Arthur in his examination of the piano concertos K413–15: a particella; string instrumentation; wind instrumentation.[23] There was a practical basis for this sequence, relating not only to the process of composition, but also to the requirements of rehearsal. The particella was a highly abbreviated score of a movement, giving (in the case of an aria) the vocal line, some or all of the bass line, and occasional hints as to the rest, for example the first (or last) few bars of the first violin part, or significant wind interjections. The purpose seems to have been to put just enough on the page to have the structure of the piece recorded. This is sometimes known as the continuity draft.[24] As we shall see later, in a significant number of arias Mozart stopped writing the particella before the concluding bars. With a nearly complete draft to hand, he could go to the singer, play it over, gain approval of the vocal line, and perhaps discuss the manner of its ending. If the changes required were sufficiently numerous or large in scale, the original particella might well have to be abandoned, but because it was only a skeleton, relatively little time would be lost.

The addition of the string lines equates to the time when string parts were required for early rehearsals with a small band of instrumentalists. In his study of the original orchestral parts for the first Vienna performances of *Figaro* and *Don Giovanni*, Edge reached the conclusion that first-desk copies of the string parts were produced directly from Mozart's autograph.[25] The parts prepared for the first Vienna performance run of *Così fan tutte* have not yet been identified, but it is likely that similar procedures would have been followed. One consequence of the early production of first-desk string parts was that the onus lay firmly on Mozart to try to ensure that his autograph was fully supplied with the necessary details of articulation and dynamics in the string scoring. These could be added to the parts during preliminary rehearsals, and no doubt changes were often needed, but if too many details were left out, rehearsal time would be wasted. When he added in the full string instrumentation, it was therefore Mozart's custom to firm up the details of the articulation and dynamics.

Before the start of the full orchestral rehearsals, duplicate string parts would be taken from the first-desk set, and the wind parts would be copied directly from the autograph. The full score produced as a reference copy for the theatre was also taken from the autograph, but independently from the parts, a procedure that inevitably resulted in two streams of textual variants entering circulation.[26]

A crucial factor in understanding Mozart's copying practices is the question of brace design. Before he put any markings on the page, he had first to estimate the likely size of the movement's scoring, so that a brace of an appropriate size could be drawn. This was necessary because of his practice of locating the string parts at the top of the page and the solo voice(s) and the bass line at the bottom. The usual choice was a brace of eight, ten or twelve staves. It would be located as far as possible in the middle of the page: that is, with an equal number of blank staves above and below. The initial selection of a brace-size reflected the broad parameters of the anticipated instrumentation by allowing three, five or seven staves for the wind, brass and timpani. Both of Despina's light *buffa* arias, for example, were copied on eight-stave braces. However there was a great deal of flexibility within this framework. If the wind parts were obbligato in character, Mozart might allocate a separate staff for each instrument of the usual pairs, but if the writing were more accompanimental in character, he would often write two parts on one staff, or in extreme cases even four. He would make full use of any unused staves above or below, before eventually having recourse to a separate leaf, usually indicated with the words 'extra Blatt'. Paradoxically, although he had to make the basic decision about brace size early on, it is very evident that the detail of the wind instrumentation was often decided quite late. It is striking how often the development of the full wind scoring led to late changes that are very obvious on the page.

In the majority of cases, what survives in the autograph are pieces copied on paper with pre-ruled braces. As he completed the orchestration, Mozart often had to adapt. There are examples of braces that in the end proved to have too many staves ('Non siate ritrosi') or too few ('Donne mie') for the required instrumentation. On the other hand, he sometimes ruled the braces as he went along and was thus able to vary the number of staves to fit the music on each page. This is clearly indicative of the existence of an earlier perhaps quite full draft from which he was recopying, and from which he could see what was required from page to page. Characteristically, pieces of this type appear to be written in a nearly uniform ink colour, with few of the layered features and contrasting inks of the scored-up particella.

The distinction between what might be termed a consultation particella, a score which embodies a break between the writing of the draft and the completion of the orchestration, and a piece copied at a single sitting (from a pre-existing version) is central to the interpretation of ink evidence in *Così*. Yet the identifications are not always clear cut. Brace design is not an infallible guide because undoubtedly there were pieces copied at a single sitting for which there was no need to vary the number of staves. Nor are ink colours conclusive. Even if copying from a fairly fully scored original, Mozart might still write out the final score in horizontal bands, producing a subtle layering effect, since ink colours often changed perceptibly during the course of copying a single movement. The extent to which a score has corrections, another feature of relevance to this distinction, is also open to interpretation. It would be wrong to argue that a heavily revised score like 'Donne mie' shows that Mozart was having particular trouble with this piece. In reality, the more problematic and heavily worked pieces might have been those for which the first draft was so drastically altered that a new version was needed.

Ink evidence is particularly useful in interpreting the copying of the scored-up particella. It is common to see a change of ink colour within the particella itself, where the composer appears to break off copying before resuming with a different ink. In such cases, there is always the pragmatic explanation that he simply switched to a new supply or even merely shook the container, yet a hiatus in copying can point to a more significant break, potentially embodying a creative decision of some kind. The frequency with which a copying break occurs at the end of the main piece but before the orchestral postlude is far too great to be mere coincidence; it points to the fact that the provision of an ending was often a distinct compositional act. On the other hand, the copying of the string lines and even more so the wind lines was almost always done at one sitting, which confirms, as we would expect, that Mozart fully scored up a piece only when he was certain that it would be in the opera and was now needed for the production of parts for rehearsals. In these later stages, it is evident that he often worked on subsections of an Act, copying the string or wind parts for several consecutive pieces at one go.

A very important moment in the preparation of an eighteenth-century opera score was the copying of the recitatives. It is sometimes assumed that this was done very late, even that they were put in only after the copying of the arias and ensembles had been completed. In *Così*, however, ink colours and other kinds of evidence strongly suggest that they were part of the continuity stage, and that the main labour of copying the full orchestration was done only at the end. Recitatives were always liable to require a certain amount of rewriting, usually to make them cadence into a key that had not originally been anticipated, and this happened several times in *Così*. Analysis of ink colours leads to the conclusion that Mozart copied several recitatives at a time – in other words, that the main plot sequences were each put together at one go, as the structure of the subsections of the opera came into place. Köhler too deduced that the simple recitatives in Acts I and II of *Figaro* were done in sequences.[27] The practice of putting together continuity sequences before scoring made good sense. To orchestrate fully a large aria with a rich instrumentation like 'Rivolgete' and then abandon it amounted to a considerable waste of precious time; but a particella for an average-sized aria could have been copied very quickly. If Mozart had to make late changes to the internal structure and position of arias and ensembles, the use of particellas meant that it would often have been as easy to write out a new version, than to attempt to doctor sections of existing scores.

Analysis of ink colours generally tends to illustrate systematic features and to draw attention to the high levels of self-discipline and professional organisation necessary to complete a substantial and complex creative enterprise like an opera, often in the space of only a few weeks. It is pleasing to be able to report that ink colours (and ink colours alone) also illuminate apparently more relaxed moments in the compositional process. An interesting feature is that when Mozart was working on a recitative, he sometimes filled in a few details on the first page of the following piece. When copying the recitative before 'Smanie implacabili', he apparently went on to complete the second violin part

and to add in the slurs of the first violin on the first page of the aria. The attitude
of mind represented by this habit is that of the person who, faced with a series
of tasks, tries to get ahead with future jobs by preparing the ground at every
possible opportunity, so that when the main task is finally confronted, some
of it has already been done. It is psychologically a very effective way of working for anyone daunted by a blank page. At other times, Mozart seems to have
sat back from the rigours of writing large sequences and to have reviewed his
work. Rather like a painter adding a few dabs of colour to a half-finished can-
vas before leaving for the night, he would insert, almost at random, seemingly
unrelated details, a tempo designation here, a phrase mark there. In this frame
of mind, Mozart was not in consistent mode, and he would make a change without worrying whether there were any consequential alterations, for example in
repeats of the same material. A useful illustration of the less systematic aspects
of Mozart's working methods is to be found in the first part of Act II. Little
use is made here of the warm brown, golden-tinged ink seen in parts of Act I,
and so the few elements that there are in an ink of this colour stand out rather
clearly. They include: the wind part labels, the wind clefs, their key and time
signatures, and rests (on the first side only) of 'Prenderò quel brunettino'; the
substitute instruction 'attacca' and the crossing out of the final cadence note of
the recitative before 'La mano a me date', and the inserted bar-lines and crossing
out of redundant bar-lines on the first page of this piece; the tempo designation
'Allegretto' and the instruction 'lietissimo' at the start of 'Ah lo veggio'; the note
'Atto 2do' at the head of 'Per pietà'. This is not to imply that these changes and
additions were all made at the same time, but they are characteristic of the way
in which Mozart would advance work on a piece by making a decision, changing something, or adding a detail, without at that moment working out the new
idea fully.

## A Two-stage Genesis?

Any attempt to date the start of work on *Così fan tutte* from the evidence of the
composer's usage of different paper types in 1789 is problematic. No matter how
refined the chronology, it can only deal with what is extant. Lost items, such
as the missing autograph of the clarinet quintet, might well alter the position
significantly. Moreover, it would be very rash indeed to assume that Mozart the
musician and teacher had no use at all for music manuscript paper other than for
writing down his own compositions. The central chronological question with
*Così fan tutte* is whether the opera was written in two distinct stages, and, if so,
how long the work was in abeyance. It is clear enough that Mozart began work
on the opera using one paper type and then completed it on another, but comparison with the papers used in other compositions of this period is of limited

value because he wrote so little during the critical period from the late spring to the early autumn of 1789. At least there can be no doubt that work on the three Prussian quartets overlapped with the composition of the opera. The first of the quartets (K575) was composed during the composer's absence from Vienna and is copied on a batch of Bohemian paper, thick and greyish, of inferior quality.[28] It was entered in the catalogue of works in June. The first movement and the opening bars of the second movement of the next quartet (K589) were copied on the remaining sheets of this paper, probably some time after Mozart's return to Vienna. This quartet was then continued on the second of the two main types used in *Così*. Following an examination of the inks at the point at which Mozart switched between the two paper types, Tyson concluded that there was probably no break in copying. Thereafter, work on the quartets appears to have become much more sporadic. Tyson observed that the first movement of the third quartet (K590) shows signs of having been written in many stages, the colour of the ink varying greatly from one section to the next.[29] Other commissions undertaken by Mozart in the second half of 1789 included a number of substitute arias for singers in Vienna, the paper type of some of which matches the first of the two main papers in the opera, and one important chamber work, the clarinet quintet, the autograph of which is lost. Overall this presents a picture of rather sporadic compositional activity, with the composer accepting such small commissions as were offered, and perhaps continuing on and off with the quartets. The evidence of the paper types thus neither precludes a start on *Così* earlier than the autumn of 1789 nor particularly suggests it.[30]

However, the theory that the opera had a two-stage genesis is supported by textual evidence. Tyson's view that there was an early layer consisting of the material copied on the first of the two main paper types, was reinforced by three features that are not found in anything copied on the later paper: the placement of Dorabella's part above that of Fiordiligi; the use of the spelling 'Guillelmo' rather than 'Guilelmo'; and inconsistency in the ordering of the parts of Don Alfonso and Guglielmo.[31] The conjunction of these features with the use of the earlier paper type suggests not merely that there was a preliminary phase of work, but that some elements of the opera were changed before Mozart resumed work on it.

The first distinctive textual feature of the early layer of *Così fan tutte* was reported by Tyson thus: in the ensembles in which the sisters sing 'the soprano staff that stands higher in the score originally bore the name Dorabella and the lower one Fiordiligi, but a correction reversed the names in each case'.[32] In all material copied on the later paper, Fiordiligi's line was entered on the upper staff. The decision to reverse the sisters' names had been made by the time that some of the early Act I recitatives were being copied, as shown in

Table 1. The second diagnostic sign of the early layer is the spelling 'Guillelmo', as shown in Table 2.

With the notable exception of the start of the first trio, all the pieces in the early layer which name this character (Nos. 2, 3, 6, 7, 13, 15a and 16) use the form 'Guillelmo', and this is the way the name is given in the first two recitatives as well. In all of the Act I music copied on the later paper and on isolated

TABLE 1  The order of the sisters in Act I

|  | Dorabella above Fiordiligi (subsequently reversed) | Fiordiligi above Dorabella |
|---|---|---|
| Ah guarda, sorella | ✓ | |
| Stelle! per carità | | ✓ |
| Sento oddio | ✓ | |
| Non v'è più tempo | | ✓ |
| Di scrivermi | | ✓ |
| Soave sia il vento | ✓ | |
| Alla bella Despinetta | ✓ | |

TABLE 2  The spelling of Guglielmo's name in Act I

| Aria / Ensemble | Recitative | Paper type | Autograph |
|---|---|---|---|
| La mia Dorabella | | 66 | Guilelmo |
| | Fuor la spada | 66 | Guillelmo |
| È la fede delle femmine | | 66 | Guillelmo |
| | Scioccherie di poeti! | 66 | Guillelmo |
| Una bella serenata | | 66 | Guillelmo |
| | Mi par che stamattina | 66 | Guilelmo |
| Sento oddio | | 66 | Guillelmo (×4) |
| Al fato | | 66 | Guillelmo |
| Di scrivermi | | 66+100 | Guillelmo |
| | Signora Dorabella | 100 | Guillelmo |
| Alla bella Despinetta | | 66 | Guillelmo |
| | Ah non partite! | 100 | Guillelmo |
| Rivolgete | | 66 | Guillelmo |
| Rivolgete (stage) | | 66 | Guillelmo |
| Non siate ritrosi | | 100 | Guillelmo |
| E voi ridete? | | 66 | Guillelmo |
| E voi ridete? (stage) | | 66 | Guilelmo |

left-over sheets of the earlier paper type, the form is consistently 'Guilelmo', as it is throughout Act II. Stage directions added to ensembles already copied also use the later spelling. The inconsistency in the spelling of this name was not corrected by Mozart, but in the libretto Da Ponte always uses the spelling 'Guilelmo'. The likely explanation is that Mozart began with a draft libretto in which the name was spelt 'Guillelmo', and that when a revised version became necessary (doubtless for other reasons), he continued to use the original version to work on the relatively settled early part of the opera, pending the arrival of the revision. It is thus by no means necessary to assume that all the pieces using the early spelling were at this stage completed, merely that the libretto text was available.

The copyists of the Vienna Court Theatre score (**V1**) standardised the spelling to 'Guilelmo', except at the start of 'Una bella serenata', always assuming that this trio was not copied before the decision to change had been made. One sign that the copyists had been instructed directly to make this change comes at the start of 'Al fato' where a second 'l' is erased. One further occurrence of the spelling with a double 'l' comes in Act II at the start of 'Il core vi dono', perhaps a simple slip.

In the two recently discovered settings of trios by Salieri the spelling is 'Guilelmo'. In chronological order, there thus appears to have been a progression from 'Guilelmo' to 'Guillelmo' back to 'Guilelmo', as shown in Table 3. It seems reasonable to conclude that the spelling in the original libretto for Salieri was 'Guilelmo', that during the first phase of Mozart's work it was changed to 'Guillelmo', and that there was then a reversion to the original spelling.

The third characteristic feature of the early layer is the inconsistent ordering of the bass parts as shown in Table 4. In the earliest ensembles to have been written, including all three opening trios, the part of Don Alfonso appears above that of Guglielmo. It seems that there was then a short period when Mozart decided to

TABLE 3 Changes in the spelling of Guglielmo's name

| Spelling | Location |
| --- | --- |
| Guilelmo | Salieri's libretto |
| Guilelmo | *Così*: La mia Dorabella |
| Guillelmo | *Così*: all other arias and ensembles written on the earlier of the two main paper types and the recitatives connecting the opening trios |
| Guilelmo | *Così*: everything written on the later of the two main paper types, and recitatives written on left-over sheets of the earlier paper type |
| Guilelmo | **V1** |
| Guglielmo | the modern spelling, which dates back to the 1791 Dresden libretto |

TABLE 4  The order of the bass parts

| Placed higher in the score | Item |
| --- | --- |
| Don Alfonso | La mia Dorabella |
| Don Alfonso | È la fede delle femmine |
| Don Alfonso | Una bella serenata |
| Guglielmo | Sento oddio (up to bar 47) |
| Don Alfonso | Sento oddio (from bar 48) |
| Guglielmo | Di scrivermi |
| Don Alfonso | Alla bella Despinetta |
| Guglielmo | E voi ridete? |
| Don Alfonso | Finale |

move Don Alfonso to the bottom of the score. This idea apparently did not last very long, as only 'E voi ridete?' and the first part of 'Sento oddio' of the early ensembles are ordered thus. The original order was re-established, apparently during a copying break in 'Sento oddio'. That there was some uncertainty in Mozart's mind over this issue from the start is clear from Guglielmo's first entry in 'Una bella serenata', a few notes of which were entered on Don Alfonso's staff and then smudged out before being copied in the correct position. Late in the Act II finale, Mozart, doubtless by accident, again reverted to the order with Don Alfonso lowest (on fols. 297v and 298). He noticed the error when putting in the string parts, and added in names to identify the correct lines. One exception to the general pattern is 'Di scrivermi', which was undoubtedly copied much later. Its reversion to the order with Guglielmo above Don Alfonso was either a mistake or else a deliberate reflection of its musical character, in which the suave quartet formed by the two parting couples finds an astringent counterpart in the cynical asides of the old philosopher. In the Vienna Court Theatre score no attempt was made to standardise the order of the two lowest vocal lines. The copyists merely followed Mozart, even duplicating the switch in the middle of 'Sento oddio', a feature that is consequently seen in many other early copies

An interesting legacy of the change of mind over the ordering of the bass lines occurs in bars 38–44 of 'Alla bella Despinetta', where the parts of Don Alfonso and Guglielmo appear to have become muddled. Don Alfonso's memorable opening phrases in this ensemble use characteristically spiky rhythms, while the two officers enter singing in mellifluous thirds. However, in bar 38 Mozart briefly forgot in which order he was placing the lower voices, and as a result Ferrando and Don Alfonso start to sing in thirds, while Guglielmo has the more sharply dotted interjections. Ferrando's text 'non ci ravvisa' was put in by Mozart, but he did not repeat it under Don Alfonso's part, again a slip as the philosopher should sing 'non li ravvisa'. Guglielmo at the bottom has his correct 'ci'. This lapse should probably be corrected in modern performances. The two lines can be switched easily, provided that the pronouns 'ci' ('us') and 'li' ('them') are exchanged in bar 41. An early copy of *Cosi fan tutte* (**Be1**) actually suggests this change.

The successive changes of mind over the ordering of the bass parts should alert us to the dangers of over-simplifying the nature of the early and late layers of this opera. For example, it is an entirely plausible scenario that in the spring of 1789, full of enthusiasm for a new operatic project, Mozart purchased a substantial batch of paper but drafted only the first three ensembles before discontinuing work. When resuming in the autumn in response to a firm contract, his first compositional acts would then still appear to belong to the early layer, as writing would continue on the original pile of paper allocated to the project, and the spelling 'Guillelmo' would be changed only after Da Ponte's revised libretto had become available. The brief switch of the bass lines could thus be seen as representing a preliminary casting in Vienna followed by a reversion to what was to be the final casting. Two features which mark out the first three ensembles as a distinct unit, perhaps earlier than anything else in the first layer, are the faint numbers added in red crayon only to these pieces (before apparently being overwritten) and the use of 'Guillelmo' in the connecting recitatives.

One further possible change of mind concerns the name of the maid: Despina or Despinetta? The latter is a normal diminutive of the kind that can occur at any time for reasons of humour or affection. Indeed, at the start of the opera, having just sealed their bet, Ferrando and Guglielmo jokingly refer to their opponent as 'Signor Don Alfonsetto'. Yet there are occasional usages of 'Despinetta', including once each as a stage direction and as a *segue*. These are given in Table 5.

The maid always refers to herself as Despina, and so, apart from the tutti in the Act II finale, do the sisters and the officers. As she does not appear in the first part of the opera, the only occurrence of her name in material copied early is Don Alfonso's memorable introduction of her at the start of the sestetto: 'Alla bella Despinetta'. Apart from this, there is a significant concentration of the use of the name Despinetta in the early scenes in Act II. Possibly this was the first subsection of the opera involving the maid that Mozart worked on.

Of the various changes that occurred between this hypothetical early layer of *Cosi fan tutte* and the main period of work, perhaps only the alteration in the spelling of 'Guglielmo' could be considered a possible indicator that a different venue for the opera was under consideration. It is certainly striking that

TABLE 5 The use of the name 'Despinetta'

| | Item | Text | Comment |
|---|---|---|---|
| Act I | Che silenzio | ... per Despina ... Despinetta! ... Despina mia ... | The first time in the opera that the maid's name is heard. |
| | Alla bella Despinetta | Alla bella Despinetta | Very likely the first piece of text set by Mozart containing the maid's name. |
| | Oh la saria | ... poi Despinetta ... | The stage direction to this recitative in the autograph refers to the diminutive form of the maid's name. The libretto has 'Despina'. (Possibly this recitative belonged originally to Act II.) |
| Act II | Andate là | Segue l'aria di Despinetta | The continuity direction at the end of this recitative has the diminutive form, perhaps the strongest hint that this name was in Mozart's mind. |
| | Il tutto deponete | Despinetta | Don Alfonso refers to the maid thus. |
| | Finale | Della cara Despinetta | The chorus adopts Don Alfonso's preferred form. |

'Guilelmo' was preferred both in Salieri's brief encounter with the libretto and in Mozart's final version. Tyson makes the tentative observation that this spelling could have been intended as a literal rendering of the German 'Wilhelm'.[33] It could therefore be argued that 'Guillelmo' was adopted with a geographical usage in mind, although this is a very slender piece of evidence on which to claim that Mozart's original interest in the libretto came in the context of a location outside Vienna. The other differences between the two layers seem to relate to the process of casting and to conceptual changes made to the opera as it developed. These are important issues and will be discussed later in this study.

A two-stage compositional process might have left one further imprint on this opera: the late inclusion of contemporary references for the benefit of the Viennese audience. In the absence of the version of the libretto originally prepared for Salieri, it is obviously impossible to know to what extent this happened. Much discussed features that might qualify include: the theme of war as expressed in the chorus 'Bella vita militar'; the change in the port of embarkation from Venice to the imperial port of Trieste; the choice of Ferrara as the home of the two sisters, possibly out of deference to Da Ponte's mistress Adriana Ferrarese del Bene; and the skit on Mesmerism. The replacement of Da Ponte's title 'La scuola degli amanti' was surely Mozart's idea. Its musical and textual reference to *Figaro* is widely accepted.

## *The Chronology of Composition*

For insights into the internal compositional order of *Così fan tutte* we can turn to the evidence of ink colours. The sheer complexity of the overall chronology will defeat any attempt to construct a detailed order of work for the whole opera, yet much useful information can be found. One feature that can be identified with a fair degree of certainty is the first layer of material to be written by the composer. It was copied in a black-looking ink and begins, as one might expect, with the particellas of the opening ensembles. This layer seems to include the first four ensembles sung by the men (Nos. 1, 2, 3 and 7) and perhaps also the first section of the sestetto (No. 13). What this material has in common is the absence of the two sisters. This layer could represent an early phase of copying, chronologically distinct from what came later, but immediately we encounter the most significant limitation of ink evidence. A change in ink does not necessarily imply a lengthy break in composition; it could easily signify nothing more interesting than the fact that the composer's ink-well had just run dry. Although a break in composition of some duration is usually implied by a change of ink colour, its length cannot be determined. An inventory of what seems to have been done during this first stage of copying is given in Appendix 1.

A study of the inks used to copy the continuity sequences of recitatives leaves many questions unanswered, but it throws up some remarkably suggestive findings. As far as they are identifiable, a summary list of these sequences is given in Table 6. Comparing the ink colours of isolated sheets of recitatives is, of course, a rather subjective undertaking.

It is reassuring that that there is an exact match in Act I with the use of the two main papers types. Further palaeographical details of these recitative sequences are given in Appendix 2. For all the uncertainty surrounding their identification, the broad outlines at least are clear, although around the departure scenes in Act I are several recitatives which do not appear to belong to any obvious sequence. The most interesting feature is the identification of copying breaks within several recitatives between the departure of the men and the Act I finale. This highlights the general point (reinforced by many other kinds of evidence) that this section of the opera was one of the last to be put in order, only after many changes had been made.

One other point of real interest is that the apparently isolated recitative 'Oh la saria' seems to have been switched between Act II and Act I. Uniquely for a recitative in this opera, it is marked 'atto primo'. Its original location was probably in the first part of Act II. As a result of what seems to have been a rather hasty rewrite, there are a number of loose ends and other ambiguities in this recitative. In reply to Don Alfonso's question as to what Despina's two

TABLE 6  Hypothetical recitative sequences

| | Sequence | Recitative |
|---|---|---|
| Act I | sequence 1 | Fuor la spada |
| | | Scioccherie di poeti! |
| | sequence 2 | Mi par che stamattina |
| | | Stelle! per carità |
| | | Non pianger |
| | | La commedia è graziosa |
| | unclear | Non v'è più tempo |
| | | Dove son? |
| | | Non son cattivo comico |
| | | Che vita maledetta (6 bars and 3 beats) |
| | sequence 3 | Che vita maledetta (from bar 6, beat 3) |
| | | Signora Dorabella |
| | | Che silenzio |
| | | Che sussurro (up to bar 7) |
| | | Che sussurro (from bar 7) |
| | sequence 4 | Ah non partite! |
| | | Si può sapere |
| | | Oh la saria |
| Act II | sequence 1 | Andate là |
| | | Sorella, cosa dici? |
| | | Ah correte al giardino |
| | | Il tutto deponete |
| | | Oh che bella giornata |
| | sequence 2 | Amico, abbiamo vinto! |
| | | Bravo: questa è costanza |
| | | Ora vedo |
| | sequence 3 | Come tutto congiura |
| | | L'abito di Ferrando |
| | | Vittoria, padroncini! |

mistresses are doing ('e che fan le tue padrone'), Mozart had the maid reply: 'le povere padrone / stanno nel giardinetto / A sognarsi coll' aria ...' ('The poor mistresses are in the garden, sighing with the breeze ...') However, in Da Ponte's libretto, the response is much sharper, reflecting the language of complaint: 'le povere buffone / stanno nel giardinetto / A lagnarsi coll' aria ...' ('The two buffoons are in the garden, complaining with the breeze ...') With appropriate gender revisions, this phrase could have applied to the two officers at the start of Act II, complaining of their lack of success. In the next section there are further divergences between the autograph and the libretto, perhaps also deriving from the repositioning of the recitative. As though changing the subject from the two officers to the two sisters, Don Alfonso asks about them: 'but in the meantime, these madwomen? ...' Here Mozart had 'quelle [those – the former] pazze', while Da Ponte had 'queste [these – the latter] pazze'. Despina responds that the two sisters will in time act as required, observing that it is good that they have been made aware that they are loved by the Albanians. But then Don Alfonso wants to know how Despina will bring them back, since they have left, referring from the context to the sisters. In the libretto, however, 'partiti' implies the Albanians, while in the autograph Mozart appears to have changed 'partite' to 'partiti'. There is thus a persistent sense of ambiguity as to which pair (the men or the women) is under discussion. The earliest manuscript copies show an awareness of this problem. The score **Ca** which may well represent the text of **V2** containing Mozart's revised version, has a compromise: 'le povere padrone ... lagnarsi'.

Ink colours provide some telling clues about the sequence in which the orchestration was done. In the middle part of Act I, a distinctive, faded, greyish-brown ink was used for the string orchestration and a slightly warmer brown one for the wind parts, as shown in Table 7.

It seems that Mozart scored up the string parts of the ensembles of this whole sequence (excluding the chorus) at one time. The late entry of the unnumbered quintetto 'Di scrivermi' appears to be confirmed: the voice and string parts are both in this ink. Much the most surprising feature to be highlighted in this table is the hint that only the first part of 'Alla bella Despinetta' was copied as a particella at this stage. Apparently there was a gap before the subsequent sections were done, perhaps around the time that the string parts in this faded ink were being added to the other ensembles. This finding has a bearing on arguments about where the original of Ferrando's missing recall was to have been located, and it may well explain the presence of an isolated bifolium of another paper type. Mozart had perhaps allocated too little paper in the first place.[34]

TABLE 7  The sequence of orchestration of some Act I ensembles

| | Sento oddio | Al fato | Di scrivermi | Soave sia il vento | Alla bella Despinetta | Alla bella Despinetta (3/4→) |
|---|---|---|---|---|---|---|
| *Particella* | | | ▒ | | | ▒ |
| *Strings* | ▒ | ▒ | ▒ | ▒ | ▒ | |
| *Wind* | | █ | █ | █ | | |

Key

▒ = faded greyish ink

█ = warmer brown ink

A similar scoring sequence can be identified for the succession of ensembles in the early part of Act II. The particellas of these are generally in medium-brown inks, while the wind instrumentation is in a much darker, blackish-looking ink. This pattern breaks down completely in the following aria 'Ah lo veggio'. The wind scoring thus defines this sequence of ensembles at the start of Act II, just as does the recitative ink colour.

As famously described by Da Ponte, an operatic finale could function as a self-contained dramatic unit with its own structure and sub-plot. To a degree then, it was sometimes possible for the copying of the finales to proceed in parallel with the rest of the opera. In the case of *Così fan tutte*, the Act I finale was copied in sections, and there was a change of plan with regard to the positioning of the part of Despina. As shown in Table 8, her line is (very briefly) highest in the score, but then her part was copied below those of the two sisters.

The ink colours and other palaeographical features hint at an interesting possibility: that the opening duet for the two sisters at the start of the Act I finale could have been conceived originally as a separate piece before being integrated into its present position. The whole score of this section appears to be in one ink colour, as opposed to the layered particella seen throughout the rest of the finale, a fact consistent with Mozart's having recopied it from a draft. The existence of an earlier draft might even help to account for the fact that in **V1** the copyist momentarily wrote Dorabella's name on the higher of the two staves allocated to the two sisters, before scratching it out, perhaps a final legacy of an earlier draft in which Fiordiligi had occupied the lower line, as she had once done in all the other early ensembles.

TABLE 8  The inks of the particella of the Act I finale

|  | Ink colour | Despina's line |
|---|---|---|
| Ah che tutta in un momento | brown with golden tones | |
| Si mora | slightly less warm brown with a finer tipped pen | |
| Gia chè a morir (at Despina's entry words 'Cosa vedo?') | medium brown, slightly scratchy looking with a tendency to blotch | Despina shares Fiordiligi's staff. |
| Eccovi il medico | medium brown | Fiordiligi and Dorabella share a staff with Despina on the staff below. |
| Dove son? & Dammi un baccio | blackish with fine nib | All three women have a staff each with Despina lowest. |

In the autograph there are several unusual features on fol. 136, just before the start of the new section 'Si mora'.[35] Mozart first drew a brace and wrote in the character names, their clefs and the bass clef, and a G major key signature. Apparently this largely blank page was then set to one side until he had finished recopying the D major duet with which the finale now opens. The last three bars of this were added in to the start of fol. 136. It was necessary to amend some details. An extra sharp now had to be added to the G major key signature originally in the parts of Fiordiligi, Dorabella and in the bass line. When working on this join, however, Mozart did not change the names of the two pairs of wind instruments he had first noted on the brace ('2 fagotti' / '2 corni'). This instrumentation thus equates neither with what now was to come before, in the opening duet section of the finale (two flutes, two horns, two bassoons) nor with what now was to follow in Scene XV (two flutes, two oboes, two bassoons, two trumpets). This adds to the sense that in its original state fol. 136 consisted merely of the brace and the part labels, clefs, key signatures for the sisters, and the bass line. In other words, this sheet had been prepared as the start of a particella.

When Mozart resumed work on this juncture of the Act I finale, he added in a G major key signature to all the voice parts and the bass line in the first bar of the new section (the fourth bar on fol. 136). For such a seemingly simple addition to the page, this produced a surprisingly complex palaeographical knot to untangle. The first symbols to be entered in this bar were the F♯s in the vocal lines and in the bass part. In the parts of Fiordiligi and Dorabella these had to be added in before the final note of their last phrase of the previous section. In the parts for the three male characters, Mozart realised almost immediately that this would be a redundant signature, since no C♯s had been added to their G major signatures at the start of the page. These were accordingly smudged out. Next, Mozart decided that the new section should be marked by a change of time signature to (C stroke). He added this in all the parts, but as there was no space between the key signature and the first note in the parts of Fiordiligi, Dorabella and the bass line, he had no alternative but to put the time signature in before the key signature. At some point during the copying of the particella and certainly before the string parts were added in, Mozart made one further significant change by turning the first bar of the new section into two bars. He had to ensure that the existing rests in the vocal lines and the bass part were changed. Some of the existing symbols were modified, others were crossed out. A figure 'i' above the newly written semibreve rests clarified that a whole bar's rest was intended.

In the next phase of work, string parts were added in, and for these Mozart decided that it was necessary to provide the new key signature in the form that cancels the previous one (F♯ and C♮). In the case of the upper string parts, he put the new signature in before the time signature (the correct place), but for the bassi (which already had an F♯) he simply added in the C♮. Finally, rather than copy in the wind parts, Mozart decided to write them on an additional sheet. Subsequently, however, an assistant crossed out the reference to this and copied in the parts for flutes and bassoons, placing the conventional cross-reference to the parts not copied in the score ('NB oboe, clarini sono scritti a parte') at the top of the page. This copyist apparently did not think it necessary to add in any key signature.

All this detailed forensic evidence points to the conclusion that Mozart did not copy out the first two sections of the Act I finale in order. It seems clear that fol. 136 was in existence with its brace and part labels before the first section was recopied in its present position. Although it is not possible to identify with certainty what caused this, an accumulation of minor details suggests the intriguing possibility that this duet and its preceding recitative were originally to have been located in the early part of Act II. The preceding recitative part label gives the maid's name as 'Despinetta', and the only other place where this happens (other than in the text of the opera) is at the start of Act II, where there is a 'segue l'aria di Despinetta'. More significantly, the recitative itself ('Oh la saria') bears the inscription 'Atto primo', which certainly seems to imply the possibility that an original Act II location was being countermanded. Also worth noting is that a copyist (rather than Mozart) wrote in 'Finale 1°' and 'Andante' at the start of the finale in the autograph. The editors of *NMA: KB* further note that at the start of the second section in bar 59, the name 'Guilelmo' appears to have been rewritten.[36] It is not clear what was there before, but one obvious possibility is the name in its earlier spelling of 'Guillelmo'.

One other interesting point to emerge from study of the ink colours of the Act I finale particella is that a break occurred not at the start of the section in which Despina enters, but at her first words. This is concordant with the idea that Despina's text was the last to be revised, perhaps also that the comic Latin was Mozart's idea.

The ink colours of the Act II finale are more consistent throughout: the particella was done in a very dark brown ink, the strings in a somewhat lighter brown, and the wind in a darker ink. As always, some fragments of the wind parts were put in at the particella stage. At the start of Scene XVI, Mozart wrote (in dark ink) parts for '2 clarinetti in B'. Later, in a lighter brown ink resembling that used to copy the string parts, he added in parts for oboes on the same staff, with the necessary caveat '2 oboe um i ton tiefer'. Thereafter (in the same lighter brown ink) he identified passages for 'clarinetti soli'. The use of German in the autograph of *Così* is unusual. In his report on the first two Acts of *Idomeneo*, Heartz noted a number of German instructions relating to the wind instrumentation of the march that were not replicated in the early Munich copy.[37] It is probable that Mozart used German when he wished to convey a written instruction to his copyist that he did not want to appear in the score. The absence of obvious horizontal copying breaks in the Act II finale suggests that it was copied in a fairly short space of time, but, as in Act I, Despina's line appears to sink down the score. When she enters as the notary, she shares a staff with Fiordiligi. After the recall of 'Bella vita militar', however, she is demoted to share a staff with Dorabella, and when eventually all six soloists have their own staves, her line is below that of the two sisters.

One further copying sequence worthy of note is that of the *accompagnato* recitatives in Act II. The particellas of 'Barbara! perché fuggi?', 'Il mio ritratto' and 'In qual fiero contrasto' were all written in black ink with a fine nib (after the first part of 'Barbara!'). The completion of all three pieces was done in a very much lighter brown, with some hint of metallic bronze (but not warm) colour. It is possible that the short trio 'Tutti accusan le donne' also belongs to this phase. It too has a particella in black ink and a completion in lighter brown ink (at which point the time signature was changed from C to ₵). The clarity of this colour division reveals a distinctive and perhaps rather surprising feature: Mozart's failure to add in many of the necessary accidentals during the first phase of the copying process, when little more than fragments of the string accompaniment were added. The missing symbols were usually added during the second stage of copying. Edge discusses an accompanied recitative attributed to Mozart in which harmonic sense is only achieved by assuming the omission of several accidentals. If Mozart's copying practices as seen in *Così fan tutte* were typical, it is easy to see how such cases could arise.[38]

Ink colour analysis is by no means the only source of potential information about the chronology of this opera. Tyson demonstrated that the foliation numbers and the continuity directions added by Mozart to his scores can provide very interesting clues. The composer's practice was to number pairs of leaves (bifoliation). Act I consists of two series: a single bifoliation sequence from 1 to 60 (the end of the Act); smaller bifoliation sequences used to number the overture, the chorus, and individual arias. As Tyson remarks, the long series could hardly have been added before the general order of the Act was settled. It includes all the extra sheets containing the recitatives.[39] Because the arias were the pieces most likely to have to be changed at the last minute as a result of demands from singers, Mozart always started them on a new bifolium with an individual number sequence, even if there was considerable space to spare at the end of the preceding page. Even at the stage of putting together the main continuity sequence, Mozart still could not depend upon the arias being in their final form, or sometimes even their final place.

The Act I bifoliation was published by Tyson.[40] Two bifoliation numbers, No. 26 ('Signora Dorabella') written in darkish brown ink and No. 27 ('Che silenzio') written in warm brown ink with a thick brown nib, seem to stand outside the general run. This perhaps indicates that these were replacement sheets. The bifoliation sequence of Act II was not given by Tyson and it is presented in Appendix 3.

The basic method of adding bifoliation numbers is that of Act I: a long sequence incorporating the recitatives and the ensembles with individual sequences for the arias. It is interesting that the number 15 in this series seems to be a slightly different colour, an indication perhaps of a late change of plan with regard to 'Tradito'. The fact that the Act II finale has a separate bifoliation system whereas the Act I finale is part of the main sequence, suggests that Mozart started work on it before the preceding seduction scenes were finalised. There are some interesting exceptions to the general pattern. Although now a quartet, 'La mano a me date' received individual bifoliation numbers, doubtless added to the blank sheets during the period when the piece was still an aria. The duet 'Fra gli amplessi' was also numbered as though it were to be an aria, whereas the parallel seduction duet between Dorabella and Guglielmo is part of the main sequence. The bifoliations of the individual aria sequences are all in brown ink, except for Ferrando's two Act II solos, both numbered in red crayon, which appears to confirm that it was Mozart's practice to work on all the arias for a single singer at one time. In several arias the last number of a series is missing. Mozart normally pre-numbered up to four double sheets for each aria, but when he went over this limit and had to add another bifolium, he sometimes forgot to add the number 5. (This is a good example of the aforementioned concept of paper allocation.) In Act I, the chorus 'Bella vita militar', even though an ensemble, received a separate numeration, unusually with one number for each sheet. In Act II, the chorus 'Secondate' is missing from the autograph, but it clearly could not have been accommodated on a single sheet after 'Ah correte al giardino', and so it too must have had a separate sequence.

Unused sides at the end of a piece were usually left blank, but sometimes a sheet was removed, as happened after recitatives (on fols. 183, 190 and 191) and arias (on fols. 228 and 241). The absence of the number 17 from the long bifoliation sequence suggests that the two recitatives in the hand of a copyist were replacements for a single bifolium previously copied by Mozart. On the other hand, there is no number in the long sequence for the missing *accompagnato* 'Ei parte', which comes between the numbers 12 and 13. Perhaps it was drafted on the spare space at the end of a particella of something else, an earlier version of

'Ah lo veggio' or an alternative aria for Ferrando, in which case it might not have needed an additional sheet. In the event, there was plenty of space at the end of 'Ah lo veggio' had Mozart wished to enter it there. Undoubtedly the most interesting aspect of the Act II bifoliation is the unusual nature of the sequence at the start of 'Fra gli amplessi'. This will be discussed in detail later.

Further chronological clues may be obtained from a close examination of the numbering system and the continuity directions. Mozart's usual practices are quite clear: the number at the head of the movement is copied on the top left, above the start of the top staff; *segue* or *attacca* instructions usually follow horizontally after the double bar at the end of a movement, even when this means using a rather cramped margin, rather than space available below; the ink colour of a *segue* indication is almost always that of the end of the preceding recitative; and the ink colour of a *dopo* instruction (copied in the top left corner of the page) is usually that of the start of the recitative above which it appears. While the ink colours of the *segue*, *attacca* and *dopo* instructions normally link them to the continuity stage of composition (when particellas were being put with their recitatives), the addition of a number at the head of each movement in Act I occurred at a later stage, when Mozart was orchestrating, or correcting errors. It made little sense to put these in until the order of the opera was truly finalised. There was evidently still some uncertainty over the numbering at the start of Act II, where the *segue* indications for 'Prenderò' and 'Secondate' have 'N°:' in brown ink without number. A red crayon (not in Mozart's hand) was used to add them. By inserting the numbers '25' and '24' after the instructions following 'Barbara! perché fuggi?', Mozart clarified the order, while the appearance of a red crayon '26' on the earlier *segue* to Guglielmo's Act II aria shows how late the revised *attacca* to 'Donne mie' (which has a brown 'N°: 26') was inserted.

The addition of a 'dopo' indication (literally 'after') was a fail-safe device for the copyist, to confirm what the order should be. In the settled first part of Act I, no use was made of 'dopo' indications, but they appear in profusion during the aria sequence before the first finale, a very telling sign that this part of the opera saw wholesale reorganisation. Apart from the instruction following 'Barbara! perché fuggi?', with its unusual formulation 'dopo questo ...', there are two such indications in Act II. The first serves to locate the recitative 'Il tutto deponete' after 'Secondate'. As this chorus was a late addition, there is no surprise here. The second *dopo* indication confirms that the recitative 'Bravo: questa è costanza' comes after Ferrando's 'Tradito'. This inaugurates the approach to the climactic duet of Act II, a section of the opera that undoubtedly saw late and very major changes.

Mozart's use of the terms 'segue' and 'attacca' deserves some further consideration, as they were sometimes changed. The distinction is not always clear cut.

Greater urgency is usually implied by the imperative 'attacca' ('continue without a break') than the more neutral 'segue' ('there follows'). The basic musical distinction is that a *segue* normally follows a perfect cadence in the recitative, while an *attacca* cadences directly from the recitative into the new piece, the V – I progression transcending the divide. While the usual conventions are clear, Mozart's employment of them is sometimes flexible. For example, he often uses a *segue* to indicate an *accompagnato* which develops directly out of a recitative, as in 'Segue Rec: istromentato' (leading into 'Ah scostati') and 'Segue stromentato' (leading into 'Stelle'). Mozart uses the *attacca* direction for several purposes. One is to link together groups of pieces, somewhat in the manner of a finale. This happens with the first three trios, and with 'Non siate ritrosi' / 'E voi ridete?' A second use of the *attacca* is to accelerate the forward momentum at particular moments for dramatic effect. Yet there can be no general presumption that an *attacca* implies a moment of greater tension, because Mozart also uses it at more reflective moments as at the start of 'Soave sia il vento'. The qualifying word 'subito' ('suddenly') enhances the urgency of a particular moment of transition. When added to a *segue*, it probably means that the following piece should continue without a break. Its application to the instruction *attacca* seems at first glance tautological, since the cadence as written produces an immediate transition to the new piece. However, even though written as an unbroken cadence, there was perhaps at least the possibility of an unwritten pause before (or even conceivably after) the dominant chord, slightly delaying the harmonic resolution at the start of the next piece. In the autograph, Mozart uses 'attacca subito' only twice – once to dramatise the start of Don Alfonso's 'Vorrei dir', the other time to ensure that the unconventional 'In uomini' flows without a break from the preceding recitative.

When drafting the particella of an aria or ensemble, Mozart usually took no account of the possibility of its being an *attacca*. If a piece was later made *attacca* (as in the case of 'Una bella serenata'), he completed the last syllables of the vocal part in the recitative (even though they were to coincide with the downbeat of the following piece), but he added no tonic chord. In the following piece, he left the rests undisturbed in the vocal line, and, of course, ensured that there was a tonic chord on the first beat (or a dominant chord in the case of a $V - I(V) - I$ progression) if there was not one already there, as he did at the start of 'Donne mie'. Everyone knew what this convention was, and there was no need to notate it precisely. The *attacca* leading into 'Di scrivermi' – it is actually given as 'segue coi stromenti' as in the other accompanied recitatives – is an exception. At first glance, ink colours appear to suggest that Mozart completed the previous simple recitative on the recto, turned over the page, ruled out the brace, put in the part labels and added in the remaining syllables sung by the two women ('-fanno'), returning later to copy the substance the movement. But this overlooks the fact that in Fiordiligi's first bar, her two syllables were written over the minim rest that would have been necessary if the syllables had not been there. Dorabella's semibreve rest remained uncancelled, despite the addition of her syllables.[41] The origin of this unusual feature perhaps lay in Mozart's decision to turn what had been intended as accompanied recitative into a fully concerted piece. The text of 'Di scrivermi' is in the seven- and eleven-syllable free lines (*settenari* and *endecasillabi*) characteristic of recitative.[42] On one of the last remaining left-over sheets of the earlier paper type, Mozart ruled out a nine-stave brace for five singers and strings, heading it 'Recitativo'. Either he was intending a conventional *accompagnato* with the usual exaggerated staccato chords and rushing scales, or something rather closer in style to a concerted piece (resembling, for example, the accompaniment to Don Alfonso's words 'Nel mare solca'), but the significant point is that he drew the brace on the verso of the sheet – in other words, he knew that a short simple recitative would lead into this piece, but perhaps not yet what its text would be.

In a memorable change of plan, Mozart decided to turn 'Di scrivermi' into a fully concerted piece, which he then continued on sheets of the later paper type but without wind parts as yet. Visible symbols of this change of plan are the absence of an F major key signature at the start and the lack of a piece number or the generic title quintetto.[43] The use of a wrong or rather an inappropriate key signature is by no means unusual in long multipartite movements such as finales, but it is rare at the start of a free-standing aria or ensemble. The final step in turning 'Di scrivermi' into a concerted piece was the addition of wind instruments. The clear implication of the overwritten rests at the start of this piece is that Mozart added the preceding simple recitative (or at least its ending) only after composing the start of the ensemble, for which the original rests were necessary. For clarity, he decided to add the cadence syllables sung by the two women at the start of the movement, rather than leave them at the end of the previous recitative. Brown comments that the appearance of a rhymed couplet at the end of the simple recitative ('stanno' / 'affanno') may possibly be taken as 'a signal that a concerted piece was to follow'.[44] This allows for the possibility that Da Ponte deliberately composed the end of this simple recitative to smooth the transition into what would now be a weightier ensemble than had originally been intended. One final point to note is that in the first bar of 'Di scrivermi' only Fiordiligi's two notes are in black ink. Her syllables '-fanno' and Dorabella's notes and syllables are in a browner ink. It is as though there were two stages, with Mozart first adding in Fiordiligi's notes, pending the arrival of the recitative text from Da Ponte, and then completing the join once he had the text to hand. When one turns over the sheet to see the recto, it is immediately apparent that Mozart originally drew the brace for the last line of simple recitative with the usual two lines. When he saw from Da Ponte's text that the recitative would end with two very short duets between the officers and the sisters, he had to change this to a three-stave brace. Only then were syllables added to the start of 'Di scrivermi'.

Key relationships between recitative and aria or ensemble also have the potential to provide chronological information. In this opera they are mainly the conventional ones: tonic–tonic; dominant–tonic; (infrequently subdominant–tonic). The link into Guglielmo's aria 'Donne mie' is a fine example of what Heartz has termed a 'double recitative cadence', one which moves from the V of the recitative cadence directly to the V of the new key, the arrival at the new tonic being delayed.[45] Minor key movements are rare in the Da Ponte operas, and so it is hard to know whether the relative key relationship leading into 'Tradito' is unusual. The one real anomaly is the mediant relationship between the recitative and the chorus 'Secondate'. This might be a sign of its late addition here, or even that it was originally in a different key. There is a striking instance of a late decision to change the key of a chorus in *Idomeneo*. Mozart originally intended 'Placido è il mar' to be in C major and composed the link from the previous recitative with the instruction 'attaca subito il Coro'. In an inspired revision, however, he decided upon the key of E major. He crossed out and recomposed the last four bars and at the same time changed the continuity instruction to 'Segue il Coro'. Heartz makes the very reasonable practical point that this change was probably to allow the chorus singers time to adjust to the pitch of this more remote key.[46] The failure to rework the recitative in the case of 'Secondate' could have been a simple oversight. Also worth noting in this context are two 'wrong' joins. Mozart himself corrected one, the lead into 'Donne mie', but the other embracing a tritone (the lead into 'È amore') was only amended in the Vienna Court Theatre score **V1**.

A possible sign that Mozart was working on a piece at a late stage is the use of an Act designation. In Tyson's view, the fact that Nos. 14 and 15b have 'Atto Iᵐᵒ' on their first pages, implies that Act II was already well under way by the time that they were being written. The Act indications for 'Una donna' and 'Donne mie' are positioned on the left of the page; those for 'Per pietà' and 'Fra gli amplessi' are in a different ink and are situated on the right of the page. It should come as no surprise that Act indications were added mainly to arias, because they clarified for the copyist, perhaps before the final numbering had been allocated, which piece (usually from a choice of two) should follow an indication such as 'Segue l'aria di ...'. There would rarely be any need to identify the Act of an ensemble. 'Fra gli amplessi' was an exception, conceivably because of the potential confusion of its opening orchestral flourish with Ferrando's Act I aria 'Un' aura amorosa', but much more likely because this instruction was unnecessarily copied from the start of an earlier draft of an aria beginning 'Fra gli amplessi'.

*Così fan tutte* would work perfectly well without the chorus, as it provides no essential musical or dramatic function. The march 'Bella vita militar' and its recall in the Act II finale could just as easily have been a piece of military band music, and the two other passages for chorus both repeat material sung by the solo characters. In fact there are several indications (including their separate bifoliations) that the music for chorus was integrated at rather a late stage.

One sign of the late entry of the chorus into Act I is the duplication of a Scene V indication in the autograph. It seems that when Mozart inserted the chorus, he forgot to cancel the already existing scene indication at the head of the following recitative. At the start of the Act II finale, the chorus seems not to have been anticipated. In the autograph, Mozart first wrote under Scena XV 'Despina poi D: Alfonso' with no mention of the chorus. He ruled a nine-stave brace for the first three pages. On fol. 274v the chorus enters, and Mozart enlarged to a twelve-stave brace. At that point he apparently returned to the start of the finale to add in 'Coro di servi e di suonatori' on the staff often left blank between the character list and the top of the brace. (The reference to the chorus is not aligned with 'Despina poi D: Alfonso' – it is well to the right.) This seems to imply that Mozart, notwithstanding the fact that servants must be on stage as Despina addresses them in her first line, was not intending them to sing in Scene XV. The libretto does not mention the chorus at the start of Scene XV, although from the scene setting with its references to an orchestra and richly clad servants, it is obvious that there are servants and musicians on stage.

If the chorus was a late addition to the opera, then the same was perhaps true of the boats. Indeed, it is possible that the maritime location of the opera was firmed up only quite late on. The autograph sets Act I, Scene II in a 'Giardino sulla spiaggia', the libretto subsequently making clear that it is a beach by the sea by adding 'del mare'. The boat in Act I does not appear in the stage directions at the start of any scene. Don Alfonso refers to its arrival (which he could easily have done by looking off-stage), and then at the end of Scene V the sisters remain on the shore ('sulla sponda del mare'), while the 'barca' sails off. This is not entirely consistent with the fact that Don Alfonso has in the meantime referred to a smaller skiff ('legno') which the officers, having literally missed the boat, must now use. The seaside location of the garden in Act II ('alla riva del mare') was perhaps decided only when the duet and chorus 'Secondate' was added.

Insights into the debate over the geographical location of the opera are to be found in the Vienna Court Theatre score (**V1**). Although achieving a fair level of accuracy, copyists inevitably departed from their source in some respects. Often these hardly count as errors at all: variations in the use of capital letters, punctuation marks, accents, elisions and the occasional slip with a single vowel or consonant. Minor discrepancies of this sort appear throughout, but more significant variants are far from randomly distributed; they occur in a small number of recitatives. It is quite possible that in such cases the copyist was working from an earlier draft of a piece which for some reason the composer himself then recopied, incorporating as he went along a few amendments. This situation could well have arisen when Mozart copied a recitative on the remaining space of an aria particella, which then had to be revised so substantially that a new draft was needed. The Vienna Court Theatre score gives the port of departure for the men in the recitative 'Signora Dorabella' as Venice. This is no mere slip or misreading; it is a significant change, and a very interesting one. If this version had indeed been copied from an earlier draft, it would show that the original place of embarkation was to have been Venice, with the opera being located in northern Italy, appropriately enough for two sisters from Ferrara. The choice of the port was certainly under active consideration, because Mozart first had it as Trieste before finally opting for sunnier climes in Naples (for which a new rhythm was required). Other than the libretto title-page, this was the only geographical reference in the whole opera that would have needed to change. As there was obviously no substantive reworking of this recitative in Mozart's final version, the copyist did not need to redo it, but for some reason the change to 'da Napoli partiti' was overlooked.

Another example of this kind of discrepancy – an amusing error – occurs at the end of the same recitative. In response to Despina's cynicism, Dorabella hotly defends the officers as 'models of fidelity' ('Di fedeltà ... essempi'). In the autograph, however, Mozart accidentally had her referring to them as models of 'infidelity' ('d'infedeltà') – a Freudian slip? Given the circumstances, it is hardly likely that Dorabella was indulging in irony. The mistake was later spotted by the composer and corrected in the autograph. (Fig. 1.) A useful clue is given by the ink colour with which Mozart crossed out the offending 'n' and the apostrophe. It closely resembles that with which the previous change to 'da Napoli partiti' had been made. These identifications are assisted by the rather fuzzy, blurred quality of the ink.

For most of the compositional period of *Così fan tutte*, the autograph remains our sole source of potential chronological information. In the run up to the première and after it, however, many other useful sources come into play. A draft libretto was produced, quickly followed by a final version. The changes made are often interesting. An invaluable source is the Vienna Court Theatre score **V1**, the text of which can be compared both with that of the libretto and that of the autograph. The variants often provide fascinating glimpses, not just of the compositional process itself, but also of the way the opera was revised. This topic will be considered in greater length in Part 3 of this study.

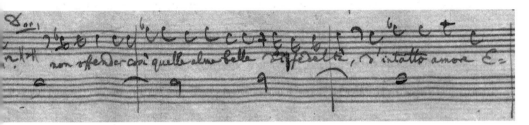

FIG. I  The autograph of *Così fan tutte*, Act I, Biblioteka Jagiellońska, Kraków, fol. 70v, 'Signora Dorabella' (bars 50–2), detail. Mozart originally had Dorabella claiming that the two officers were models of infidelity ('d'infedeltà'). This was corrected to 'di fedeltà'. (Reproduced by kind permission of the Biblioteka Jagiellońska, Kraków.)

# [ 2 ]

# *Singers and their Arias*

I T I S A F A I R A S S U M P T I O N that Mozart expected to be in contact with his singers during the process of aria composition. In a famous passage concerning a piece he was composing for the singer Anton Raaff, he wrote:

> I asked him to tell me candidly if he did not like his aria or if it did not suit his voice, adding that I would alter it if he wished or even compose another one. 'God forbid', he said, 'the aria must remain just as it is, for nothing could be finer. But please shorten it a little, for I am no longer able to sustain my notes.' 'Most gladly', I replied, 'as much as you like. I made it a little long on purpose, for it is always easy to cut down, but not so easy to lengthen.' ... When I took leave of him he thanked me most cordially, while I assured him that I would arrange the aria in such a way that it would give him pleasure to sing it. For I like an aria to fit a singer as perfectly as a well-made suit of clothes.[1]

In his letters Mozart made detailed appraisals of several of his singers, and it is clear that he studied carefully the strengths, weaknesses and vocal characteristics of anyone for whom he wrote. In Raaff's case, he noted with approval several positive features, such as his impressive diction and good breath control.[2]

In order to ensure that the singer was happy with what he had written, Mozart's usual practice was to run through an aria with its performer before committing himself to a conclusion, leaving open the possibility of lengthening or abbreviating the piece. In several arias in *Così*, there is in fact a break in the ink colour of the particella shortly before the end of the singer's material. Conceptually, such a draft would be more open-ended than, for example, an aria particella which merely lacked its final orchestral ritornello.[3] After glancing through the draft or trying it out with the composer accompanying at the keyboard, a troublesome singer might reject the proposed aria entirely, in which case Mozart would be left with several sheets of paper, lightly scored but unusable. Once the aria had been accepted, Mozart could make final adjustments and then set the particella aside to be orchestrated, but probably not before sending it to a copyist to produce a rehearsal score for the singer. Salieri's early biographer Ignaz von Mosel described how he composed scenes even as Da Ponte brought them to him, sometimes with just the vocal line and the bass. These would be sent off to a copyist so that the singers could start to learn their parts.[4] Whether the draft of the aria seen by the singer could be used for the final full score would depend on the state of the manuscript. If many changes were required, it might well be necessary to recopy. Distinguishing between the scored-up particella (seen and approved by the singer) and the fair copy (made after a significant number of alterations had been agreed), is an essential prerequisite for a discussion of aria revisions.

A review of the substantive changes made to arias in *Così* during the process of composition reveals one very striking fact: like the particella ink breaks, they are heavily concentrated around the climactic points, just prior to the orchestral postludes. This confirms the idea that it was Mozart's usual practice not to complete an aria until he had checked it with the singer.[5] In a distinct (though not necessarily long-delayed) phase of composition, he would then round off the piece. Some of the changes made at climactic points concern a matter about which any singer would have had views: the range of the vocal line. An example of this comes towards the climax of Benucci's discarded Act I aria 'Rivolgete'. Mozart had originally included an extra fifteen bars, but he crossed these out at the particella stage. The most notable feature of the rejected material is that Benucci was apparently to be asked for a high F♯ to add to the three (one immediately before the cut passage, two after it) which give this conclusion its power.[6] As has been pointed out by Rushton, 'Rivolgete' has an unusually high tessitura for this singer.[7]

Requests for changes to arias could continue even during final orchestral rehearsals. One problem that might emerge only at this stage is the overall demands that the performance of the whole opera might place on a singer's voice. Cuts in the length of an aria might indicate that its performer felt that he or she was being asked to do too much, even though admiring what had been written. The abbreviation of Ferrando's arias could be an example of this. The largest 'agreed' cut to any aria in *Così* was made to 'Ah lo veggio'. Calvesi perhaps found this aria just too demanding on his voice with its high tessitura and repeated high B♭. Two shorter 'agreed' cuts were also made in his Act I aria 'Un'aura amorosa', perhaps again a compromise between singer and composer.

Another area of potential concern to a singer might be the start of a piece. In Act I, Scene II, Fiordiligi and Dorabella appear together in a garden to the mellifluous sound of clarinets and horns. Their A major duet 'Ah guarda sorella' in fact begins with a substantial solo for each of them in turn, before they join together in a duet of beguiling charm. Analysis of the ink colours suggests that Mozart worked on this piece in two halves, possibly even completing the second section before the first. The justification for so doing would have been the elaborate character of the solo writing in the first section. As the first appearance of the two leading ladies was a diplomatically sensitive moment, it was necessary to ensure that both women were happy with what he had written for them. In a dark-looking ink, Mozart crossed out several bars of the first phrase sung by Villeneuve as Dorabella and substituted a new version below. (Fig. 2.) The change in musical character is clear: the revision eliminated the octave leaps. (Example 1.) As always, it is possible that the composer made this alteration for purely musical reasons, yet the singer could have requested it, with the intention of avoiding leaps early on, even though they are not especially daunting ones. It might equally have been the case that he wrote the solo sections with two particular singers in mind, and then found that, having decided to switch the lines between the two characters, the performer of Dorabella's line was no longer happy with aspects of what he had written for her predecessor in the role.

The reason for supposing that Villeneuve herself could have been present when the changes to her musical line were made lies in a palaeographical feature which is hard to explain as anything other than the result of a rehearsal. Mozart did not usually write out twice in his autograph any text sung by more than one singer; especially in finales and large ensembles this saved a great deal of time. As one looks through the ensembles in the first part of Act I including 'Ah guarda sorella', it quickly becomes obvious that many sections of text sung by Dorabella (which merely duplicate Fiordiligi's words one line above) were inserted later in a black-looking ink, distinct from anything else on the page. It is hardly likely that this was done to assist a copyist, as it is plainly evident that the two sisters are singing the same words. A more likely explanation is that Mozart had a preliminary rehearsal of these ensembles with Villeneuve, during which, for the ease of her reading, he added the text below her line. The ink used to make these additions looks very similar to that used to remove the early octave leaps.

FIG. 2 The autograph of *Così fan tutte*, Act I, Biblioteka Jagiellońska, Kraków, fol. 30, 'Ah guarda sorella' (bars 39–43), detail. Mozart crossed out the original passage for Dorabella with its descending octaves and wrote a revised version on the blank staff below the bass line. (Reproduced by kind permission of the Biblioteka Jagiellońska, Kraków.)

EX. 1 Near the beginning of 'Ah guarda sorella' (bars 40–2), Mozart revised Dorabella's line at the words 'se fiamma, se dardi non sembran scoccar' to eliminate the octave leaps.

Whilst the principal concern of singers was undoubtedly with their arias, they might also express views on ensembles, particularly duets with solo passages. An example of a passage in a duet being revised probably for reasons of tessitura may found in 'Fra gli amplessi', where Mozart reworked bars 121–3 and the varied repeat in bars 126–8. As originally conceived, Calvesi and Ferrarese would have been asked to sing an unprepared high A four times in quick succession. (Example 2.) On the other hand, the composer might, paradoxically, have been looking to extend the climax of the duet, since the figure originally sung by the two singers here (a concluding motif) appears at the end of the movement in violin 1. In the revised version, there is a steadier build up to the climax.

EX. 2 In 'Fra gli amplessi' (bars 121–3), Mozart revised the vocal lines to eliminate the repeated entries on the high tonic note A. Perhaps this was found to be too taxing for the singers, or perhaps he felt that this pre-empted the closing figure.

## Adriana Ferrarese del Bene's 'Per pietà'

Fiordiligi's magnificent rondò contains a significant piece of rewriting. What would have been a rather understated climax was transformed into a spectacular display of vocal agility. The three bars containing Mozart's original version of the climax, have full obbligato wind instrumentation, lines which must have been put in before Mozart carried on to write the seven replacement bars in the particella. (Fig. 3.) The copyist of this movement in **V1** apparently started to write out the shorter original version before being instructed by Mozart to

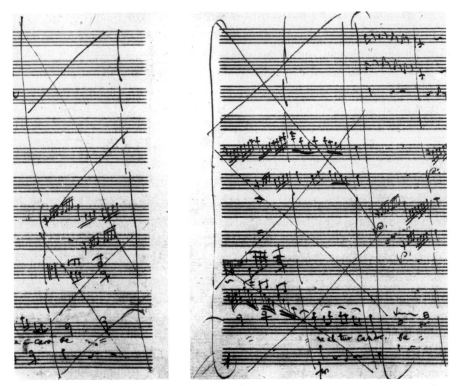

FIG. 3 The autograph of *Così fan tutte*, Act II (Mus. ms. Autogr. W. A. Mozart 588, vol. 2, fols. 227–227v), Staatsbibliothek zu Berlin, Preußischer Kulturbesitz, Musikabteilung mit Mendelssohn Archiv, 'Per pietà' (bars 113–17, original version), detail. Mozart had already completed the wind instrumentation before crossing these bars out. He replaced this passage with a much grander climax for Fiordiligi. (Staatsbibliothek zu Berlin – Preußischer Kulturbesitz, Musikabteilung mit Mendelssohn-Archiv. Mus.ms.autogr. W. A. Mozart 588 vol. 2)

change it. The bar is scraped out, but it looks as though there were two ascending minims (B and E), possibly each with a trill and a final turn. The cancelled version in the autograph has no trills. The much greater virtuosity of the final version enhances the impact of the vocal cadence. Other improvements include the loss of the routine chugging bassoons and the gain in clarity from separating the flute scales from the horn arpeggios.[8] More importantly, the range required from Adriana Ferrarese del Bene was extended upwards by a minor third. Fiordiligi was now liberated to ascend to her thrilling top note, where in the first version she was to remain relatively earth-bound a minor third lower. (Example 3.) It is quite likely that Mozart took this particella to show to Ferrarese once he had completed it up to the original climax, and that it was she who requested the higher note, the better to show off her top register, and perhaps also a more generally showy ending with which to make a memorable exit.[9]

Earlier in his career Mozart famously wrote of having to 'sacrifice' a little to the 'flexible throat' of the singer Cavalieri, which apparently resulted in the inclusion of a greater amount of virtuoso passagework in her aria than he would have liked.[10] Throughout 'Per pietà', mindful of the deeply personal qualities of Fiordiligi's soliloquy, Mozart kept the amount of overtly florid writing under very strict control. It would be interesting to know whether he regarded the more virtuoso replacement ending as in any sense a concession to his latest *prima donna*. In the case of Cavalieri's aria he appeared confident that he had still been able to express the character's feelings as far as an Italian 'bravura' aria would allow. If the revised ending of 'Per pietà' came about as the result of a direct request from Ferrarese, it presumably satisfied her needs, but it is also a memorable musical improvement which adds an appropriate sense of climactic power to this great display of deeply felt penitence, without any apparent sacrifice in the characterisation of Fiordiligi. With good reason, Mozart was proud of his ability to make a virtue out of necessity.

EX. 3 The partial draft of Mozart's original three-bar climax for Fiordiligi in 'Per pietà' later expanded to seven bars (bars 114–21) was rather understated. The revision allowed Adriana Ferrarese del Bene to display her virtuosity to the full.

## Dorotea Bussani's 'Una donna'

A similar extension to vocal range occurs at the end of Despina's Act II aria 'Una donna', and there is also a splendid improvement to the dramatic characterisation of its climax. The additional material is copied on hand-ruled extensions to the staves at the end of the recto and the start of the verso of the last page. (Fig. 4.) The first two additional bars extend the upper range of the vocal line, this time by a major third. Up to that point, Bussani had only been required to sing a high G, but now the addition of a high B adds punch to the climax. The second pair of extra bars introduces a charming idea: the brief false start of the final phrase. The autograph shows that these four bars cannot have been inserted after

FIG. 4  The autograph of *Così fan tutte*, Act II (Mus. ms. Autogr. W. A. Mozart 588, vol. 2, fols. 182–182v), Staatsbibliothek zu Berlin, Preußischer Kulturbesitz, Musikabteilung mit Mendelssohn Archiv, 'Una donna' (bars 83–9), detail. Mozart added two extensions to the braces, first to lengthen the climax of Despina's aria, and then to include a brief false start of the final statement of the main theme. (Staatsbibliothek zu Berlin – Preußischer Kulturbesitz, Musikabteilung mit Mendelssohn-Archiv. Mus.ms.autogr. W. A. Mozart 588 vol. 2)

the completion of the aria. If Mozart had continued on the verso in the usual
way (before adding the extra bars), one would expect to see signs of an erased
tonic chord. On the other hand, although the word 'ubbidir' in the vocal line
had been intended to end on the first note of the two extra bars on the recto, the
syllable '-dir' is in fact written over a typically Mozartean double-dash hyphen,
which shows that it was originally to have come on the verso. There is no sign of
it here in the first ordinary bar, but it does appear at the start of the first of the
two extra bars. This implies that the first pair of additional bars (extending the
range) was put in after the second. In reshaping the end of this charming aria,
Mozart, as ever sensitive to the needs of his singers on stage, incorporated an
opportunity for Bussani to flirt with the audience.

In a perceptive analysis, Goehring identifies several unusual features of this
aria.[11] An examination of the autograph and early manuscript copies confirms
that these features were under consideration during the compositional process
itself. Although there is insufficient information to construct anything more
than a provisional chronology, there are several telling indications of the issues
involved. One slightly surprising feature of the text concerns a sung aside in
which Despina observes that her doctrine appears to be having an effect on
the two sisters – a slightly optimistic reading, perhaps, of their responses so far.
Whatever reservations Mozart might once have entertained about the role of
the aside, they were evidently no longer a problem by the time of *Così*, in which
there are several examples. In such a plot it was a very useful dramatic device.
Goehring, however, pointed out that a tension exists between the rhetorical
considerations implicit in its use (best as a one-off, throw-away remark) and
musical and structural requirements which might necessitate a repetition.

Another striking feature of 'Una donna' noted by Goehring is the way that
towards its climax it quits the musical world of comic opera to embrace the
heroic style. Mozart changes the mood of the piece at the final statement of the
quatrain beginning with the line 'E qual regina': like a queen on her throne, a
woman can get her way with an 'I can' and an 'I want'. Elements of this 'heroic'
build-up include octave leaps, semiquaver anacruses and a dramatic pause. These
are followed by 'an equally grand Mannheim-style cadence and a wide ranging
vocal line'.[12] Features of the autograph score confirm that this was indeed the
direction in which Mozart was heading. In bars 74–5 he was already thinking of
an octave leap for the singer, which he decided against in favour of a more gradual build-up. Moreover, on fols. 181v and 182 which contain the climax, he ruled
out ten-stave braces (the rest of the aria has eight-stave braces) apparently in the
firm expectation of an increase in orchestral forces. As these were not in the end
required, he clarified the continuation of the existing wind instrumentation by
writing in the names of the woodwind instruments again. Having constructed a

rather serious climax in elevated style for what had started out as a delightfully light-hearted *buffo* aria, Mozart apparently felt the need to restore the original mood, which he did with the extra two-bar false start. He was entirely capable of fashioning the climax according to purely musical and dramatic criteria, but it is as likely that the aria was developed in the light of views expressed by the singer, desirous perhaps of something rather more substantial than originally planned.

A close reading of the earliest copies of this aria allows some fascinating glimpses into the workshop of the composer. Table 9 presents a hypothetical reconstruction of the various stages that the Allegretto of this aria seems to have gone through during its composer's lifetime. We can only speculate as to why the structure of this aria caused Mozart some trouble. One interesting possibility is that the stanza containing the aside was itself a late addition to the aria text. If, for example, 'Una donna' had originally been intended as Despina's Act I entrance cavatina, then its change of position to Act II might well have been accompanied with the thought that some textual addition was necessary to turn a soliloquy into an aria of persuasion. Mozart considered it more difficult to expand than abbreviate an aria.

TABLE 9  A compositional history of the Allegretto of 'Una donna'

|  | A | B | transition | A | B | climax | false start | conclusion |
|---|---|---|---|---|---|---|---|---|
| *Bar* | 21–36 | 36–44 | 44–51 | 51–66 | 66–79 | 80–7 | 87–8 | 89–99 |
| *Key* | G | D | G | G | G | G | G | G |
| *Text* | Dee in un momento | E qual regina | (Par ch'abbian) | Dee in un momento | E qual regina | Col posso e voglio | | (Par ch'abbian) |

Mozart was considering a cut from bar 36. It is marked (although later countermanded) in **V1**, and the last three quavers of bar 35 were crossed out in red crayon in preparation for it. The score **Ca** (via **V2**) also omits these three quavers. Page-break analysis of later copies showing disturbance to the orderly pattern of transmission, suggests that the cut perhaps lasted until bar 51. This would have removed the first occurrence of the climactic lines 'E qual regina ...' as well as Despina's aside ('Par ch'abbian gusto ...').

It is possible that the (temporary) loss of the aside at this point in the aria persuaded Mozart to reinstate it at the end, using what had been intended as the closing orchestral postlude to accompany Despina's exit.

For some reason, Mozart decided to reinstate the lost music, and **V1** was amended (and in part recopied), leaving only traces of the cut.

Apparently Mozart was still not satisfied with the structure of this aria. When he was making other changes associated with the **V2** version, he decided to make a different cut by removing the tonic repeat of the words 'E qual regina' (bars 66–79). This had the musical consequence of bringing forward the climax and removing Despina's *seria*-style approach to it. The disadvantage was that the text made less sense, with 'Col posso' lacking the previous lines.

By the time of the Prague production of 1791, it had been decided that this aria should be performed without cuts, as shown in the score **C1**.

## *Francesco Benucci's 'Donne mie'*

One aria almost certainly revised after consultation with its singer is 'Donne mie', the main showpiece for Benucci. The autograph suggests that Mozart took great pains to get it exactly right, as there are many small-scale alterations to instrumentation and figuration. There are other more significant changes. At a late stage its orchestration was expanded, and parts for '2 Clarini in C' and 'Timpany in C' were written above and below the ten-stave brace. There are also clear hints that its form was expanded. As he had told Raaff, Mozart was quite prepared to lengthen a piece if need be, even though this was the more difficult option. For all these reasons, 'Donne mie' makes a very good case study of how Da Ponte went about revising an aria.

The text of this rondo-form aria went through a lengthy process of refinement. One of the discarded fragments has a significant variant; the libretto text does not match that of the autograph; and the autograph text itself was amended. In Table 10 these variants are given in the order in which they probably occurred. The subdivisions follow the layout in the libretto.

The text is in *ottonario* with alternating eight-syllable lines (*piano*) and seven-syllable lines (*tronco*). There is also one pair of nine-syllable lines (*sdrucciolo*). Da Ponte began with two quatrains, followed by a pair of refrain lines, the first of which clearly links back to the first line of the aria without repeating it exactly. The refrain leads naturally into the next quatrain and this pattern is repeated. The final return of the refrain (now expanded to three lines) refers back to the opening quatrain. The punch-line is a characteristically memorable epithet. As conceived by Da Ponte, this structure was perfectly suited to a rondo-form aria: ABACADA or ABACABA. Indeed, it is quite likely that Mozart himself requested a rondo text.

There are many subtle features in Mozart's handling of the form. He reserved the first of the refrain lines for a $V^7$ pedal, enhancing the tension with patter repeats of the word 'tanti', so that when the musical return to the tonic comes, it always coincides with the second refrain line, the one containing new text and leading on to the next quatrain. This places great emphasis each time on the completion of the phrase: 'but that you do this to so many and so many'. Furthermore, because only a single line of text is allocated to the tonic, all the intermediate statements of the musical material of the rondo are very brief indeed. This imparts a powerful forward momentum to the piece, and the new keys of the episodes (subdominant, tonic minor) appear with almost breathless haste at the start of each new quatrain. The musical form of the piece is given in Table 11, which identifies the section that appears to have been added later.

TABLE 10 Variants in the text of 'Donne mie'

| Libretto (variants) | Mozart's first text (variants) | Mozart's final text |
|---|---|---|
| 1 | | Donne mie la fate a tanti |
| 2 | | Che se il ver vi deggio dir |
| 3 | | Se si lagnano gli amanti |
| 4 | | Li comincio a compatir. |
| 5 | | Io vo bene al sesso vostro, |
| 6 | | Lo sapete, ognun lo sa, |
| 7 | a voi lo mostro | Ogni giorno ve lo mostro, |
| 8 vi do marche | vi do marche | Vi do segno d'amistà. (Mozart was inconsistent, writing 'Vi do marche' twice.) |
| 9 a tanti e tanti | | Ma quel farla a tanti a tanti |
| 10 | | M'avvilisce in verità. |
| 11 | | Mille volte il brando presi |
| 12 | | Per salvar il vostro onor |
| 13 | | Mille volte vi difesi |
| 14 | | Colla bocca e più col cor. |
| 15 a tanti e tanti | | Ma quel farla a tanti a tanti |
| 16 | | È un vizietto seccator |
| 17 | | Siete vaghi, siete amabili |
| 18 | | Più tesori il ciel vi diè |
| 19 | | E le grazie vi circondano |
| 20 fino i piè | | Dalla testa fino ai piè. |
| (These lines are missing.) | Ma la fate a tanti a tanti | Ma la fate a tanti a tanti |
| | Che credibile non è, | Che credibile non è, |
| | 17 Siete vaghe siete amabili | 5 Io vo bene al sesso vostro, |
| | 20 Fino ai piè, | 7 Ve lo mostro |
| | 11 Mille volte il brando presi | 11 Mille volte il brando presi, |
| | 13 Vi difesi, | 13 Vi difesi, |
| | 18 Gran tesori il ciel vi die, | 18 Gran tesori il ciel vi die, |
| | 7 Ve lo mostro | 20 Fino ai piè. |
| 21 a tanti e tanti | | Ma la fate a tanti a tanti |
| 22 | | Che se gridano gli amanti, |
| 23 il lor perchè. | | Hanno certo un gran perchè. |

TABLE 11  The structure of 'Donne mie'

| | A | | B | A | | C | A | | D | | | added? | added? | A |
|---|---|---|---|---|---|---|---|---|---|---|---|---|---|---|---|
| *Bars* | 1 | 5 | 13 | 29 | 49 | 53 | 60 | 77 | 79 | 85 | 103 | 108 | 129 | 136 |
| | V⁷ | I | I | V | V⁷ | I | IV | V⁷ | I | I minor | V⁷ | I | V⁷ | I |
| | pedal | | | | pedal | | | pedal | | | pedal | | pedal | |

A nice touch is the varied treatment of the refrain V⁷ pedal (derived from the first bar of the piece) that re-establishes the tonic each time. In the final tonic section, there is a brief incursion of sonata-form procedure, when Mozart reuses a prominent motif from the B section (bars 41–3), transposed from the dominant to the tonic and stated twice (bars 152–4 and 158–60).

In support of this musical structure Da Ponte carefully fashioned a sophisticated pattern of rhyme. Each of the quatrains has an x–y–x–y scheme. Only the pair of lines 17 and 19 (nine-syllable *sdrucciolo* lines) breaks the mould. With each pair of refrain lines, Da Ponte matched the rhyme of the second line with lines 2 and 4 of the preceding quatrain, for example: 'Lo sapete ognun lo sa' / 'Vi do segno d'amistà' / 'M'avvilisce in verità'. Thus the rhyme scheme transcends the musical division. Although the final refrain has three lines, it too works on this principle, its final syllable '-chè' matching 'piè' which ends the previous quatrain. Overall, the text of 'Donne mie' has an elegant, precise construction, with small asymmetries.

There are signs that at some point Mozart decided to expand the aria, quite possibly at the behest of Benucci, who was no doubt anxious to have a large showcase aria for his vocal talents following the loss of 'Rivolgete' in Act I. An obvious response to any request to expand a rondo was to add in another episode, which is what Mozart apparently did. The additional text for the new section departs from Da Ponte's original structure, although the new line 'Che credibile non è' adheres to the rhyme scheme. An entirely new technique is introduced with lines from the episodes being recapitulated, full lines alternating with half lines. This was exactly how the last aria written for Benucci by Mozart and Da Ponte, the magnificent 'Aprite' in *Figaro*, had been structured. Its technique of fragmenting and telescoping previously heard text sets up an intense drive towards the final section. It may be that Mozart, possibly even at Benucci's suggestion, had this piece directly in mind, and that he was hoping to recapture something of its exciting climax. Da Ponte may not himself have come up with the first version of the extra text, because it is something of a jumble. There were several problems. First, the lines were not recapitulated in order. Secondly, one of the lines chosen was one of the nine-syllable (*sdrucciolo*) lines, the distinctive rhythm of which comes across best as one of a balancing pair. Thirdly, the fact

that the new text ended with the word 'mostro' contradicts Da Ponte's carefully worked-out rhyme scheme. The revised version cleverly solved all these
problems at a stroke, placing the lines in order, cutting out the nine-syllable line
altogether, and ending with the word 'piè'. The impression left by this piece of
additional text is that it was hastily concocted during the heat of composition,
and was only later polished by Da Ponte. It is therefore possible that Mozart or
even Benucci himself could have come up with the one entirely new line 'Che
credibile non è'. It is a punchy epithet of the kind that this singer excelled in
delivering. When the revised version of the extra text was put in the autograph,
Mozart found that he had to alter several line endings in the music to cope with
a different number of syllables, for example, replacing 'amabili' with 'vostro'.

Mozart's task in expanding his musical setting was considerably eased by two
factors: the rondo form of the aria, and its intensely concentrated motivic language. A possible choice of tonality for the added episode would have been the
subdominant. This would have resulted in a tonal structure: tonic – dominant –
tonic – subdominant – tonic – tonic minor – tonic – subdominant – tonic. An
added advantage of the subdominant is that it would allow a further (and balancing) incursion of trumpets and drums, a feature very probably to the taste of
Benucci. However, Mozart chose instead to keep it in the tonic, albeit stressing
subdominant-chord triadic writing. In selecting motivic material for the new
section, Mozart decided not to make any specific references to the music of
the fragments of text in their original locations. Instead, in a clear gain for the
overall unity of the aria, he made use of the little contrapuntal working of the
semiquaver motif first heard after the opening line of the aria and then in the
first episode in the dominant but not thereafter.

A further sign that this section was added later comes in the refrain lines
which surround it. Da Ponte used the line 'Ma quel farla a tanti e tanti' as the
first line of each refrain couplet, the second line starting with a verb. But the
additional text is introduced by the line 'Ma la fate a tanti a tanti' which in its
two other occurrences (at the start and the end of the aria) is followed by 'che'.
This rather implies that it was originally intended to lead on to the end of the
piece, and the pair of lines starting 'che se gridano'. When the extra section of
text was put in, the choice was either to revise the refrain line, or to ensure that
the extra text began 'Che ...' The latter option was chosen. After the additional
episode, the line 'Ma la fate a tanti a tanti' was naturally repeated.

For evidence about earlier stages in the development of the text of 'Donne
mie', we can turn to the libretto text. It is clear that this aria was inserted late
into the libretto, because the usual linking syllable on the previous page ('Don-')
is missing. Moreover, there is space to spare after the last line, which would not
be the case if the aria had been type-set with the rest of the text. The fact that

the new text does not appear even in the revised libretto shows how close to the première all this was being worked out. Another sign of this is the fact that small copyists' numbers appear on the autograph rather than in **V1**. What we have in the libretto is probably the version of the text that immediately preceded the final one. Da Ponte perhaps knew that a substantial revision was imminent, and this may be why he did not correct the draft text, which does not match exactly that given in the autograph. A small improvement was the substitution of '... a tanti a tanti' for Da Ponte's '... a tanti e tanti' in the first refrain line. Mozart perhaps felt this gave him more flexibility in the three-, four- and five-fold repetitions of 'a tanti' that he was planning. He could be fussy about the choice of a single word. An example of this occurs in line eight: whether to refer to a sign ('segno') or a 'mark' ('marche'). In the libretto it is 'marche', but in the autograph it is first 'segno' and then 'marche' twice, as though Mozart had not fully resolved the issue in his mind. In the extra text, Mozart used 'Gran tesori' instead of 'Più tesori' in the source line. If 'Gran' was now his preferred choice, 'Più' was not corrected in the earlier location.

A still earlier version of the text of 'Donne mie' is hinted at in one of the two particella fragments. It has only a line and a half of text, but there is a variant: 'a voi lo mostro / vi dò marche d'amistà'. Although its musical style is very different, nonetheless the cadence into the dominant at 'd'amistà' matches the dominant cadence of the final version. The use of 'marche' here suggests that this was the original word and that Mozart was considering a change to 'segno' but lapsed back to 'marche' for the text repetition in his autograph. The other draft fragment has the text of the first two lines (up to 'deggio'). Already Mozart was using 'a tanti a tanti'.

An examination of the inks used for the last few pages of 'Donne mie' is unusually revealing. The changes to the inserted text are done in a fuzzy brown ink. Because this ink is rather distinctive in character, it is possible to identify further changes made with it. One short passage was altered significantly when Mozart had second thoughts about the *sotto voce* precursor to the climax. The character of the revision suggests that he wanted a more sostenuto version. His keen eye for a harmonic improvement is also evident in the replacement of the rather fussy original with a bolder cadence, and the dull melodic ending was also enlivened. (Example 4.) Again one senses a distinct acknowledgement of 'Aprite', which similarly has a hushed precursor to its final cadence.

Mozart's practice of leaving the ending of an aria in abeyance is shown with particular clarity in this particella. He seems to have stopped writing in bar 163. What follows is Benucci's resounding climax, the bass line of which (bars 164–70) was copied in the fuzzy brown ink, probably around the time that the preceding textual and musical revisions were done. Only then was the

EX. 4 Mozart's revision of the quiet pre-climax passage in 'Donne mie' (bars 155–8) was more direct, both melodically and harmonically.

concluding orchestral postlude put in. Its particella seems to be in a third ink, rather blacker in colour. From the point of view of the study of compositional process, it seems evident that the moment when Mozart 'rounded off' an aria was a significant one. Through the careful shaping of climax, he was able to achieve an appropriate sense of closure, and in this he was very much acting in the interests of his singers. For the performer on stage, ending on the right note was something that mattered very much.

The nature of these changes allows us a rare glimpse of the collaboration between Mozart and one of his most admired interpreters. It is not hard to imagine a preliminary run through using an incomplete particella. If by then Benucci's showpiece Act I aria had already been replaced with the lightweight 'Non siate ritrosi', he would have had good reason to argue for a bigger piece, to request the addition of trumpets and drums, or to consider carefully how the *sotto voce* statements of 'un gran perchè' would work best. Mozart would have taken very seriously any change suggested by an artist of his stature, especially as he was now in danger of having nothing with which to recapture his run-away success in 'Non più andrai'.

# [ 3 ]
## Refining the Musical Text

ALTHOUGH there are relatively few major structural alterations in the autograph of *Così fan tutte*, there are numerous examples of small-scale changes which Mozart made as he polished his work. These included revisions made to enhance the dramatic effectiveness of the score as well as the purely musical detail of figuration and orchestration.

### The Musical Representation of Drama

Mozart's concern with the effectiveness of the stage action in his operas is very apparent in his letters about *Idomeneo*. Once the structure of the plot, its detailed working out and the text itself had been agreed to his satisfaction, he set himself the objective of ensuring that his score enhanced the on-stage drama as effectively as possible. A significant category of revisions in the autograph score illustrate the musical dramatist at work.

One of the most powerful mechanisms for the musical expression of on-stage drama was the recall of which there are several well-known examples in the earlier Da Ponte operas.[1] In introducing a musical recall to his score, Mozart's aim was instant recognition, almost always with a clear dramatic purpose in mind. The chorus 'Bella vita militar' sung as the two officers depart is recalled towards the end of the opera, where the repeat of its military strains shocks the two sisters by heralding the imminent return of their betrayed lovers. There are some indications that the decision to have this chorus performed twice in its original location was made at a late stage. Mozart indicated its repeat after the quintet 'Di scrivermi' with the instruction 'attacca il coro', the result of which, as noted in the *NMA*, is a 5/4 bar.[2] The wording of this rubric, however, leaves some uncertainty as to whether the repeat of the chorus should be preceded by the twenty-five bar instrumental introduction heard on its first appearance. The additional words 'da capo' suggest the inclusion of the orchestral introduction, but these were smudged out. An assistant attempted to clarify matters with the further instruction: 'NB qui si ripete il coro bella vita militar', but again this left open the possibility that the repeat should omit the orchestral passage. In V1 there is much confusion at this point. A copyist wrote out the wind introduction followed by the chorus, but this introduction was apparently cut and reinstated several times. Later copies usually omit it.

An intervention to ensure memorability is also seen in the third of the three musical recalls at the climax of the Act II finale. Ferrando and Guglielmo seek to embarrass Despina (who is still ignorant of their real identities) by recalling her 'magnetic' music in Act I. At a late stage, after the copyist of **V1** had done the Act I finale, Mozart apparently decided that the recall would be more effective if it were to be elaborated in its original location. The passage of six bars accompanying Despina's mesmeric ministrations with a trill in the string orchestra was repeated in a still more overtly comedic version for wind instruments. Mozart himself noted the place with an NB sign, and an assistant copied it out. In **V1** an added leaf was inserted only after the small bar-count numbers for the finale had been put in. When this moment was recalled in the Act II finale, it was with a single statement of the six-bar trill passage (bars 513–18), accompanied by both strings and wind. Mozart could simply have added wind instruments to the original location in Act I, which would have produced a better match of sonorities, but he chose instead a repetition. The guiding principle was memorability. The recall could be fleeting, provided that the original was well enough established in the memory. In this case the result is conceptually precise and instantly recognisable, although the scoring and indeed the time signature are different. A secondary reason for the addition, as pointed out in the *NMA*, could have been that Dorotea Bussani required more time on stage to burlesque her duties as a magnetic doctor.[3]

An interesting example of the use of a textual recall in a recitative occurs late in Act II when in 'Ah poveretto me!' Ferrando recollects with pointed irony Guglielmo's earlier boast about superiority. Mozart seems to have decided that the reference back to the earlier material was too brief. In the revised version of the libretto an additional line of recall was added ('un poco di più merto'), just to reinforce the connection. However, even with this additional line, not everyone thought that the reference worked. In the early Bohemian score **D1**, produced for the Dresden première in 1791, this whole passage was cut.

The provision of the right amount of instrumental music to accompany on-stage actions sometimes necessitated a musical extension or even an extra section. In a letter dated 3 January 1781, Mozart discussed several such additions to *Idomeneo* needed for reasons of stagecraft.[4] Uncertainty over the length of time that characters might need to make an exit was another reason for leaving the precise length of an orchestral postlude undecided until late on. The trio 'Una bella serenata' seems a case in point. The extension to the ending of this piece required the addition of an extra sheet, which was put in too late for it to be incorporated into the long bifoliation sequence. The original particella ended with the conclusion of the vocal lines, at which point the three men leave the stage. In an ink unlike that of the rest of the particella, Mozart completed six more bars, using up the space remaining on the originally allocated sheets. There was apparently a further break here, because he resumed copying the particella of the final eight bars (on the extra sheet) in another ink again. The addition of this relatively long postlude might well have been occasioned by requirements on stage. Tyson cites a similar example in *Don Giovanni*, a very late extension to Zerlina's aria 'Vedrai carino'.[5] In general the composer seems to have made a regular practice of delaying the completion of the orchestral postlude. Another example is the last seven bars of 'Alla bella Despinetta'.

Scenes involving a chorus were especially liable to be extended to allow additional time for the stage action to be completed. It was usually possible to repeat material already composed. An interesting case is the Act II chorus 'Secondate', about which someone associated with the first performances, perhaps even Mozart himself, had a significant change of mind. This rethink may well have been occasioned by considerations other than those of stagecraft, but one consequence was to increase the amount of time the chorus was on stage. The autograph is lost, but the piece appears in **V1**, where Tyson noted that there is an additional section of music. This was apparently crossed out at a very early stage, because it appears in no other source.[6] There are good reasons for believing that this abandoned segment of music had once been intended as a ritornello to the chorus rather than as an extension to the introduction to the duet, and that it was wrongly incorporated in **V1** and then crossed out.

The autograph itself suggests that Mozart had a change of mind, because at the end of the previous recitative he first wrote 'Segue scena IV / coro' and only subsequently added 'Duetto con'. It is likely then that 'Secondate' was originally conceived as a short chorus with an instrumental ritornello, rather like 'Bella vita militar'. Musically, the cancelled section in **V1** does indeed match the chorus with its distinctive ending cadence. At some point Mozart apparently took the decision to expand the chorus by starting it with a duet version for the two officers. This was either newly composed, or else it was previously a duet version for the male members of the chorus. Either way, the lateness of the decision to have the two officers sing this serenade seems to be confirmed in **V1**, in which the copyist originally drew up a nine-stave brace for two clarinets, two bassoons, two horns (on one staff) and the four chorus parts. Only later did someone add in a very much smaller hand the names 'Ferrando' and 'Guglielmo' below the original chorus part labels for tenor and bass. It is more than likely that the original chorus lacked flutes and that when the structure of the piece was expanded, these were added in to change the sonority at the entry of the full chorus. The very late inclusion of Ferrando and Guglielmo in this piece might go some way towards explaining why its text seems slightly strange coming from them. In some ways, a chorus imploring the friendly breezes to carry their feelings to their loved ones might seem more appropriate if sung by or on behalf of the two sisters.[7]

A less welcome by-product of this revision was that it left the stage instructions in this part of the opera in a rather confused state. The libretto is unclear as to whether Fiordiligi and Dorabella should be on stage to hear this lyrical offering. Both they and Don Alfonso ostensibly leave at the end of Scene III according to the stage direction 'partono' (which is not, however, in the autograph), but the stage direction for Scene IV mentions only the two officers and Despina. It quickly becomes clear from a subsequent internal stage direction that Don Alfonso and the two sisters are part of this scene. A slight uncertainty remains as to whether they should enter at that moment (i.e. after the chorus) or whether they should be present to hear the two officers sing 'Secondate'. In the stage direction for the officers there is an apparent reference to the cut passage of music, the chorus ritornello: 'Nel tempo del ritornello di questo coro, Ferrando e Guilelmo scendono con catene di fiori'. Some early productions of the opera attempted to sort out this legacy of confusion, in one instance by having the sisters disembark.

Late changes to the form of this piece would certainly be sufficient to explain the uncertainty over its structure in **V1**. Another possibility is that Mozart entrusted an assistant with the task of putting this piece into its final form. Although this music is unquestionably authentic with its rich orchestration and beautiful harmonisation, there is, as it stands, a looseness in its structure, with different endings to the various occurrences of the second part of the A section. Moreover, as the editors of *NMA* noted, bars 33–4 (in the cut section) are corrupt.[8] Edge agreed that bar 34 was incorrect, and he suggested an alternative reading for it, while arguing that 'the difficulty of finding a fully satisfactory solution that could plausibly reflect what was in the copyist's *Vorlage* ... may in itself be taken as evidence against Mozart's authorship of these measures'.[9] It is conceivable that an assistant, working from materials supplied by Mozart, misunderstood the structure of the piece by incorporating the chorus ritornello in the introduction. This section should probably be omitted in modern performances. If it is included, it should come as shown in Table 12 after the chorus. Probably the only justification for including it is the possible reference

TABLE 12 The structure of 'Secondate'

| | A | A1 | B | A | C | A2 | A3 | ritornello |
|---|---|---|---|---|---|---|---|---|
| *Bars* | 1–8 | 9–16 | 17–24 | 38–45 | 46–61 | 62–71 | 72–84 | 25–37 |
| | I–V | I–I | V–V7 | I–V | V–V | I–I | I–I | I–I |
| | | | duet | duet | duet | duet | chorus | |

to it in the stage instruction accompanying the disembarkation of Ferrando and Guglielmo, although here 'ritornello' could just as easily refer to the instrumental introduction.

Some changes in the autograph score are suggestive of the care that Mozart took over the question of dramatic pacing. In finales and large ensembles, there were many opportunities for fast-moving action. Sequences of smaller ensembles, too, could have their dramatic pacing controlled through the judicious use of *segue* or *attacca* indications. When Mozart drafted the first three trios, he left open the manner in which the sequence as a whole was to be linked together by leaving the endings in abeyance. Once he was in a position to complete this sequence with the intervening recitatives, he took the opportunity to develop it into a fast-moving progression of ensembles. First he completed the last five bars of the particella of 'La mia Dorabella' (the first violin and bass lines) in a light brown ink, and wrote out the following recitative 'Fuor la spada', at the end of which comes the instruction 'attacca il Terzetto'. At the end of 'È la fede delle femmine', he had apparently been considering an accompanied recitative, as shown by the appearance of the heading 'Recitativo' in the ink of the particella. To facilitate this, he had added neither rests nor even a double bar. Having decided to continue in faster-moving simple recitative, Mozart added in the rests and the double bar, but retained the direct link. The third trio 'Una bella serenata' similarly begins as an *attacca*, and again it is clear that this decision was only made at the continuity stage. The effect of adding in these *attacca* instructions was to increase the pace of the drama.

On a small scale, Mozart could always exert some control over dramatic pacing at the start of an aria through the choice of a *segue* or an *attacca* instruction. That this was a decision to be taken with care is suggested by Ferrando's Act I aria. At the end of the previous recitative 'Si puo sapere', Mozart appears for a time to have been undecided about whether it should continue as an *attacca* or not. In the last bar he wrote Ferrando's final word 'vita' followed by crotchet and minim rests (leaving open the possibility of a *segue*). When he put in the bass part, however, he added only a crotchet on the dominant (implying that an *attacca* was under consideration). Having decided that it was indeed to be an *attacca*, he added a double bar half-way through the last bar. It is possible that the opening of the aria was changed at this point. Although the ink colours are not especially conclusive, it seems that the opening two-beat orchestral flourish might have been put in only when the orchestral postlude was done. Perhaps Mozart first envisaged a quiet start (with muted violins) following a *segue*, and added the dramatic forte flourish as an *attacca* (still with muted violins) only at the continuity stage. A move from a *segue* to an *attacca* is also seen in Act II in 'La mano a me date' and 'Donne mie'. There may well have been other factors contributing to these changes, yet the decision to choose the sharper, more urgent option, is in line with Mozart's usual way of revising.

Another clear sign of Mozart's interest in the pace of the drama on stage is the consistency with which he went for a snappier rhythm when making a change in a recitative, usually in order to facilitate a livelier rendition of the words or a sharper riposte from another character. Occasionally a whole line is replaced. In 'Amico abbiamo vinto', Mozart changed Da Ponte's classical reference 'O mio fedele Mercurio' (eleven syllables) to the sharper 'O mio fido Mercurio' (seven syllables). Undoubtedly the most interesting case of this kind occurs in 'Di scrivermi'. Don Alfonso was originally to have entered with his aside ('Io crepo se non rido') on the last crotchet of bar 4 in the halting rhythm of the other voices. In an inspired piece of thinking, Mozart realised that Don Alfonso's asides needed to be more sharply characterised, and he supplied a dotted rhythm.

It is also probable that Mozart continued to look for small improvements in the libretto text even as he worked with it. From his correspondence during the composition of *Idomeneo*, it is clear that even minor details of the text were carefully considered. Matters of interest included the meaning of individual words, their accentuation, line divisions, and even, following a complaint from a singer, the number of 'i' vowels in a concluding phrase. There are examples of small-scale changes to words in each of Fiordiligi's two arias. In 'Come scoglio' Mozart crossed out 'Far che cangi questo cor' and replaced it with 'Far che cangi affetto il cor'. Twice in 'Per pietà', a small mistake indicates that the original first line of this aria could have been different. In bar 2 Mozart apparently started to write an 'm' before substituting the 'b' of 'ben mio'. Again in bar 23, he wrote 'Per pieta mi' before crossing out 'mi' and writing 'ben mio' above the staff.

Other changes point to Mozart's concern that his orchestral writing should have precision at moments of musical drama. A small but interesting example of this comes in 'Una bella serenata'. To accompany the rising wind chords in bars 46–7, Mozart originally wrote a sustained roll in the timpani, but he changed this to simple crotchets at minim intervals. The likely reason is that he did not wish to pre-empt the timpani roll in bar 49, which gives the required punch to the second bar of the orchestral trill. In 'Donne mie' he made two revisions to improve the clarity of the return of the main theme of the rondo. In bar 47 he attempted a horn entry but smudged it out, so that the horns could mark the precise moment of the return of the $V^7$ pedal. Similarly, in bar 75 his first thought was to write a sustained minim C in the bass, but this was crossed out, again to ensure a precise match between orchestration and musical structure two bars later. This search for precision produced a small change in bar 51 of 'La mano a me date', even though the difference is apparently negligible. At the particella stage, Mozart wrote 'Allegro' in the bass line at the start of the bar. When putting in the instrumentation, this was moved forward to the *forte* entry of the strings.

In late eighteenth-century style, the bass line was one element of the score liable to be treated in rather a routine fashion. Mozart, as ever, was alert to the dangers of unthinking repetition, and there are quite a few examples of small but telling changes. In bars 11–14 of 'Alla bella Despinetta' he originally repeated the bass figure from the opening of the movement but replaced it with the simple and elegant series of five quavers now in the score. In bar 29 of 'La mia Dorabella' he originally continued with the figuration of the previous bars but changed it to mark the new musical paragraph. In bars 33–4 he replaced the slurs over the pairs of crotchets with staccato marks, the better to characterise Don Alfonso's interjection. In bar 11 of 'Tutti accusan le donne', there were originally four crotchets, the first of which was later amended to a quaver followed by a rest in order to impart greater clarity to the change of direction in the orchestration.

## Wind Instrumentation

The mere fact that Mozart copied the wind parts last does not necessarily imply that the basic character of the instrumentation was not conceived as early as other fundamental elements. The composer rarely mentioned details of instrumentation in his letters, but in one telling passage in which he discussed his favourite aria for Adamberger in *Die Entführung*, he recalled with evident satisfaction how he had been able to characterise the text through the use of muted violins, a flute, and a crescendo marking.[10] Especially if a movement opened with a wind ritornello, then at least some wind instruments would be identified on the brace from the start. Nonetheless, there are many indications that Mozart sometimes refined his original choice during the later stages of composition.

Two factors limited the selection of wind instruments: one was technical, some instruments being ill-suited to certain keys; the other was conventional, particular orchestral timbres having strong associations with topics such as the military or the pastoral. Mozart was typically adventurous in his attitude to such categorisations, regarding them neither as prescriptive nor exclusive. In *Così* he extended the traditional function of the trumpet in C or D major finales and other large ensembles to include B♭ trumpets (without drums) in some aria accompaniments. In a large multi-movement work like an opera, there was also the question of sequence. A detailed overall plan seems unlikely, although common sense suggests that Mozart would normally aim for variety, avoiding, if possible, successive numbers with too similar an instrumentation, but not being overly concerned by occasional exceptions. On purely practical grounds, he would probably also need to avoid the over-use of brass instruments in successive movements.

Table 13 shows a list of pieces in which there appears to have been a change of plan with regard to the wind instrumentation. Several changes were apparently made for sequential reasons, that is, to avoid successive numbers with identical or very similar orchestral timbres. A good example is the Act II duet for the sisters. Mozart decided initially upon '2 oboe, 2 fagotti and 2 clarini in B' for the wind instrumentation. Only later, when completing the wind scoring, did he cross out 'clarini' and add 'corni' and 'alti'. There was thus a break between the initial choice of wind instruments and the subsequent change from trumpets to horns. Perhaps the proximity of the quartet with D trumpets and Ferrando's aria with B♭ trumpets caused this change of mind. Another example is the trio 'E voi ridete?', apparently at first scored only with flutes and bassoons. The late incorporation of Benucci's replacement aria, which is in the same key and similarly scored with one flute and one bassoon, perhaps encouraged Mozart to add oboe and horn parts to the trio.

More interesting than changes made on sequential grounds are those which appear to have been made for conceptual reasons. As we have previously seen, Mozart went through several stages in transforming the unnumbered quintetto 'Di scrivermi' from an accompanied recitative to a fully concerted piece.

TABLE 13   Changes in wind instrumentation

| Item | Change |
| --- | --- |
| Act I | |
| Di scrivermi | Parts for two clarinets and two bassoons were added at a later stage to what had apparently been intended as a string accompaniment. |
| Alla bella Despinetta | Two clarinet parts were added to the score of the first section, when Mozart began writing out the 3/4 section. |
| Rivolgete | Two horn parts were composed until bar 134, but then crossed out. |
| E voi ridete? | Two oboe and two horn parts were added to the original scoring. |
| Act II | |
| Una donna | Mozart considered increasing the wind instrumentation from bar 70, but decided not to do so. |
| Prenderò quel brunettino | Two 'corni alti in B' were substituted for two 'clarini in B'. |
| Ah lo veggio | A part for second bassoon was envisaged but not composed. |
| Donne mie | Parts for two trumpets and drums were added. |
| Tradito | Parts for two oboes were added. |
| È amore | The string bass line was removed from the wind theme, and parts were added for two oboes. |

The change of identity was finally sealed with the addition of sonorous lines for pairs of clarinets and bassoons. These are in a different ink and were copied later than the string and vocal lines, which were themselves done quite late. In **V1** 'Di scrivermi' was first copied with string accompaniment only. The copyist then added the bassoon parts on the blank staff *above* the score, possibly implying that Mozart had decided upon the addition of bassoons first. When clarinets were also added, the copyist did not use the two blank staves below the score, but put them on a separate sheet.

A significant and perhaps quite late change of instrumentation occurs in Dorabella's Act II aria 'È amore'. The most obvious sign of a change of plan here is the removal of the string bass line from the wind ritornellos, as shown in Table 14.

With the possible exception of bars 19–31, the bass line was copied in a dark ink in the particella up until the final vocal refrain and the orchestral conclusion which were added later in a lighter brown ink resembling that used to copy the string parts. At some point Mozart decided to change the instrumentation. The ritornello passages now scored for wind instruments alone originally had a string bass line. This was crossed out on each occurrence. (Fig. 5.) Apparently some consideration was given to leaving in the cellos. The instruction 'senza basso' in bar 10 was accompanied by the addition of rests below the staff for the double bass part. In the end, however, another assistant added the word 'tacet', removing all the string bass instruments. For some reason the note-heads in the passages in the bass line to be left in the score were enlarged. This feature also occurs in the bass line in the overture and in the replacement for the canon

TABLE 14 Alterations to the bass line in 'È amore'

| Bars | Dark ink | Light brown ink | Noteheads enlarged | Rests added | Bass part deleted | Added instructions (1) | (2) |
|---|---|---|---|---|---|---|---|
| 1–9 | | | | | | | |
| 10–18 | ✓ | | | ✓ | ✓ | senza basso | tacet |
| 19–31 | | ✓ ? | ✓ | | | | bassi |
| 32–40 | ✓ | | | ✓ | ✓ | senza basso | tacet |
| 41–62 | ✓ | | ✓ | | | | |
| 63–71 | ✓ | | | ✓ | ✓ | senza basso | tacet |
| 72–97 | ✓ | | ✓ | | | | |
| 98–106 | ✓ (98) | ✓ (99→) | | ✓ | ✓ | senza basso | tacet |
| 107–12 | | ✓ | ✓ | | | | bassi |

FIG. 5 The autograph of *Così fan tutte*, Act II (Mus. ms. Autogr. W. A. Mozart 588, vol. 2, fol. 250v), Staatsbibliothek zu Berlin, Preußischer Kulturbesitz, Musikabteilung mit Mendelssohn Archiv, 'È amore' (bars 10–13), detail. The string bass was removed from the wind ritornello passages in this aria. (Staatsbibliothek zu Berlin – Preußischer Kulturbesitz, Musikabteilung mit Mendelssohn-Archiv. Mus.ms.autogr. W. A. Mozart 588 vol. 2)

quartet in the Act II finale, both probably among the last items to be composed. A plausible explanation might be that the note-heads were enlarged for the practical purpose of allowing a string bass player to read off the score at a rehearsal, the requisite part not yet having been copied.[11]

The alterations to the bass line are very obvious, but there are subtler features of the copying process that shed further light on Mozart's changing intentions. At the start of the aria, Mozart drew the opening twelve-stave brace and listed the violins, viola, flute, clarinets in B♭ (on two staves), Dorabella, the bass line, and perhaps he also added the 'Allegretto vivace' over the singer's line. There were at this stage four free staves. The particella is very clear up to bar 98, with only very fragmentary indications in the other parts, for example, the flute theme in bars 17–18 and the first violin theme in bars 80–1. However, there is no clear sign of a particella on the first side (fol. 250), largely because there is no material for voice or bass. It is possible that the first clarinet melody represents the particella on this page, but another feature suggests that Mozart could have left the page blank apart from the brace and part names. This is the fact that a single B♭ quaver appears at the start of Dorabella's part, which was immediately smudged out, and (perhaps later) overwritten with a rest. It seems that Mozart had some previous intention of beginning this aria directly with the singer, but then decided upon an instrumental introduction, and moved on nine bars to start the particella with the vocal entry, leaving the first side to be filled in later. It is therefore far from certain what instrumentation Mozart originally had in mind for this introduction. The particella of the first statement of the theme by Dorabella had the vocal line and the bass part (before it was crossed out) with the flute's melodic doubling in bars 17–18. A texture with wind ensemble and string bass is possible, but it is as likely that Mozart was not yet thinking of this style of orchestral sound for the main theme. In the next section (bars 19–31) it appears that he wrote nothing in the bass line during the particella stage. Although it is particularly difficult to tell because of the subsequent enlargement of the note-heads, it looks as though the bass line was done in a light brown ink. Mozart could thus have been intending the arrival of the dominant to be marked with wind instrumentation, with the bass of the harmony in the bassoons or horns, an entirely normal procedure. If so, this adds weight to the idea that he fully developed his conception of the instrumentation (with wind sonority marking the ritornello theme) only after the particella had been started. Another sign that the first page could have been left blank is a small slip in the copying of the clarinet melody. The melody itself falls into two phrases: the upbeat to the first phrase is Bb; the upbeat to the second phrase (over a V$^7$ chord) is F. In subsequent returns of the main theme, however, Mozart was sometimes obliged to write the upbeat of the first phrase as an F or a C (because the note came over a V$^7$ chord). When he started to write the clarinet part at the beginning, he accidentally put in an F, but he crossed it out and replaced with the correct Bb.

One further slip on the opening page calls for an explanation. When Mozart wrote a pause in any part, he would usually add one to all the other parts, even those in the middle of a long rest. This was necessary for practical reasons to identify for the orchestral players those moments when added embellishments were expected. In bar 7 (the repetition of 'La pace' in the vocal statement of the theme) he added the appropriate rests and pause signs in the string parts. In the bass part alone, he wrote a similar set of rests with a pause in the next bar, but then smudged it out. This would seem a very simple error, one which might suggest that Mozart copied the pause in the bass line before the clarinet melody was there and simply mistook the bar, but a surprising addition at the end of fol. 250v suggests that there may be more to it than that. The first bar of fol. 251 contains the particella of bar 17 with the flute melody, but for some reason Mozart crossed it out (and a copyist added further heavy crossing out). Later, he decided to restore the bar, but did so not by countermanding the crossing out, but by squeezing the same bar in at the end of fol. 250v. This was done in the lighter brown ink of the orchestration, and significantly it omits the string bass line, which clearly demonstrates that it was Mozart himself who decided to cut this from the ritornello sections. Yet the original reason for crossing out what is a very necessary bar seems obscure. There is no apparent copying break, and no attempt to cut the equivalent bar was made in any subsequent statement of the ritornello. A hypothetical explanation might be that, when returning to complete the particella, Mozart briefly considered the idea of repeating bar 7, perhaps as an echo effect of 'la pace' in typical *buffo* manner, but quickly decided against it. An example of the insertion of an echo effect into an already drafted piece can be seen in a sketch for 'Torna la pace' from *Idomeneo*.[12]

Pure wind sonority provided Mozart with some memorable soundscapes, but on several occasions he apparently had second thoughts and added a string bass line. It is possible that this was done after a preliminary rehearsal in which greater support was found to be necessary for one or more of the singers. The decision to add a cello line to the wind instruments in the middle section of 'Alla bella Despinetta' (bars 82–103) was a late one. Similar late reinforcement is seen in 'Soave sia il vento', where the cellos were added to the bassoon line doubling Don Alfonso in bars 28–30. Bussani was not so strong a singer as Benucci, and the reinforcement of his line could have been a pragmatic decision.

A question about which Mozart often had second thoughts was whether to score for oboes or clarinets or to use both pairs of instruments. In view of the strikingly original form of Ferrando's cavatina 'Tradito' and the part played by wind scoring in articulating its structure, it is interesting to see that Mozart did not allocate any space for '2 oboi' on the original brace. Other than in multi-movement finales (where pragmatic space considerations determined the positioning of wind instruments on the brace), his normal practice was to note the full instrumentation at the start. In this case, however, it seems as though he was not yet anticipating the need for oboes. This could signify that he had not yet planned (or at least fully conceptualised) the C major concluding section, which is beautifully characterised by the substitution of oboes for clarinets. A bar before the C major key signature, Mozart wrote '2 oboi' but then smudged it out, writing 'oboe' above each of the two staves hitherto used for the two clarinet parts. This reflects his decision to exclude the clarinets for a while to achieve a distinctive change in wind sonority. When the clarinets eventually reappear before the tutti wind slurred chords, Mozart wrote '2 oboi' and '2 clarinetti' above the appropriate staves. The correct key signature for the two clarinets in the final section would have been D major, but Mozart preferred to keep it as D minor, adding accidentals where necessary.[13]

If Mozart decided to add extra wind instruments during the composition of a piece, the question always arose as to how they should be integrated into the first part of the score. The sestetto 'Alla bella Despinetta' provides a case in point. Only when starting work on the 3/4 Allegro (probably after a significant break in composition) did Mozart decide to add clarinets. In a distinctive warm brown ink he added '2 clarinetti' at the beginning of the oboe staff and he then proceeded as follows: in bars 1–36 the existing oboe parts were shared out with the clarinets, with bars 14–22 being transferred to the new instruments; between bars 37 and 53 Mozart added new clarinet parts on the oboe staff (in the same warm brown ink); finally, from bar 54 the ink of the clarinet parts is that of the other wind parts, and from this point Mozart began to write idiomatically for them, as in the passage from bars 81 to 102.

The idea that in large multipartite ensembles Mozart sometimes backtracked to incorporate wind instruments not originally envisaged allows for the possibility that their integration into the first sections was done less completely than it would have been if the full instrumentation had been decided from the start, even that one or two tricks were missed. Again 'Alla bella Despinetta' might be a case in point. The trumpet and drum parts were not copied in the autograph, but on this occasion Mozart did not write in his customary cross-reference.[14] In the absence of an additional wind score in Mozart's own hand, the trumpet and drum parts have to be supplied from secondary sources. Their regular appearance in early copies suggests that they are probably authentic, yet the question arises as to whether the composer ever entrusted routine work of this nature to an assistant. One curious feature of 'Alla bella Despinetta' is that there is no writing for timpani in either of the first two sections, whereas two trumpets in C play throughout. It is conceivable that in the rush, timpani parts for the first section of the sestetto were somehow lost, and that Mozart was expecting a good thwack from his timpanist in bar 2.

## Polishing the Detail

The basic parameters of a movement, its key and time signature were decided before Mozart began writing, and were not often changed thereafter. There are occasional examples of a rethink. An earlier fragment of the start of 'Donne mie' was drafted with a time signature of ₵. In the autograph score, Mozart actually wrote ₵ at the start of the autograph particella on the part of Guglielmo and the bass line, before smudging it out and replacing it with 2/4. He appears to have changed his mind at the very moment of starting to write. Another example is 'Il core vi dono'. In the bass line and both voice parts, Mozart originally entered 3/4 which he then amended to 3/8. In this case the explanation may be that the first few bars of the duet were used as a recall in the Act II finale in 3/8. It is conceivable that he changed the time signature at the start of 'Il core vi dono' to align it more closely with the recalled material.

Tempo designations (put in at varying stages in the compositional process) were perhaps more commonly changed, usually the result of a wider structural rethink. At the particella stage of 'Alla bella Despinetta' Mozart crossed out the word 'assai' from his original choice 'Allegro assai' at the start of the 3/4 section, doubtless because there was now to be an 'Allegro molto' for the final section.

Here the addition of the word 'molto' to the existing 'Allegro' in the bass part is very clear. The alteration had been done by the time that Mozart added the string parts. (A sign of the uncertainty is that these tempo designations were put into **V1** in three different hands.) Another example is to be found in 'Come scoglio'. The final section was originally to have been 'Allegro'. The modifying term 'più' was added later, again before the instrumentation was done.

If Mozart decided to change the key of a piece after starting to write it, he would, of course, begin again. The only remaining evidence might be the survival of a fragment or sketch in a different key. An intriguing case is Ferrando's 'Ah lo veggio' which is in B♭. The opening also exists as a fragment for clarinet quintet in A major. In view of the exceptionally high tessitura of the aria, the possibility of an upwards transposition of a semitone must be considered.

Much has been made of Mozart's 'wrong' key signatures during the course of multi-section movements, but there is little justification for elaborate theories of symbolism. Two factors diminish the significance of these unorthodox signatures. First, it is easy to overlook the fact that Mozart's practice was not to rewrite the key signature on every new page. He therefore lacked the constant visual reminder of the key, that might have provoked him into changing the signature more often. Secondly, his habitual practice of beginning with a particella meant that he would not yet have been bothered by the need to enter large numbers of accidentals. In both respects, a modern score provides a very misleading representation of the original autograph in its early stages. A well-known case is the first section of Scene XV in the Act I finale (bars 62–137), written throughout in the key signature of one sharp, even though the keys include B♭ major.[15] In the Act II finale, Mozart used a B♭ key signature for a lengthy period, during which there are many key changes: B♭ major, E♭ major, C minor, B♭ major, D minor, F major, C major. By the time that he reached the F major section (Guglielmo's 3/8 recall) Mozart was adding in flats to the note B as though the key signature had none. Only after the recall of the magnetic music did he finally put in a new signature (A minor).

One measure of Mozart's essential fluency in opera composition is the rarity of harmonic or contrapuntal changes. In bar 46 of 'In uomini' Mozart rethought a $V^9$ chord. His original ascending arpeggio for Despina implied such a chord, but he then decided upon the simpler $V^7$ chord. Part-writing in an *opera buffa* was only exceptionally as elaborate as that which might be found in a string quartet or quintet. On the rare occasions when complex polyphony was needed (such as the canon quartet in the Act II finale) Mozart would make preliminary sketches.[16] The autograph score of *Così* contains few changes made for reasons of part-writing. In bar 4 of 'Una donna' he eliminated a small infelicity in the viola line, which would have produced parallel fifths with the bassoon, while in

'Donne mie' he smudged out a G♯ in the second oboe in bar 72 which was about to result in a parallel octave with the bass line. That there are so few such corrections is testimony to his fluency in part writing. One contrapuntal choice to be made in the case of a sustained, richly orchestrated V⁷ chord was whether to have pairs of wind instruments moving in parallel thirds or in contrary motion. In bars 79–86 of 'Il core vi dono' Mozart changed his mind and scored the bassoons in contrary motion against the clarinets.

One of the great mysteries of musical composition is melodic memorability: why, out of ten thousand eighteenth-century themes based on the simple arpeggio, is that of *Eine kleine Nachtmusik* so instantly memorable? A moment's thought suggests that memorability is a function of all aspects of a tune, including its rhythm, dynamics, articulation and orchestration. Moreover, once heard, we clearly remember the four-note motto of Beethoven's Fifth Symphony, not just for its own qualities, but as an encapsulation of a much greater whole. Mozart clearly had the gift of writing tunes which everyone could whistle in the street, and so it is particularly interesting to observe places where he appears to have been dissatisfied with what he first wrote. It is likely that he had the melodic theme in his head before starting work on any particella, as there is certainly no sign of wholesale reworking, but in the process of making a draft and then returning twice to fill in the strings and the wind parts, he at least provided himself with an occasion for a rethink of the detail. To judge by some of the minor amendments made at this stage, Mozart had the very useful gift of being able to spot a seemingly trivial weakness in the detail. He was even willing to rethink the first note(s) of a melody if necessary. The upbeat to 'Una donna' seems to have been copied first as two semiquavers, though this is not entirely clear. The quavers are more measured. A more significant example is in bar 67 of 'Per pietà', where the phrase originally descended only to B, a weaker melodic shape than the note one tone lower that replaced it. Exploitation of the singer's strong lower register could have been a factor.

There are indications that Mozart thought with particular care about small sequential phrases within a melody or the two balancing halves of a melody. The question was in what circumstances exact repetition was the most expressive option, and when variation would serve that purpose better. In 'Per pietà', Mozart altered the end of Fiordiligi's phrase 'oh Dio, sarà', substituting a B♮ for the original E. Perhaps in this case it seemed fussy not to repeat the fall back down to the B. In the third repetition of Dorabella's hesitant opening phrase in 'Il core vi dono', Mozart first varied the pattern by writing a B♭ as the last note of bar 13, later choosing the more exact repetition E. On occasion Mozart changed the final note of a phrase to achieve a more dynamic continuation into the next phrase. In bar 47 of 'Come scoglio', for example, he replaced Fiordiligi's

F with a C to connect with the continuation. Precision was as much a consideration in Mozartean melody as in other aspects of his compositional style. He removed the appoggiatura in bar 61 of 'Ah guarda sorella' from the final statement of the words 'che alletta', in order to signal with exactitude the dramatic incursion of the dotted figuration. The fact that Mozart first wrote a 'sighing' appoggiatura and then removed it – he did the same at the end of the Act II canon – tells against the idea that this feature should be unthinkingly added to any such context where it is not given.[17] This concern with dramatic precision is seen on a slightly larger scale in the well-known revision in the quartet in *Idomeneo*, in which Mozart seemed worried that the transitions to the D♭ and C♭ sections were rather laboured as they stood. Both passages were reworked, but the crucial change was the omission of what had been the last bar of each transition, allowing a direct and exceedingly dramatic cadence into the new key.[18]

Undoubtedly the most interesting melodic revisions are those made in the duet 'Fra gli amplessi'. The start of Ferrando's 'Volgi a me' is the only example in this opera of a substantial change to melodic identity after the particella stage. (Fig. 6.) The original version seems altogether less effective, rather hesitant in character. Mozart did not make the changes until he had added in the first violin line which doubles the singer's melody. The revision turns an undistinguished first draft into a gloriously flowing musical assault on Fiordiligi's integrity. (Example 5.) A telling example of Mozart's flair for spotting where a small

FIG. 6 The autograph of *Così fan tutte*, Act II (Mus. ms. Autogr. W. A. Mozart 588, vol. 2, fol. 266v), Staatsbibliothek zu Berlin, Preußischer Kulturbesitz, Musikabteilung mit Mendelssohn Archiv, 'Fra gli amplessi' (bars 76–9), detail. At the start of Ferrando's 'Volgi a me', Mozart made unusually substantial revisions to the melodic character of the vocal line. (Staatsbibliothek zu Berlin – Preußischer Kulturbesitz, Musikabteilung mit Mendelssohn-Archiv. Mus.ms.autogr. W. A. Mozart 588 vol. 2)

EX. 5 Mozart changed the melodic character of the opening of Ferrando's theme in 'Fra gli amplessi' (bars 76–9) to an unusual extent.

detail could be changed with great gain, comes in the famous oboe melody, which soars above the orchestral texture, expressing Fiordiligi's fall from grace. This began originally with a dotted-minim E, but Mozart was inspired to add a touch of chromaticism with the quaver E♯, a highly expressive reference to a similar phrase sung previously by Ferrando. Such changes show the craftsman polishing his creation, now with a detail simplified, now with a touch of added richness.

Refinements in the detail of the orchestration are often seen. These changes are not spread randomly throughout the score: rather they appear to reflect some areas of particular interest to the composer. As a viola player himself, Mozart was at pains to get the part of this traditionally undervalued member of the string orchestra exactly right. More than most composers of the age, he acted to free the viola from its restrictive 'col basso' status. Occasionally he had to remind himself to do this. In bars 59–60 of 'Donne mie', the viola was at first 'col basso', but later the line was changed to join in the more interesting triplet semiquavers of the violins. Similarly, in bars 33–6 of 'Fra gli amplessi', the viola was changed from 'col basso' to a livelier syncopated rhythm. Another decision that often had to be made was whether to opt for a string chord spacing with the viola line high (as in Bach chorale style) or with it low down (as in the texture memorably exploited at the start of the Clarinet Quintet). In bars 84–5 of 'Donne mie', the viola line was originally an octave higher than it is now. When he added in the wind parts, Mozart chose the richer sonority with the viola an octave down. In *Così fan tutte* a texture with *divisi* violas is regularly selected. In bars 30–3 of 'Il core vi dono', the lower G was added to the viola line only when the wind instrumentation was done.

One question over which there is occasionally some uncertainty is whether the viola line should be muted or not. Typically, Mozart wrote the instruction 'sordino' over the first and second violin lines, but tended to omit it over the lower string parts. Presumably in 'Un'aura amorosa' and at the start of the Act I finale, all the strings should be muted. It is rather less clear in the case of 'Soave sia il vento', where the viola has a distinctive sostenuto line. It is interesting to see several early changes of mind over this issue in some viola parts associated with K.[19]

A question about which Mozart sometimes had second thoughts was whether to double the melodic line of an aria. In 'È amore', he briefly considered doubling the start of the vocal line in the first clarinet part. Three notes were put in before being smudged out.

By common consent 'Per pietà' is one of the most beautifully orchestrated arias in the opera, with elaborate obbligato writing for wind instruments. Several features of the autograph, the variable brace size (12 → 10 → 12 → 11), the essential unity of the ink colours, and the degree to which the replaced bars leading to the climax had already been orchestrated, point to the existence of a previous draft. Some of the refinements in the orchestration could thus have come about as he was recopying. The first significant rethink occurs in bar 13, where the *dolce* ascending semiquaver figure was originally in the flute line. By the time that he reached its third occurrence, Mozart decided to give it instead to the clarinet, and he smudged out the two entries already written on the flute staff. When the opening theme returns in bar 21 accompanied now by horns rather than violins, Mozart originally wrote a full bar's rest in the string parts at bar 22, as though the accompaniment was to continue in the wind instruments. This too was smudged out to allow for the insertion of minim rests. The result was greater fluidity of orchestral sound expressed by the more rapidly alternating wind and string fragments. An interesting change occurs in bar 29. The first bassoon originally entered this little trio only with its semiquaver figure. The first part of the bar had a minim and a crotchet rest. The addition of the quaver G♯ and the crotchet F♯ completes the harmony. A revision allowing a more effective build up to an orchestral climax is seen in bars 71–3 where Mozart first had the bassoons entering in octaves with the clarinets in bar 73. By bringing them in sooner to double the violins in bar 71, he achieved a steadier increase in the richness of the orchestral texture. A simple change in bar 79 saw Mozart filling in the note-heads of the two minims in the bass line and adding in crotchet rests. This small change gives added effect to slurred figure in the strings in the following bar. In general, the need not to pre-empt a particular articulation or dynamic level (again this concern with precision at moments of change) underlies quite a few small revisions. Finally in the third of the revised bars of the climax (bar 116), Mozart decided that the flutes should sustain their notes for two bars and a beat. The stems of the original minims were crossed out and also the minim rests, and ties were added across the bar-lines.

Another aspect of orchestration sometimes refined as the composer worked on the score is figuration. If he felt he could do better, Mozart would rewrite the figuration of an entire aria accompaniment.[20] In 'Donne mie', the intention throughout was to sustain intense forward momentum, and in several instances Mozart revised to achieve this end. In bar 20, he first wrote a minim in the second violin, but replaced this with the semiquavers which imitate the first violin figure in bar 21. In bar 28 the first violin originally had the semiquaver figure now in the second violin, but Mozart smudged it out, so that he could use the first violin to double the voice in the next bar. Alertness to the role of orchestral figuration in reinforcing dramatic character is nicely seen in bars 65–6 of 'La mano a me date'. Mozart initially placed the bass line on the beat, but after only a bar decided upon the much wittier off-beat pattern.

The nature of some of the detailed reworkings in the score suggests that the consistency of repeated passages was an issue with Mozart, and that when he noticed an inconsistency, he would sometimes make a change to standardise, yet it is very obvious that he did not systematically eliminate variant readings in the detail. A good example is his handling of the viola line in the various occurrences of a single progression in 'Donne mie'. The main cadential approach ($II^b – I^c$  $V^7 – I$) usually occurs with the viola line high (bars 24, 26, 55, 58, 81 and 110). In bar 84, however, by changing the viola to the lower register, Mozart removed the seventh from the $V^7$ chord on the last quaver and left the following chord without a third. No doubt this was to signal the transition to G minor. On a subsequent occurrence in bar 113, he started with the two low notes and then realised that there was a problem, because he took up the last two notes an octave. Meticulous craftsman though he was, Mozart was not neurotic about the achievement of total consistency. Judicious modern intervention in such cases is theoretically possible, but once an editor embarks upon this kind of improvement, it is very hard indeed to know where to draw the line.

Musicians and scholars point to certain passages in *Così fan tutte* as representing an especially high level of perfection. The lexicon of superlatives has long been exhausted.[21] It will be interesting to conclude this discussion of Mozart's working methods with a brief account of the 'finishing touches' made to two such pieces: the Act I terzettino 'Soave sia il vento' and the canon quartet 'E nel tuo, nel mio bicchiero' in the Act II finale. Although not sharply differentiated in colour, the inks used to copy the three stages of 'Soave sia il vento' are distinguishable: the string parts were added to the particella in faded ink; the wind parts were done in a slightly warmer, more focused brown. When he drafted the particella, Mozart was not anticipating the use of pizzicato in the bass line. Only when he put in the violin and viola lines did he make this inspired change, adding the final touch of perfection to the orchestral sonority. When he reached bar 28, he had second thoughts about the orchestration, deciding to double Don Alfonso's line in the cellos. All the necessary instructions, 'violoncelli', 'col arco' and 'bassi' are in the ink of the string orchestration, as is the subsequent 'pizzicato'. Another significant detail changed by Mozart is to the upbeat to bar 27 in the two sisters' lines. Fiordiligi originally had B and Dorabella D♯, arguably quite expressive leaps, but the final version is smoother. Lastly, Mozart changed the clarinet parts in bar 28 from a minim / minim rest to a semibreve tied to the following semibreve to increase the sense of timeless sostenuto.

The sketches for the canon quartet show an intensive working out of the three-part canon with fragments also of Guglielmo's interjections.²² The closest version to the autograph starts about half-way along the top of the page. In its disposition, this working matches the fourth and final statement of the canon in the finished version but without Guglielmo's interjections. A variant in the first section was not changed in subsequent workings, but one in the second was. The next brace of three staves (nothing on this page is actually ruled as a brace) together with two corrected staves below shows Mozart attempting and in some cases rejecting potential improvements. That this was a conceptual exercise at this stage seems clear from the fact that all three staves are for women's voices. Finally, a four-part version is begun, with two fragments of Guglielmo's line, but the disposition of this working is different from that of the final version, with the canon restarting in the tenor clef. This could imply that Mozart had thoughts of starting the quartet with Ferrando. Significantly, this working leads directly into what would have been the start of a fifth statement of the canon. In his autograph, Mozart started to copy such a section, but abruptly crossed out the one bar he had begun.

Small changes in the autograph score continued the process of refinement begun in these sketches. In bar 181, the four semiquavers at the start of the second section (in Fiordiligi's line) were written over something else that was scraped out. In the sketches these four semiquavers were given in several different versions. The chosen pattern appears twice in the sketches, but Mozart only selected it after trying an alternative. The autograph also gives the original version of the melodic arpeggio as descending to a low D♭ in bar 178. This was changed to an F. As in 'Soave sia il vento', Mozart chose to make the last section pizzicato, only when scoring up the piece. He had to change the final A♭ minim in the bass to a crotchet. Finally, when he crossed out the last bar leading to a further statement of the canon, he changed the sighing appoggiatura in Fiordiligi's line to a reiterated note, introducing the new mood with precision.

From all the examples discussed above, it is possible to draw some general conclusions about Mozart's working methods. The basic elements of a piece – its melody, structure, harmony and part-writing – were changed only infrequently, once a particella had been accepted. The extent to which a process of preliminary sketching preceded this moment is hard to know. The existence of two abandoned draft fragments for Guglielmo's 'Donne mie' shows that Mozart was perfectly prepared to start again and again, and the existence of several arias, apparently copied in a single sitting also points to the existence of earlier drafts too heavily corrected for actual use. There are two leaves of true sketches, both from the Act II finale. For a full-length opera, this seems a surprisingly small amount, yet such material is by nature ephemeral, and perhaps large amounts of it were immediately consigned to the bin, the paper being unusable for anything else. Even after a particella had been drafted to Mozart's general satisfaction, substantive changes could still be made, and the evidence of the *Così* autograph strongly points to the two areas in which these were most likely to occur: the fashioning of the climax of an aria, through consideration of such matters as its highest note or its last musical paragraphs; and the development of the score as the most effective possible support for the drama on stage, through changes made to ensure the memorability of recalls, to improve the dramatic pacing, or to facilitate stage exits. The most significant purely musical feature to evolve late was the wind instrumentation, and in deciding upon this, Mozart considered not only the character of the individual piece but also its place in a larger scheme. At the level of the detail, he refined his melodic lines, worked out the best figurations, improved orchestral chord spacings, and polished figurations, but there was no systematic review to achieve total consistency. If one final piece of evidence were required to show that Mozart never ceased to look for improvements, the final bars of the opera would do. Even after so much labour, the composer was still ready to improve what he evidently thought too routine an ending.

# PART II

## The 'School for Lovers': An Enigma Revealed?

# Casting the Roles

CONSIDERING the influence that the process of casting could have on an opera's reception, it is surprising that so little is known either about how it was done, or about who had responsibility for making the decisions. The theatre management under the direction of Joseph II himself (until his withdrawal from active involvement) had the final say over which singers were recruited in the first place and their salaries, but it is not clear that this overall control extended to the allocation of roles. By the time that *Così fan tutte* was being composed, Da Ponte had established a position of some influence in the company, and he later claimed that he had written this libretto specifically for Adriana Ferrarese del Bene, his mistress. But Francesco Bussani, himself a member of the cast of *Così fan tutte*, apparently also took some responsibility for casting decisions. When reorganising the theatre in the summer of 1791, the new emperor Leopold argued for the dismissal of that 'rascally intriguer' and demanded that: 'Bussani will from now on no longer have any say in the direction of the theatre or in the distribution of roles.'[1] An important context in which the casting of *Così fan tutte* took place was thus the rivalry between Da Ponte and Bussani over whose was the responsibility for allocating roles.

Some (doubtless very one-sided) glimpses of this struggle for influence are to be found in the series of memoranda that the librettist wrote following his dismissal in 1791. In one of these he singles out Bussani as his 'third adversary' ('il terzo nemico'), the first two being Salieri and Thorwart, who was involved in the financial management of the Viennese theatres. He claims that this enmity arose because he had not given Bussani prime roles when he had first come to sing in Vienna, the implication being that he (Da Ponte) had control over this. Since then, he had recruited 'La Villeneuve' and had attempted to hire 'La Casparini', both appointments being opposed by Bussani. Da Ponte asserts that the management of the opera had explicitly given to him the duty to propose performers and to contact them, but it is clear that recently the balance had been changing. Da Ponte had argued for the reinstatement of his mistress Ferrarese, while Bussani had allocated her roles to his wife Dorotea. The librettist reiterates his contemptuous view of Dorotea Bussani as singer unfit for the roles of 'la prima donna' in Vienna.

It is not clear how this long-running dispute affected the casting of *Così fan tutte*. According to Da Ponte's well-known account of the preparations for

*Figaro*, Mozart had become involved when Bussani ('inspettor del vestiario e della scena') informed Count Rosenberg that the opera was to include a ballet (the Fandango in Act III). Mozart's reaction to the news that the dance would probably have to be removed was to express a desire to 'rough up' ('strapazzar') Bussani. [2] When it came to casting decisions, Da Ponte would very likely have argued the case for his own mistress Ferrarese and his new protégé Villeneuve, while Bussani would have naturally supported the claims of his own wife. By 1791 Da Ponte was in the grip of a more general paranoia. He had now fallen out with Villeneuve, whom he accused of forgetting his earlier favours after not being allocated a role in *L'ape musicale rinnuovata*. He was apparently even in dispute with Calvesi and Benucci. In the absence of any concrete information as to what went on during the casting of *Così fan tutte*, scholars have focused on the final outcome, how the roles were suited to the singers who actually sang them. Yet there are at least hints in the original sources that the allocation of roles may not have gone smoothly, even that the casting could have been changed at some point before the première.

In the hypothesis that follows, it will be suggested that two pairs of singers were recast: that Benucci and Villeneuve were first allocated the roles of Don Alfonso and Despina, later switching to become the second pair of 'amanti'.

## *Francesco Benucci: Don Alfonso or Guglielmo?*

The problems experienced by Mozart in the run up to the première of *Così fan tutte* undoubtedly involved Benucci, the star singer of the Vienna troupe. Shortly before the first performance, he took the drastic step of cutting from the opera this singer's great set piece aria 'Rivolgete', replacing it with the charming but lightweight 'Non siate ritrosi'. Throughout his years in Vienna, Benucci had been the dominant performer in the Italian opera company. Joseph II thought him worth 'two Storaces', and Mozart quickly recognised his quality. The idea that Benucci's casting as Guglielmo caused Mozart some difficulty was developed by Heartz. In his book on the operas, he wrote:

> Guglielmo's part gave Mozart and Da Ponte more trouble than any other. Benucci, as the veteran primo buffo of the troupe and its mainstay, clearly deserved every possible consideration. Indeed, they may have been over-eager to please him and to use his great acting abilities; it is otherwise difficult to explain how Mozart's shrewd discernment about texts failed him when he permitted Da Ponte to let stand such a motley collection of oddities as the original Guglielmo aria (No. 15a), in which Da Ponte careens wildly from myth, to history, to geography, to Boiardo's *Orlando innamorato*, throwing in references to bird song and a contemporary

dancer for good measure. Mozart composed it from beginning to end and fully orchestrated it before he brought himself to admit how wrong it was where it stood. The piece is in D major with trumpets and drums – features of the impending first finale. Yet Mozart had always reserved trumpets and drums as well as the key of the finale by not using them in the immediately preceding numbers.[3]

This idea was developed further in a later essay in which Heartz suggested that Mozart's problem was that his *basso buffo* would have to take a role rather different from his accustomed one as the larger-than-life servant Figaro / Leporello:

> Mozart's mature operas each contain at least one scene or one role that was particularly difficult to compose. In *Così fan tutte* that role, surprisingly, was Guglielmo's, written for the one singer whom Mozart knew the best, and who outclassed the others in stage presence. But this was perhaps at the heart of the problem. Benucci *qua* Benucci cut such a figure as a *basso buffo* that it was no easy task to scale him down and remodel his persona into that of a Neapolitan gentleman, or ever to forget that he was the living incarnation of Figaro.[4]

The difficulty in casting the star singer of the troupe was perhaps that it was not clear whether he would be best suited to the role of Don Alfonso or Guglielmo. In some ways, the part of the old philosopher, a dominating stage presence, might have fitted him rather well. [5] If this singer was actually cast for a time as Don Alfonso, the question would then arise as to whether his famed charisma affected any aspect of the development of this role while he was in it, or conversely whether the characterisation of the role of Guglielmo was in any way muted by his late arrival. As to who might have been the original choice for the second officer, the loss of the Court Theatre records for this period hinders discussion. But perhaps the Bussani couple simply swapped with Benucci and Villeneuve. The ongoing rivalry between Da Ponte and Bussani over the control of casting decisions could have provided the context for such a switch, but there is a more pragmatic explanation: that for some reason the casting of a real-life couple as a pair of on-stage 'amanti' did not work.

A possible sign of the recasting of the bass roles could be the switching of the order of the bass lines in the early ensembles. As was suggested earlier, the first pieces to have been composed (the three opening trios) could even pre-date the casting of the opera in Vienna altogether. In these early ensembles, the line of Guglielmo appears lowest in the score. There was then a period when Mozart apparently changed the order, placing the part of Don Alfonso on the lower line. The decision to revert to the original order with Guglielmo lowest in the score was taken during the composition of 'Sento oddio', as shown by the fact that the order of the bass parts was changed by Mozart half-way through. The switch occurs thus. After the old philosopher's memorable words 'saldo amico: finem lauda!' (bar 48), Mozart wrote 'Guillelmo' and 'Don Alfonso' above the two staves, reversing the previous order. (There was little point in going back to the start of the movement to cross out and copy on the correct staff the individual lines sung by the men to that point – the issue was who should take the lower line when the two were singing together.) The names, still with the early spelling of 'Guillelmo', were added to the two following pages as well. The two men sing for a while in thirds, and then in unison from 'Ah chi mai' (bar 54). In bar 63 Mozart originally had the two men still in unison, but he changed the lower of the men's lines (at first intended for Don Alfonso) so that the singer (now Guglielmo) would sing an octave lower.

Ink evidence supports the idea that there was a break in composition at this point. The particella of the first part of the quintetto was copied in brown ink. It includes the vocal parts, the basso, some fragments of the first violin, and perhaps also some of the wind interjections. Black ink makes a dramatic appearance in bar 64 and is used in the remainder of the particella, including the vocal parts, the bass, and the final bar of the first violin part, without its first dotted quaver. The change of ink colour in the particella thus coincides with the place where the composer decided to revert to the original order of the bass lines. The implication is that the first part of this quintet represents the end of the phase in which the character of Don Alfonso was allocated to the lower line and that Mozart paused, either because he wished to consider the issue of the bass lines, or for some other reason, during which time his views on their order had changed.

If Mozart began work on *Così* before confirmation of a commission, then the early ensembles could have been composed with no particular singers in mind. The placement of Don Alfonso's as the lower of the two lines might then represent the first stage of actual casting, and the reversion to the previous order, the final casting. This would allow for the possibility that Benucci was briefly considered for the role of Don Alfonso. Evidence about the vocal tessitura of Francesco Bussani, who eventually sang Don Alfonso, is rather ambiguous, but on this occasion Mozart clearly wanted to place him above Benucci in ensembles.[6]

Any suggestion that Benucci was recast must take full account of the circumstances surrounding the loss of his aria 'Rivolgete'. It is not inconceivable that Mozart's first draft could have been for another singer altogether. The entry for this aria in the composer's catalogue 'für Benucci' is unambiguous enough, yet some shadows of suspicion perhaps remain. Heartz considered its text to stand rather outside the usual Benucci canon[7], while Rushton thought its tessitura untypical for this singer.[8]

Another way of looking at this question is to consider what Mozart might have composed for Benucci in Act I as Don Alfonso, a necessary high point, given the singer's dominant status. One intriguing answer is that it was his Act II aria 'Donne mie'. The autograph score contains a clear hint that it was not originally intended for its present location.[9] As pointed out by Tyson, the preceding *accompagnato* originally cadenced in the key of C minor with Ferrando's words 'Abbi di me pietà, dammi consiglio'. This was followed by the instruction 'segue l'aria di Guilelmo'. The layout of the page shows that this was the intended conclusion of the recitative, but on an additional leaf, Mozart then composed a new link to cadence into 'Donne mie' as an *attacca*. Tyson suggested that the original idea had been to continue with Ferrando's cavatina 'Tradito', and everything about the character of this recitative suggests that it was indeed the intended precursor of an anguished piece of this nature.[10] However, as the editors of the *NMA* point out, there is then the question as to why there is no *segue* indication for an aria for Ferrando.[11] A sign of the composer's uncertainty on this point is that when he wrote down the C minor cadence, he did not put in the minim rests or the double bar to complete the piece, even though it was a *segue*. It is as though he was anticipating that this join might require further work.

The autograph shows how 'Donne mie' was incorporated into Act II after Ferrando's *accompagnato*. Mozart first wrote ¢ time signatures on the part of Guglielmo and the bass line, which he then quickly smudged out. (There is a ¢ signature at the start of the draft fragment of the opening of this movement.) Also during this first stage, he wrote 'pia' under the bass line in bar 1. The particella stage of the opening of this movement was written in light brown ink, and it included the name 'Guilelmo', the part labels for the strings, the held bass notes, the 'Allegretto' marking, and the first violin part from bar 2. The movement was later completed in a blackish-looking ink. Only at this later stage did Mozart add the chord in bar 1 to the upper strings to make it an *attacca* from an *accompagnato*. When he did this, he overwrote the original 'pia' in bar 1 under the bass line with 'for'. The intended lead into the piece was therefore probably an *attacca* from a simple recitative, and this appears to be confirmed by one of the draft fragments which has the words 'in cadenza' at its head. When Mozart chose its final location, he needed to change it to an *attacca* from an *accompagnato*, and so string chords were added in the first bar and the dynamic was changed to *forte*.

Whatever the original continuation was going to be, it is certain that 'Donne mie' was a very late addition to this place in the opera. The piece belongs to what is virtually a sub-category of arias which address the shortcomings of women in general, but there seems no particular reason in its present position for Guglielmo to respond to Ferrando's plea for advice in such a manner. Indeed, in a recent production by John Eliot Gardiner, the singer playing Guglielmo strides dramatically off into the audience, in a striking visual demonstration of the point. Arias in which singers stand aside from the action on stage to address a general commentary to the audience, are by no means uncommon, and indeed by its very nature this is a function of the 'Donne' aria.[12] Yet there is another place in the opera where 'Donne mie' fits strikingly well as part of the plot action itself. This is the location in Act I where 'Rivolgete' was placed before being cut. In the recitative 'Ah non partite' the initial approach of the Albanian suitors is rebuffed firmly, yet Guglielmo makes one last plea to the women, lest 'the most faithful of lovers' die in front of them. This could have been the moment for Benucci as Don Alfonso to sing his first big aria, addressing the women on stage and through them women more generally. In this location, the text would have contained a pointed irony: as Albanians, the two 'amanti' have immediate grounds for complaint because of the sisters' resolute fidelity; later, as the real lovers, the problem will be the too ready infidelity of their original partners. A small but significant change to the text as given in the libretto might have resulted from this repositioning. In the libretto the last line reads: 'Hanno certo il lor perchè'. If your lovers complain, 'they for certain have *their* reason'. What in Act I could have been a direct reference to the complaints of the disguised Guglielmo and Ferrando, became in Act II a less specific statement: lovers in general have good reason ('un gran perchè') for complaint. Brown reasonably suggests that there is a deliberate reference here to Susanna's similar lines in *Figaro*: 'Se l'amano le femmine, Han certo il lor perchè'.[13] If so, then the change in 'Donne mie' takes on further significance.

'Donne mie' was certainly of an appropriate scale for Benucci's first appearance as a soloist. It has an even larger orchestration than 'Rivolgete' with flutes, oboes, clarinets, horns, trumpets and drums, and it perhaps contains a musical allusion to his earlier triumph in *Figaro*. As Heartz put it, 'Donne mie' gave an opportunity for Benucci 'to recapture the electricity' of the moment in 'Non più andrai' when he reaches the same note E (at the words 'Cherubino alla vittoria; alla gloria militar').[14] In 'Donne mie' this comes in the subdominant passage, when the trumpets and drums are suddenly introduced at the thrice repeated words 'Mille volte'.

Perhaps the most telling clue to the possibility of a connection between 'Rivolgete' and 'Donne mie' comes in the earlier of the two extant sketches for the latter. As pointed out by Heartz, it contains a figure resembling one used in 'Rivolgete' at the approach to the climactic mid-point cadences in the dominant at the phrase 'Da Vienna al Canada'.[15] In the sketch for 'Donne mie', this figure similarly heralds the arrival of the dominant. (Example 6.) It does not seem very likely that Mozart would have countenanced two arias for Benucci incorporating this same motivic element, and so the possibility that 'Donne mie' was an alternative Act I aria for Don Alfonso is a real one. One unintended consequence of any initial positioning of 'Donne mie' in Act I could have been that Benucci ended up with two arias in G major – a slightly unusual circumstance in a Mozart opera. 'Rivolgete' would have pre-empted the key of the finale, and perhaps this is why, when he had the opportunity to provide a last-minute replacement, Mozart decided against the key of D major. For the composer, avoidance of the key of the approaching finale was perhaps a more important consideration than the need to provide arias in contrasting keys for a singer.[16] Other signs of the late composition of the linking passage are that, whereas the spelling 'Guillelmo' is used at the start of 'Rivolgete', the stage direction 'ferando e guilelmo cominciano à *ridere*' uses the later spelling, and the direction 'attacca No. 16' indicates that the link was still in the opera when the arias and ensembles received their final numbering.

Another consequence of 'Rivolgete' having been brought back into *Così* at a late stage might be the rather surprising fact that it continues without a break into the next trio. Heartz has developed the interesting idea that Mozart sometimes indulged in applause management. When writing an aria for Raaff, he first fashioned an ending in which the singer 'could hope for applause'.[17] The revised version plunges straight into the following recitative. Similarly in the case of 'Rivolgete', Mozart cast it as a large scale piece, following which Benucci had every reason to expect a 'thunderous ovation', but he then seemed to want to forestall this by continuing with a short link via a $V^7$ chord into 'E voi ridete?'[18]

The musical connection between the draft of 'Donne mie' and 'Rivolgete' could thus be explained as a consequence of the recasting of Benucci. In the following hypothetical sequence, no attempt is made to guess at the character, status or location of 'Rivolgete' in any earlier form.

1   Benucci, cast as the philosopher Don Alfonso, was to have sung 'Donne mie' in the location where 'Non siate ritrosi' was eventually placed. He would have admonished the two sisters on stage (and through them women in general) about their behaviour towards men. A fragment of a particella of this is extant, suggesting an aria with a musical character close to 'Rivolgete', but with the text of 'Donne mie'.

2   When Benucci was recast as Guglielmo, Mozart and Da Ponte faced a clear choice: either to insert an aria for Guglielmo here (the same singer in a different character) or one for Don Alfonso (the same character but a different singer).

EX. 6 Excerpts from a passage in 'Rivolgete' (bars 45–58) resemble a fragment of a particella of 'Donne mie'.

Possibly they considered an aria for the new Don Alfonso (Bussani) entitled 'La mano a me date', in which he tried to encourage the two sisters to form pairs with the newly arrived Albanians.

3 The inevitable decision was made to give precedence to the star of the opera troupe, and so Mozart completed the big set-piece aria 'Rivolgete', using some melodic material from the abandoned draft of 'Donne mie'.

4 'Rivolgete' remained in the opera as a show-case for Benucci until quite close to the première. Its late removal had a range of consequences. As Guglielmo was no longer to attempt any symbolic pairing off (the most likely of the many reasons for its loss), a replacement aria, neutral on this question, was needed

and 'Non siate ritrosi' was the result. There was now a need for some moment of symbolic pairing and Don Alfonso's aria 'La mano a me date' would fulfil the function, although it would have to be expanded into an ensemble, now that actual pairings were to be effected. Benucci, now lacking a big aria, had to be provided with one in Act II, and 'Donne mie' was reworked in a style very different from that seen in the earlier particella.

This hypothetical sequence assumes one important point: that the retention of the text of 'Rivolgete' in the draft libretto (with 'Donne mie' in its place in Act II) was merely a temporary expedient, pending the composition of a replacement. In order to avoid too much disruption to the printed libretto, it was necessary that the text of 'Non siate ritrosi' be no longer than that of 'Rivolgete'. If, on the other hand, it was much shorter, it would leave a big gap. When drafting it, Da Ponte, who had control of the printing of the libretto, perhaps had space considerations in mind when he provided enough verses to fill the page. Mozart, pressed for time, simply omitted two complete stanzas.

The foregoing hypothesis could provide an explanation for several puzzling aspects of *Così fan tutte*. First is the absence of even one true aria for the commanding personality of the old philosopher, a curious omission in a tightly knit opera with its three pairs of characters and symmetrical interrelationships. The other five characters each have their ration of two, and Ferrando, indeed, has a third. With Benucci interpreting the role, Don Alfonso could have had a major aria 'Donne mie'. Its loss left this character seeking an aria, and what might have been a replacement 'La mano a me date', was itself turned into a quartet, again depriving its performer of his rightful moment as a soloist. As some compensation, Mozart composed the very short arioso, 'Vorrei dir', a late insertion into the first part of Act I, as shown by the fact that he felt it necessary to write the words of a cue at its head. This piece was composed in a clearly recognisable F minor *agitato* style, seen in one aria recently sung by Bussani himself in Paisiello's *Il barbiere*.[19] Perhaps at this late stage, Mozart wanted to be sure of something the singer could manage.

Further recompense for Don Alfonso's lack of an Act I aria was provided by short but impressive accompanied recitatives. Features of the autograph suggest that the composition of these *accompagnato* passages was done in a somewhat *ad hoc* manner. In the simple recitative 'Non son cattivo comico' the words '[d'u]more: o pove[rini]' were originally written over a semibreve F in the bass line. Mozart sharpened up the rhythm now over a minim F and crossed out the misplaced bar-line, adding a second minim C♯, in order to move the music in the direction of D minor. He briefly continued copying Don Alfonso's line on the next brace as simple recitative, but after the words 'feminar giocar cento zecchini' ('zecchini' has no notes), he crossed this out and redrew the brace for an *accompagnato*. Ink colours suggest that this was all done at one time, as does the absence of the usual indication 'Segue stromentato'. The cumulative effect of *accompagnato* passages like this was to add weight to the stage presence of the philosopher. In his memoirs Da Ponte portrayed Bussani as being hostile to him, and he had played only relatively minor roles in Mozart's earlier operas – Bartolo / Antonio in *Figaro*, and the Commendatore / Masetto in *Don Giovanni*. In addition to any responsibilities that he had in allocating the roles, he had other functions in the management of the opera, being described on one occasion as 'sopraintendente sul scenario e vestiaro'.[20] Friction with Mozart as well as Da Ponte is entirely possible. Yet for a singer in the shadow of Benucci, Don Alfonso was a major opportunity even without show-stopping arias.[21]

It should not be forgotten that Don Alfonso was to have been given an aria entitled 'La mano a me date'. Would this have been for Benucci? The autograph score contains useful clues as to how this piece came to be changed into a quartet. The previous recitative ends with a V – I cadence in D major using the whole bar, which is followed by the instruction 'Segue Aria di Don Alfonso'. This piece was thus still envisaged as an aria at the first continuity stage when the recitatives were being added in. In a lighter, warmer brown ink, Mozart later added the word 'attacca' above the *segue*, crossing out the final minim, and adding a bar-line after the preceding crotchet to make a half bar. The brace of the first side of 'La mano' is laid out as though for an aria, and it has the separate bifoliation sequence appropriate for this purpose. (Fig. 7.) It is possible to say exactly how much of this particella was barred in the first phase of copying, because Mozart had to rebar the first eight bars, about a side and a half. Bars 1–2 of the final score contain erased bar-lines at their halfway points; bars 3–8 all contain bar-lines at their halfway points crossed out in ink which clearly resembles that used to add in the word 'attacca'. When the rebarring was done, some rests had to be adjusted in the part of Don Alfonso and in the bass line. All this shows that when the link into 'La mano' was turned into an 'attacca', the piece still consisted of only eight bars of particella. This certainly leaves open the possibility that the first short draft of this aria had been begun for another location, before being adapted for this point in the opera. Other signs that 'La mano' did not start out as an ensemble include the absence of the genre title 'quartetto' and the selective insertion of stage directions in the first eight bars. These refer only to Don Alfonso's actions, and there is no reference to Despina taking Fiordiligi's hand (as she has to in the libretto). As the copying proceeded, Mozart made pragmatic decisions to cope with the additional singers. For the echoes sung by Ferrando and Guglielmo he used the staves allocated to the trumpets and the part of Don Alfonso. Later, Despina uses the trumpet staff.

FIG. 7 The autograph of *Così fan tutte*, Act II (Mus. ms. Autogr. W. A. Mozart 588, vol. 2, fol. 192), Staatsbibliothek zu Berlin, Preußischer Kulturbesitz, Musikabteilung mit Mendelssohn Archiv, 'La mano a me date' (bars 1–4), detail. While this piece was still an aria for Don Alfonso, Mozart changed it from a *segue* to an *attacca*. As there was now a chord on the first beat, he decided to rebar the opening measures, scraping or crossing out the original bar lines, which had been positioned for a half-bar start. A similar change was made to 'Bei Männern' in *Die Zauberflöte*. (Staatsbibliothek zu Berlin – Preußischer Kulturbesitz, Musikabteilung mit Mendelssohn-Archiv. Mus. ms.autogr. W. A. Mozart 588 vol. 2)

What could have led to a change of roles for Benucci? The creation of an eighteenth-century *opera buffa* began with the characters. In the early stages, the considerations were generic. Adherence to basic stereotypes would allow an opera to be repeated all over Europe with many different casts of singers. But as Da Ponte wrote in his memoirs, it was also necessary to study the individual actors when they were cast, to play to their strengths and avoid their weaknesses.[22] There must often have been a tension between these two considerations. Benucci's two previous appearances in Mozart's operas had both been in servant roles of a distinctive type. Figaro and Leporello are no mere buffoons. Although acting in the context of the aristocrat-servant partnership, both are substantial figures, easily the musical equivalents of their masters, and both take an active role in influencing the course of events. In *Così* the role that approximated closest to this was that of the philosopher, potentially a dominant character, responsible with his assistant for directing and stage-managing the deception from beginning to end. Whatever the reasons for this recasting, it left Benucci, as Heartz sensed, in as role for which he was not especially well suited.

## *The Role of Despina*

There is certainly no direct evidence to support the theory that Villeneuve was originally cast as the maid, and that Dorotea Bussani replaced her in this role, but what the sources do strongly suggest is that the role of Despina was under active revision shortly before the première.[23] A substantive change of plan occurred at the moment of her first entry. After Don Alfonso's 'Non son cattivo comico!', Mozart originally put in the instruction 'Segue scena / VIII. / Cavatina di / Despina', but he subsequently crossed out the last three words. At the top of the next page containing her first recitative 'Che vita maledetta' appear further deleted words: 'dopo la Cavatina di Despina / Scena 8va'. The original intention was thus that the maid should make her entry with a cavatina, and this was still the plan at the continuity stage when the recitatives were being put in.[24] The missing piece can hardly have been her eventual Act I aria 'In uomini' as it stands, as this is clearly cast as a response to Dorabella's tirade.[25] Her first utterance might instead have been in a conventional comic mode, lightly autobiographical, a skittish commentary on her duties, or a statement of her views on love and life. An arguable hypothesis is that the piece is not in fact missing at all, but that it was merely switched to a new location in the opera. There are only three possibilities: the main section of 'In uomini' ('Di pasta simile'), which unlike the first three lines need not be a response to Dorabella; Despina's Act II aria 'Una donna', perhaps in an abbreviated form; and Dorabella's 'È amore'.

To consider the case of 'In uomini' first, it seems that the aria was originally intended to begin with the words 'Di pasta simile', as shown by the layout in the libretto. The first three lines ('In uomini, in soldati / sperare fedeltà? / Non vi fate sentir, per carità!') were apparently intended to end the preceding recitative, but Mozart chose to blur the normally clear division between recitative and aria text conventions by beginning the aria itself with these three lines. Palaeographical evidence also suggests something unusual happened here, because the way the opening of the aria was copied represents a break with Mozart's usual practice of beginning an aria on a new bifolium. The first few bars were placed below the preceding recitative, and as a result Mozart had to situate his score lower on the page (staves 4–11) than on the subsequent leaves (staves 3–10). Despina's aria is thus the only one in the opera to start on a bifolium in the long foliation sequence.

The autograph score contains further clues to suggest how 'In uomini' came to be in this place in the opera. The piece is one of two arias in Act I (the other is the undoubtedly late 'Non siate ritrosi') that were given bifoliation numbers in red crayon, suggesting that both pieces were written out when Mozart was working on Act II, in which red crayon was used more frequently. Since the red bifoliation of 'In uomini' starts only with the 2, it is possible that there was an earlier bifolium numbered '1' with a red crayon, which was set to one side when a new opening was copied on the remaining blank side and a half of the bifolium in the main sequence numbered 26. It is clear, however, that Mozart did not simply attach a new 2/4 opening to an existing copy of the 6/8 section, because 'Di pasta simile' does not appear at the start of a page. Nonetheless, it is not unreasonable to infer that there was a change of plan here. Scrutiny of the start of 'In uomini' reveals an interesting copying break. The first section of the particella consists of about a page and a half, up to the first beat of bar 18. The ink appears to have the warm colour of the preceding recitative sequence. There was at least a short pause at this point. When Mozart resumed copying in a somewhat different ink, he turned the crotchet at the start of this bar into a quaver and then continued with the rest of the piece. An explanation for the missing red crayon '1' could therefore be that Mozart selected the usual allocation of four bifolia for an aria, numbered them 1 to 4, and then began the particella, perhaps only its opening phrase 'Di pasta simile'. When a new beginning was required, he copied the particella of the new start of the aria (an interesting hybrid between accompanied recitative and concerted style) on the ample space remaining after the end of the previous recitative, and then completed the aria on his allocation of four bifolia, abandoning the first (and now useless) original bifolium and continuing on the remaining three blank sheets, already numbered 2 to 4 in red crayon. Another possible sign that a new beginning was being grafted onto an existing opening comes in the first and second violin parts in bar 25. Both instruments originally started this bar with a crotchet and quaver rest so that they entered with the voice. Mozart overwrote this with the continuation of the sustained notes from the previous bar. It may be significant that in **V1** a new copyist took over on a new gathering at precisely bar 18 of 'In uomini'.[26]

This hypothesis focuses attention on the recitative that leads into Despina's aria. Surprisingly it begins 'Signora Dorabella, Signora Fiordiligi', as though in response to both sisters, despite the highly personal nature of the former's 'Smanie implacabili'. But perhaps this recitative was to have been Despina's first response (after her cavatina) to the tumultuous entrance of the distraught sisters. Quite naturally Despina would ask what the matter was and Dorabella and Fiordiligi would give the reason for the commotion – the departure of their lovers. With this moment postponed, a new section of recitative was needed to lead into Dorabella's aria, and this was the soliloquy 'Che vita maledetta', followed by the entry of the two sisters and Dorabella's *accompagnato* 'Ah scostati'. Other palaeographic evidence that 'Signora Dorabella' was a replacement sheet includes the fact that the ink colour of its foliation number 26 stands outside the wider sequence (as does 27 after the aria 'In uomini'). There are also significant textual variants in the version of 'Signora Dorabella' in **V1** perhaps stemming from this earlier copy.

The study of the ink colours in this part of the opera throws light upon the general reordering that took place. Mozart began Despina's recitative of self-introduction ('Che vita maledetta'), but he apparently put in only six bars. There was then a break, during which the whole passage relating to the entrance of the two sisters was worked out. Once this was finalised, the recitative sequence in warm brown ink was copied, starting at the words 'è mezz'ora' in bar 6. Dorabella's *accompagnato* and aria were integrated into the sequence, as was the following recitative, 'Signora Dorabella'.

The strength of the palaeographic evidence that 'In uomini' was integrated late into its present position does not, of course, prove that it was Despina's original entrance cavatina. Indeed, given that a general reorganisation of aria positions seems to have taken place, it is just as likely that an aria entitled 'Di pasta simile' was intended for Act II. Its text presents a view about whether men can be faithful. Despina points out the general inconstancy of the sex and the necessity for women to pay them back in the same currency. This theme is present in the recitative leading into her Act II aria, with the word 'reclutate' – go recruiting yourselves.

Perhaps, then, the maid's two arias were switched between Acts. As an Act I aria, 'Una donna' would at least have been self-introductory. Despina coquettishly lists all the seductive arts a woman of fifteen should have. While there is no direct evidence in the autograph to suggest that this aria was ever designed as Despina's entrance in Act I, we have already discussed indications that the stanza containing the aside (which turns what could have been a soliloquy into an aria performed with a view to persuading the two sisters) was causing problems.

There are clear signs in **V1** of the repositioning of 'Una donna' in Act I, notably the red crayon numbers eleven and twelve at its head, with further comments (later smudged out) which include the words 'Atto I^mo'. This change was made by Treitschke for his 1804 Vienna revival of the opera *Mädchentreue*. He decided to retain the sense of the original first line of 'In uomini' ('Unter Männern, bey Soldaten'), but then to merge this opening with the translation of 'Una donna' given in his main source text, Bretzner's *Weibertreue* of 1794. The substance of Despina's self-introduction (excluding the aside) was thus transferred into Act I. In the *Mädchentreue* score **V4** one can follow through the changes in the numbering, required to take into account the many cuts of this version. Mozart's original numbers were added first. In the case of 'Una donna', however, the numbering changes (in reverse order) are 8, 11 and 12. This suggests that the aria had been transferred to an Act I position before Treitschke's decision to do the same with it. The study of retrospective evidence from early reception history is a fascinating one, but by its very nature it is difficult to establish firm facts with any degree of certainty. Whether the switch of position for 'Una donna' stemmed from received knowledge must therefore remain an open question.

An even more radical suggestion for Despina's entrance cavatina is Dorabella's 'È amore', which was undoubtedly added only at a late stage to the score.[27] If this were so, that might indeed imply that Villeneuve had first been cast as the maid and that the aria came with her when she transferred to the part of the second sister. Her aria 'È amore' could then have functioned as an initial expression of the maid's personality and views. Link has suggested that the first words of 'È amore un ladroncello' were intended to remind the Viennese audience of the fact that as Amore in Martín y Soler's *L'arbore di Diana* Villeneuve had sung the words 'Amore è un bricconcello'.[28] Although difficult now to identify, this kind of 'in-joke' did sometimes form part of the comic repertoire of authors of *opere buffe*. In London the bass singer Morelli was the butt of an on-stage joke about his previous occupation as a footman. With 'È amore' as the maid's original entrance cavatina in Act I, a joke of the 'here-I-am-again' variety could have been intended, based on this personalised musical calling-card.

The suggestion that 'È amore' could have been intended for Villeneuve as Despina is obviously entirely speculative, yet such a casting change might shed some light on the development of the personality of the second sister. The essential neutrality of the Act I characterisation of the two sisters (their arias apart) persists at the start of Act II. Only in 'Sorella, cosa dici?' are there clear signs as to which sister will first adapt to Despina's way of thinking. Once she has surrendered to her desires, Dorabella immediately takes over Despina's role as an active advocate against fidelity, culminating in her words 'Credi, sorella, è meglio che tu ceda' ('believe me sister, you'd better give in'). Her techniques are those of the maid: the appeal to a light and frivolous philosophy, made with street-wise clichés and proverbs of a less literary cast than Don Alfonso's: 'Fra un ben certo e un incerto, C'è sempre un gran divario!' ('A bird in the hand is worth two in the bush!'); and the use of quips, to brush aside counter-arguments: 'Che domanda ridicola!' ('What a stupid question!'), 'Siam donne!' ('We're women!'). By the time that she finally sings 'È amore', her attitudes are close to those of Despina, as Brown points out: 'Having adopted Alfonso's reasoning [in the citation of a proverb in the preceding recitative], Dorabella now takes up Despina's 6/8 metre and philosophy. Her almost anatomical description – reminiscent of much earlier Italian poetry – of how Love gains entry to the soul, is interlarded with several quite licentious doubles entendres.'[19] Referring to the pastoral style of 'È amore', Goehring writes of 'Dorabella's immersion in Despina's pastoral world'.[30] It is not inconceivable that the wish to retain 'È amore' for Villeneuve as Dorabella could have acted as the catalyst in this sister's character development.

While the theory that Villeneuve switched roles must remain in the realm of hypothesis, there is an abundance of evidence in the original sources that a problem arose with the character of Despina. Shortly before the première and quite possibly for a time after it, there was a concerted attempt to tone down the spicier elements of the maid's personality. There are two possible explanations: either Mozart and Da Ponte were worried that the views expressed by Despina had exceeded the boundaries of what was acceptable (or had been informed by the censor that what they were proposing was unacceptable); or the part of the maid as written was proving troublesome or inappropriate for the singer performing it. If at least part of the problem was with the performer, that might well suggest a late casting, but it would not prove that Villeneuve had switched roles. On balance, it seems likely that the late changes to Despina's role were made at the behest of the performer rather than the censor.

It is not difficult to imagine what the problem could have been, because Dorotea Bussani, who sang Despina, was in fact married to Francesco Bussani, who was cast as Don Alfonso. The appearance on stage of two singers married to each other in real life would have added a different layer of comic potential, one ripe for exploitation but perhaps difficult to control, especially if they were to be cast as a pair of lovers. To make matters worse, Dorotea was some twenty years younger than her husband, and it could well have been this that caused her problems with the flirtatious character of the maid, who constantly urges the sisters to be on the lookout for the main chance, a rich husband. Many of the changes that affect the role of Despina seem in one way or another to be related to this issue. The first sign of the problem occurs in the autograph. One line of Despina's text in the recitative 'Che silenzio' was omitted. The maid is quizzing Don Alfonso as to whether his suitors are handsome and whether they are rich, when, in an aside, she adds that this attribute is of particular significance to her ('per me questa mi preme') – a witty line, but one that might well, from the Bussani couple's point of view, have had the audience laughing for all the wrong reasons. Both versions of the libretto have the line. Mozart at first omitted it from the autograph, but then squeezed in seven notes (without the text). On the other hand, in **V1** which was probably copied before these notes were added in, the words of the text were put in as an insert without any notes. The sources thus appear to reflect ongoing indecision as to whether or not to include this line.

Continuing problems with Despina's character next resulted in two rather pointed changes in the text between the draft and final versions of the libretto. The first of these, which comes earlier in the recitative 'Che silenzio', is the moment when Despina, cheekily replying to Don Alfonso's observation that he needs her, remarks: 'an old man like you can do nothing for a young girl like me'. It would be hard to think of anything more likely to provoke laughter at the expense of the young singer and her more experienced husband. Perhaps equally difficult for Dorotea was a remark in Despina's Act II aria that 'a young girl should know where the devil keeps his tail'. Again, it is easy to see Dorotea or Francesco objecting to the ridicule this might bring upon them. The proposed replacement is entirely anodyne. Interestingly, neither the autograph nor **V1** have the revised text, which might well mean that both these pieces had already been copied by the time that the revisions appeared in the final libretto.

These textual changes could be interpreted in a variety of ways. It is possible that having cast the Bussani couple as Despina and Don Alfonso, all concerned co-operated in developing comments designed to enhance the comic potential of the situation. This seems unlikely because of the deliberate removal of several of the more pointed lines from the final version of the libretto.[31] An obvious alternative is that Da Ponte, who in his memoirs was contemptuous of both Dorotea and Francesco Bussani, deliberately set out to poke fun at the couple, only to have them object strenuously.[32] Yet the most likely explanation is that the problem arose accidentally, following the casting process, when these quips from Despina, so telling of her personality, suddenly acquired an unwanted personal slant for the performer.

There are many further signs in **V1** of problems caused by the role of Despina. In fact no fewer than four of the five 'agreed' recitative cuts seem closely related to the character of the maid. These cuts are listed in Table 25 below. The first cut comes in the recitative 'Che silenzio'. It removes not only the controversial lines 'A una fanciulla / Un vecchio come lei non può far nulla' but also the whole of the following passage about money. By recommencing with Don Alfonso's 'Prendi', the hand-over of the bribe is still allowed, but the text makes nothing of it. Another potentially difficult line for Dorotea Bussani to have addressed to her husband, 'Ed io niente di lei' ('but I have no need of you'), was also apparently under active consideration for the axe. The second 'agreed' cut in the recitative 'Oh la saria' would have removed further embarrassing lines for the maid to have addressed to her real-life partner. Boasting of her skills, she claims to have led 'a thousand men by the nose'. She follows this with a casual enquiry about the wealth of the two men. The third 'agreed' cut occurs at the start of Act II, where Despina, with growing urgency, seeks to persuade the two sisters of the merits of being unfaithful to their absent lovers. Not far into this scene, the red crayon came out and the passage from Fiordiligi's 'Che diavolo' to her 'per Bacco' was deleted. In it, Despina advocates a light-hearted approach to love, arguing that the sisters should avoid the misfortune of those who place their trust in men. Fiordiligi retorts: 'What a devil! you'd do it yourself'. Despina replies 'I already do.' Again, this was perhaps felt too risqué for Dorotea, and another possibly difficult line follows shortly, when she refers to the possibility of being able to do 'without love' but not 'without lovers'.

The fourth cut seems not to be related to this issue. In the omitted passage Fiordiligi objects that flirting with their new suitors will get the two sisters talked about, and she wonders what Ferrando and Guglielmo will make of it. The problem here was perhaps that this idea has already been discussed in the previous scene. The fifth cut once again seems to relate to the role of Despina. The cut passage required from Dorotea Bussani the potentially embarrassing lines: 'so rarely does anything [anyone] good come along for us poor girls, that we must seize our chance when it [he] comes.'

Further cuts in **V1** were not 'agreed' but may nonetheless have been under consideration in 1790. Several of them continue the process of removing from Despina's part the racier elements of her philosophy that could have raised unwanted laughs when taken to apply to the singer's own situation. From 'Signora Dorabella' was removed a reference to making love 'like assassins' and her view that if one man dies there are many others to take his place. A cut larger than the 'agreed' cut in 'Andate là' would have removed her statement in favour of coquetry and her observation that even a maid can attract the attention of two lovers. It is easy to see that this process was steadily toning down the spicy essence of Despina's character.

Whether or not this close attention to the role of the maid was the direct result of a recasting decision must remain unproven, but there is one further hint that a change of singer could have been the reason: the repositioning of Despina's line in the score of the two finales. As noted above, her part appears to migrate downwards to a lower position, as each finale progresses.

## [ 5 ]

## *Lovers Crossed or Uncrossed?*

A<small>T THE HEART</small> of the enigma of *Così fan tutte* lie changes to the plot far more radical than those attributable to the casting of singers. As one reads through the autograph score, a number of small but quite extraordinary features catch the eye. For example, when Mozart began writing the particella of 'Rivolgete à me / lui', he apparently felt unable to enter any pronoun at all and simply left a blank, into which space another hand later added the word 'lui'. (Fig. 8.) Arguably, this pronoun is the most significant word in the opera up to this point, since it signals the pairings between the disguised suitors and the sisters. Mozart's indecision is thus amazing. In the following analysis, it will be suggested that a wide range of puzzling features in this opera stem from an attempt to overcome a deep-seated flaw in the plot, an attempt that in the end

F<small>IG.</small> 8 The autograph of *Così fan tutte*, Act I, Biblioteka Jagiellońska, Kraków, fol. 105, 'Rivolgete' (bars 1–4), detail. After writing in 'Rivolgete à' Mozart left a blank. Another person added in the word 'lui'. In his own catalogue, Mozart referred to the title as 'Rivolgete à me'. Having composed almost all of the horn parts, he decided to cut them, adding in the instruction 'corni tacciono'. (Reproduced by kind permission of the Biblioteka Jagiellońska, Kraków.)

failed to achieve the desired result and was hastily abandoned. The essence of the theory is that Mozart and Da Ponte tried to make the opera work with the disguised men seducing their own women – lovers uncrossed.

Mozart never had any doubt that the composer must be in ultimate control of the libretto for an opera. Writing of a piece by Varesco, he commented that the poet must expect to have to 'change and rearrange things as much and as often as I want'.[1] The use of the phrase 'as often' is significant. It confirms that Mozart's input into a libretto was by no means restricted to a phase of preliminary discussion with his poet. It would continue and perhaps even intensify during the period of composition and rehearsal, when problems with singers and weaknesses in the drama became evident in the theatre. His initial interest lay in the basic outline of the drama, the 'Plan des stücks', and he was quite prepared to ask a poet to provide a text for a given plan.[2] Next came the detailed plotting, the working out of the plan. There are useful pointers to Mozart's likely areas of concern in his correspondence with his father during his early career as an opera composer. He was apt to discuss matters such as the timing of entrances, the credibility and coherence of individual actions, and, displaying a doubtless well-justified anxiety about the boredom threshold of the audience, how long particular elements could be sustained. Once the première drew near, the indifferent acting abilities of some singers could be a cause for concern. Finally, he claimed the right to subject the text itself to a detailed scrutiny. The choice of a single word was sometimes considered very carefully.

As a result of Da Ponte's reticence in his memoirs, very little is known of the creative process that composer and librettist went through, in order to arrive at the three celebrated operas we know today. In the printed libretto of *Figaro*, he credited Mozart with a good deal of help in his efforts to turn the famous Beaumarchais play into a libretto, admitting, however, that 'in spite of all the study, diligence and care taken by the composer and by me to be brief, the opera will still not be the shortest one ever put on in our theatre.'[3] It is not difficult to imagine the kinds of issues that are likely to have troubled composer and librettist in *Così*: how would the pairing of the lovers best be managed? would the disguises really work? how should the opera end when the original couples are reinstated?

The basic theme of *Così fan tutte* is that of a well-established archetype: the plot in which a wager is made on the fidelity of a woman who is then put to the test. Research on the literary antecedents of the opera has reinforced the view that Ariosto's *Orlando furioso* was a significant influence.[4] In this work, a tale is told in which it is the man himself who returns to conduct the deception, magically transformed, and he then experiences first-hand the bitterness of betrayal. There are many variations of the basic idea, which goes back to Ovid's retelling of the story of Cephalus and Procris. Sometimes, as in the opera, two men subject their lovers to the test.[5] *Così* is unusual in having a formulation in which two men return in disguise, each to seduce the other's partner. An important question in such plots is who learns the harshest lesson? The message is sometimes not the fallibility of women but the folly of men who, through entrapment, provoke an infidelity that would not otherwise have occurred. It may be the men who emerge chastened, the women indignant at the cruel and unjustifiable trick to which they have been subjected.

The plot that Da Ponte constructed for Salieri and revised for Mozart has attracted some admiration (at least in the modern era), but it has proved impossible to shake off the dark suspicion that below its elegant and witty surface, lies some fundamental problem. In a brief account of the opera, Niemetschek wrote: 'In the year 1789 in the month of December Mozart wrote the Italian comic opera *Così fan tutte*, or "The School for Lovers"; people are universally amazed that this great genius could condescend to waste his heavenly sweet melodies on such a miserable and clumsy text.'[6] The libretto was evidently beginning to attract opprobrium to the extent that Da Ponte's work was not only considered wretched or miserable ('elend') but also in some more fundamental sense a bungled job ('Machwerk'). A lucid explanation of the dilemma that Mozart was supposed to have faced in attempting to set a false libretto was expounded by Ulybyshev in his 1843 biography of the composer.[7] In our age, Joseph Kerman has been blunt: 'Even the most devoted Mozartean will have to admit there is something unsatisfactory about *Così fan tutte*.' He conceded the technical merits of the libretto, 'the intrigue smooth and elegant, the construction masterly, the verse delightful', but he could not reconcile the overwhelming beauty and truth of the music with the cynicism of the plot.[8]

The discontinuity between the remarkable expressivity of the music and the essentially cynical tone of the drama comes to a head in the character of Ferrando. There were two genres of eighteenth-century Italian opera: *opera seria*, haunt of kings and aristocrats, which explored lofty ideals such as duty and love; *opera buffa* or comic opera, which embraced a much wider range of social types and was more naturalistic. By the late eighteenth century, it was commonplace to incorporate *seria* characters in comic opera plots, and Da Ponte did so in each of his three dramas for Mozart.[9] The interaction between the serious, the semi-serious and the fully comic adds to the characteristic light and shade of these works, even though otherwise admirably virtuous *seria* characters can in this context appear stilted or unsympathetic. Ferrando is a *seria* tenor, his music lyrical, ardent and sincere as befits his character-type. His problem lies in the actions he has to perform, as he is required to engage in deception on two levels. The first is hardly problematic: he has to disguise himself and act a part. Physical concealment is routine in comic opera; convention dictates that the audience can see through the false whiskers, while some of the characters on stage cannot. Disguises are usually assumed for relatively short periods, and their context is often farcical, as in the episodes with Despina as doctor and notary. Vocal disguise is another matter altogether. Mozart experimented with it in *Figaro*, where Susanna (in disguise) adopts an altered voice. Figaro cannot see through the disguise and does not recognise her assumed voice, but the moment that she inadvertently resumes her normal voice, the deception (to him) is revealed. As Webster points out, disguise which 'entails a change not only of costume but of musical style, indeed often of voice, an operatic character's most intimate attribute', may be used either for comic purposes or for 'deeply poetic' ends.[10] Mozart fully accepted this convention, and, in what was to be the largest aria of the opera, Guglielmo (in disguise) was to address the two women at great length, presumably in his 'own' voice. It was taken for granted that his own woman Fiordiligi would not to be able to 'hear' who he really is.

Much more troubling was the question of Ferrando's musical voice and how it was to be handled during the long deception, necessitated by the plot construction with switched lovers. Whilst in disguise, he has to articulate feigned feelings, deploying without modification (presumably) the sincere tones of his lyrical tenor voice for an utterly duplicitous dramatic purpose: the seduction of Fiordiligi. As Rushton put it, if Ferrando is not sincere (in 'Fra gli amplessi') 'then he could instruct Don Giovanni in seduction'.[11] Attempts to distinguish sincere and insincere characteristics in the soaring lines with which he sings of his own woman and those with which a little while later he entraps his friend's lover have not met with success, and it is easy to understand why. In his cavatina, sung in anguish soon after he has heard of his own lover's capitulation, he feels 'betrayed and scorned' but still hears the 'voices of love'. A little while later in his scene with Guglielmo's lover, he sings: 'Turn your merciful eye upon me. In me alone you will find a husband, lover, and more if you wish. Do not delay, my adored one.' Most would agree with the conductor John Eliot Gardiner, that this is 'an unequivocally sincere outpouring of love to Fiordiligi'.[12] She is powerless to resist his passionate musical seduction, and the two end up singing in harmonious thirds. The musical impact of this climactic duet is so great that when, shortly afterwards, the deception is revealed and Fiordiligi has to return to her original partner, the conclusion is not only dramatically implausible but (a much more serious flaw in an opera) emotionally unsatisfying. Kerman's characterisation of the hasty restitution of the original pairings as an 'improbable and immoral' *volte face* seems well merited. As he put it: 'It took Fiordiligi three arias and a duet to change the first time, and if there was any depth to her feelings, she would require some parallel dramatic development to change back.'[13]

Indeed, critics have found it so difficult to come to terms with the restored couples that it is commonly argued, in a variety of ways, that Ferrando was always destined for Fiordiligi or that he is starting to fall in love with her 'despite himself'. Heartz, for example, wrote of their 'gradual melodic symbiosis', a sign that Ferrando and Fiordiligi were 'destined to become lovers from the beginning'.[14] In effect it is as though Ferrando's vocal type hinders him from fulfilling the dramatic role assigned to him, and this is tantamount to saying that the plot with its formulation of switched lovers was impossible to bring off satisfactorily within the musical conventions of the time.

A possible way out of this dilemma would have been for Ferrando and Guglielmo each to attempt the seduction of his own woman. This would have gone some way to resolve the problem with the character of Ferrando, as it would remove the requirement for his musical voice to represent a falsely assumed emotion, love for a woman he does not love. He would still be complicit in an unwise and cruel deception as to his identity, albeit undertaken from the best of motives and in the firm expectation that the fidelity of his lover would be confirmed, but at no point in the opera would his musical expressions of love be directed insincerely towards the 'wrong' woman. The true identities of the Albanian suitors would be revealed at the end, but there would be no need for last-minute repairing. Apologies all round would be in order, the men for their trick, the women for falling for it, but the ending would be free of the perplexing questions generated by the abrupt restitution of the original couples. It would become evident to everyone on stage that Ferrando's soaring melodic lines had been addressed to the 'right' woman throughout the opera, even though she had not been aware of the identity of her would-be seducer. But in exchange for a resolution of the difficulties over Ferrando's character and the unsatisfactory ending, a new and equally insoluble problem would in turn arise: how would it be possible for Ferrando's own lover to remain in ignorance of his identity whilst being seduced with music of such eloquent power? We have our answer in the opera as it stands today: the suspension of disbelief required during the seduction scenes (vocally rather than physically) would be too great to sustain dramatic credibility. In such a duplicitous undertaking as Don Alfonso's school, there was never going to be an easy place for a lyrical *seria* tenor. Ferrando in disguise cannot address his melodies of love to his own woman, because if their love means anything she must recognise them, but nor can he easily serenade her sister because then the musical character of his voice (sincerity) is sharply at odds with his dramatic purpose (insincerity). A dilemma thus faced composer and librettist to which there was no satisfactory solution.

The hypothesis now to be argued is that the opera as it has come down to us embodies the effects of one or more changes of mind in respect of this dilemma: specifically, that Mozart and Da Ponte favoured for a time the plot with unswitched lovers, before reverting to the alternative, but that this final change of mind came too late for them to expunge completely the evidence of the earlier state. This radical theory has the potential to shed new light on some of the most extensively discussed problems of the plot, as well as on the many small-scale changes and unresolved discrepancies that have been observed in the score and the two versions of the libretto.

At first sight it might seem very strange indeed that so fundamental an alteration to the essence of the drama could be contemplated at all. Surely there would be the necessity for wholesale rewriting? Such is the structure of *Così fan tutte*, however, that astonishingly little revision would have been required. The reason for this is that for much of the opera the sisters and the officers act in pairs. The one section of the opera that would have required significant revision is shown in Table 15.

Re-pairing would have transformed the effect of the opera as a whole, but the only major structural change required would have been in the seduction scenes. If in Act I there had been a moment of symbolic pairing off, this too would have had to be changed, but two such possible moments (Ferrando's 'A voi s'inchina' and Guglielmo's 'Rivolgete') were both cut – in itself quite a telling feature. The only clue to the forthcoming pairings left in the score of Act I comes after Fiordiligi's 'Come scoglio', when one of the officers (by implication at least her suitor-to-be) has to seek to detain her. As we shall see, Mozart himself was in a fog of confusion as to whether it should be Ferrando or Guglielmo. Remarkably, both finales could stand virtually unaltered in a plot with lovers uncrossed. A clear indication of the way things were about to go could have been given in the Act I finale when the two officers, regaining consciousness after their magnetic treatment, address the sisters individually, but Mozart did not indicate which one each of them approaches. The stage instructions ('à Dor.' and 'à Fiord.') in *NMA* are editorial.[15] Similarly, in the Act II finale, the two brief lines which Ferrando and Guglielmo, returning as officers, address to their real lovers individually ('Ma cos'è quel pallor, quel silenzio' and 'L'idol mio perchè mesto si sta?') also lack stage directions. Only at the very end, when the officers perform their musical recalls are the names of the women to be addressed actually given in the score, and these could be changed with the stroke of a pen.

TABLE 15 Section of the opera requiring revision for a plot with lovers uncrossed

| Act 1 | | | | Act 2 | | |
| --- | --- | --- | --- | --- | --- | --- |
| opening ensembles | departure of the men | return of the Albanians | finale | pairing off | seductions | finale |

One factor that must be considered in the discussion of this hypothesis is the structure of the libretto that Mozart inherited from Salieri. It is possible, for example, that he first worked with a plot outline as constructed for the older composer, and that he then asked the librettist for a major rewrite. Alternatively, the rewrite (at least as far as it concerned the pairing of the lovers) could have taken place at the start of Mozart's interest in the libretto, followed by a reversion to an earlier conception of the plot, when new problems proved more intractable than the original difficulties. Of the libretto that Salieri attempted to set, all that survives is the text of the first two trios, connected by a recitative, and so the question of whether the disguised lovers were or were not in crossed pairs is unanswerable. The ensuing analysis will focus on a hypothetical change from unswitched to switched lovers, but the idea that the pairing of the lovers in the final version marked a reversion to an original state will be kept in mind. This leaves open the possibility of alternative sequences of either two or three revisions as shown in Table 16.

In passing, it is worth pointing out that a switch from State 1 to State 2 could conceivably have had a direct impact on the hypothetical casting problems of the opera discussed above. Although impossible to prove, the Bussani couple, in theory at least, could have been quite plausibly cast as the second (real) couple in State 1, fact and fiction not at all at odds. A sudden switch to State 2, with

TABLE 16  Lovers crossed or uncrossed?

| | STATE 1 (lovers switched) | |
| --- | --- | --- |
| Ferrando / Dorabella | Ferrando (disguised) / Fiordiligi | Ferrando / Dorabella |
| Guglielmo / Fiordiligi | Guglielmo (disguised) / Dorabella | Guglielmo / Fiordiligi |
| | STATE 2 (lovers unswitched) | |
| Ferrando / Dorabella | Ferrando (disguised) / Dorabella | Ferrando / Dorabella |
| Guglielmo / Fiordiligi | Guglielmo (disguised) / Fiordiligi | Guglielmo / Fiordiligi |
| | STATE 3 (lovers switched) | |
| Ferrando / Dorabella | Ferrando (disguised) / Fiordiligi | Ferrando / Dorabella |
| Guglielmo / Fiordiligi | Guglielmo (disguised) / Dorabella | Guglielmo / Fiordiligi |

Dorotea now having to succumb to the charms of her (unrecognised) Francesco, might well have stretched credibility to breaking point and precipitated their hasty departure from those roles. By the time of a final restitution to State 3, it would presumably have been too late to consider any further recasting.

One implication of the structure with lovers unswitched is that Dorabella, Ferrando's partner throughout, would have been the *seria* woman. In rejecting this arrangement, it would have been possible to re-pair from the start with Ferrando singing 'La mia Fiordiligi'. This course of action would have necessitated some recomposition in the opening ensembles, but it would have preserved some of the character associations of the name 'Fiordiligi'. There is no evidence of this at all in the autograph, but a small slip in **V1** certainly gives some pause for thought. In 'È la fede delle femmine', the copyist first wrote for Ferrando in bars 18–20 the line 'La fenice è Fiordiligi'. This was scraped out and the correct name Dorabella put in. Guglielmo's subsequent entry 'La fenice è Fiordiligi' seems unchanged. Was this a simple slip-up, or could the copyist have been working from a score in which the names had been switched and then restored?

It is important to stress that the concept of a 'state' does not equate to a full or even a partial draft of the opera that was then dismembered. It merely implies Mozart and Da Ponte were struggling with this problem even as the opera was being composed, and that their views on the solution changed as they progressed. If this idea is correct, then it is possible, and indeed very likely, that some elements of this opera plot were changed twice, some once, with a few things left unchanged that ideally should have been changed.

The potential influence of the two plot structures on character development deserves consideration. Whichever plot was chosen, the two officers would retain their characters throughout, Ferrando as the ardent lover, Guglielmo as the swaggering braggart, but there would have been the opportunity and perhaps even the necessity for the women to switch characters. What so complicates the issue of the characters of the women is the plot structure with lovers crossed. If the lovers remain uncrossed, there is no problem: the two couples sing and act together in the appropriate musical pairings throughout the opera. But with lovers crossed, Mozart faced a critical decision. Should the serious sister be Ferrando's target of seduction (his musical partner) or his real love (his dramatic partner)? The composer could not have it both ways. Küster, citing the views of Kunze, argued that in an opera the correct musical pairing is of much the greater importance.[16] A perfect musical match is established during the seduction scenes, and the sense of incongruity at the end of the opera when Fiordiligi, the high soprano and the serious character, has to leave her natural musical partner to return to the bombastic grumbling bass is overwhelming. As

Heartz so memorably put it: 'by all the laws of opera, if not of Heaven, high voices should be paired together ... the prima donna surely deserves to contemplate going through life into eternity singing love duets with the tenor, not the bass.'[17] Küster suggested that only after he was well advanced with the composition of Act I did Mozart realise what was about to happen in Act II with the mismatched musical pairs. The theory that there was an ongoing debate about whether the lovers should be crossed or uncrossed provides an alternative explanation for this character switch.

In considering what characters the two sisters should have, Mozart and Da Ponte apparently explored three tones of musical voice: histrionic, sincere, and light-hearted. There were many possible models for the characterisation of two contrasting sisters. In Salieri's *La grotta di Trofonio*, Otelia is the serious lover of the philosopher tenor, Dori the playful lover of the fun-loving baritone. In that opera, magical transformations substitute for character development.[18] In *Così* the histrionic is represented by 'Ah! scostati' / 'Smanie implacabili' and (surprisingly) by the last lines of 'Ei parte'; the sincere by 'Per pietà' and the opening stanza of 'Fra gli amplessi'; and the light-hearted by 'È amore'. As has often been noted, there is very little in Act I to define the individual characters of the two sisters, apart from their arias. If these were put in very late, much of Act I could have been composed before a final decision was taken as to their musical and dramatic characterisation. Only in Act II does it finally start to become apparent that Fiordiligi is a character of depth and sincerity, while Dorabella is an easy convert to Despina's cynical way of thinking. One possibility is that Mozart and Da Ponte began with the two sisters as histrionic and sincere characters, *both* essentially robust guardians of their own virtue. Their personalities might then have resembled those of Donna Elvira and Donna Anna, with one sister reacting to her 'fall' with an outburst of wild grief, the other with a passionate plea for forgiveness. If the second sister had ever been intended as a histrionic personality, then at some point it was decided that she should be won over to a more frivolous view of love, and end up expressing these sentiments in the language of *opera buffa*. It is arguable that a process of lightening the second woman can also be discerned in *Figaro*, in which Mozart replaced Susanna's original Act IV aria, a piece apparently to have been in the vein of 'Smanie implacabili', with the inspired simplicity of 'Deh vieni'.[19] It is also worth recalling that Da Ponte later claimed with reference to *Don Giovanni* that he had urged upon Mozart the importance of the *vis comica*, as though the composer's natural inclinations were towards the serious.[20] If the character of the second sister evolved in this way when the pairings were uncrossed as a natural partner for Guglielmo, it is easy to see how a decision to cross the pairings would have caused difficulty, as by now the characterisations could not be easily undone. By taking up Despina's

TABLE 17  The hypothetical character development of the two sisters

|  | [State 1] | State 2 | State 3 |
|---|---|---|---|
| Dorabella | [histrionic] | sincere | histrionic → light-hearted |
| Fiordiligi | [sincere] | histrionic → light-hearted | sincere |

philosophy of love as readily as she does, Dorabella merely adds to the jarring incompatibility experienced at the end of the opera between the *seria* tenor and his fickle *buffa* partner, and the sincere sister and her braggart officer. This hypothetical development of the character of the two sisters can be represented as in Table 17.

What now follows is an analysis of how a phase with lovers unswitched could have affected the composition of the opera. This will be a lengthy and detailed investigation, and at its end the objection might be raised that the seriousness of the enquiry is somewhat at odds with the light-hearted nature of its subject. Like any *opera buffa*, this score was intended primarily to give its singers a chance to shine and to provide entertainment for a perhaps not very attentive audience. The answer to this point is that in the centuries following the night of its first performance on 26 January 1790, *Così fan tutte* gradually won a position as one of the central works of the operatic canon, and as a result of this attracted to itself a huge weight of serious scholarship. It is my contention that this critical tradition evolved without a full understanding of one of the crucial artistic decisions facing the composer and the librettist: how the lovers should be paired. In uncovering what this decision was and why it was apparently a difficult one to take, some of the problems long associated with this opera may turn out not to be problems at all, or, at least, not in quite the sense that has been assumed.

## *The Departure of the Officers*

It is appropriate to begin with a well-known feature of the two sisters' lines. In the early ensembles of Act I, Mozart originally allocated the higher of the two soprano parts to the character named Dorabella. Later he had a change of mind, and he went back over these pieces, switching the names of the two parts, so that Fiordiligi would sing the higher lines. Although the physical changes in the autograph were done late, the actual decision to switch Fiordiligi to the higher line probably occurred some time prior to this, because in the remainder of the opera her line is always above that of Dorabella. One factor that could also have influenced this switch was the casting of the singers. In the autograph of *Figaro*, the part of the Countess was originally written higher than that of Susanna. The choice is not particularly surprising, as a distinction was sometimes made between the higher tessitura appropriate for the *seria* style and for aristocratic roles, and the slightly lower range deemed suitable for parts *di mezzo carattere* and for figures of lesser social standing. It is possible that when the singers were cast in these roles, Mozart decided that, notwithstanding this convention, Storace was better equipped to take the higher line. Similarly, in *Così* the most straightforward reason for Mozart to have switched Fiordiligi to the higher line is that this happened after the casting of the parts of the two sisters. There is certainly nothing in the status of the two sisters to suggest any vocal distinction between them on the grounds of social class; only by their characters and actions are the two separable. Yet there are many indications that the reason for the switch was plot-related, and that the name change represents a character change.

This change of plan is also reflected in a feature that distinguishes the libretto from the autograph fairly consistently. It relates to the question of precedence: which sister is named first? The libretto usually places Dorabella first (Act I: Scenes II, IX and XIV; Act II: Scenes I and II). In the autograph, in which the addition of characters' names in the headings (as distinct from the part labels) was done quite late, the reverse is the case, and Fiordiligi is given precedence. Exceptions to this are the naming of Fiordiligi first in the libretto (Act I: Scene XI), and the naming of Dorabella first in the autograph (Act II: Scene I). The explanation of the former would appear to be that this scene (as located in the libretto) marked the start of the F major section of the sestetto, quite possibly among the last major elements of the opera to have been written, by which time the agreed change in the order of precedence went without question. The appearance of Dorabella's name first at the start of Act II in the autograph could indicate that this recitative text was done fairly early, and was not revised. (In this context it is worth recalling that it ends with a *segue* to an aria for 'Despinetta'.)

From the moment that the two sisters step on stage, a shadow of uncertainty hangs over their characters. Kerman viewed the initial characterisation of the lovers as 'neutral', though 'as vivid as ever' for Don Alfonso and Despina. The lovers start out 'less as serious individuals than as anonymous representatives of their sexes.'[21] Many agree over the initial lack of individuality in the two sisters, but most follow Heartz in arguing that 'Una bella serenata' is quite sufficient to differentiate Ferrando from Guglielmo.[22] John Eliot Gardiner in the booklet accompanying his CD of *Così fan tutte* argues persuasively that this initial neutrality should be left undisturbed in modern productions, allowing the characters of the two sisters to emerge in response to their situation.[23] A point often overlooked in accounts of the name switch is that whereas in most of the early

TABLE 18 The text of 'Ah guarda sorella'

| State 2 | Dorabella on Ferrando | Fiordiligi on Guglielmo |
| State 3 | Fiordiligi on Guglielmo | Dorabella on Ferrando |
| | Ah, guarda, sorella | Osserva tu un poco |
| | Se bocca più bella, | Che fuoco ha ne' sguardi |
| | Se aspetto più nobile | Se fiamma, se dardi |
| | Si può ritrovar. | Non sembran soccar. |
| | Si vede un sembiante | Si vede un faccia |
| | Guerriero, ed amante; | Che alletta, e minaccia. |

ensembles in Act I the consequential switch of text from one sister to the other is non-existent (i.e. they are singing the same words), this is not true of their opening duet 'Ah guarda sorella', in which each sister in turn has a solo stanza in praise of her own lover. By changing the names here, Mozart was in effect reallocating each sister's reaction to the miniature portrait of her lover, as shown in Table 18.

Neville views the words that Fiordiligi sings as an indication that Don Alfonso will win his bet: 'As is clearly outlined by the end of the fourth number of this opera, the wager is bound to succeed because the couples are mismatched. Fiordiligi may hold in her hand a portrait of Guglielmo but her words describe Ferrando with whom she is subsequently paired.'[24] While the two sisters' characterisations of their lovers are, of course, wholly conventional, as originally intended, the noble countenance and beautiful mouth may indeed have belonged to Ferrando, the fiery and combustible looks to Guglielmo. A further clue that some reallocation of text was taking place, comes in the discrepancy over which sister should sing 'Felice son io' and which 'Io sono felice'. The autograph and the libretto disagree over this. In a black-looking ink, apparently that with which he made late changes to Dorabella's vocal line, Mozart crossed out the original text sung by both sisters and substituted a neat little mirror image. The original text (in the brown ink of the particella) is not entirely clear, but it does not seem not be that of the libretto. It was deleted, and the mirror-image words inserted:

Dorabella [later Fiordiligi]

pel / mio son fe - / li - ce pel / mio son fe - / li - / ce    [brown ink]
fe - / li - ce son / io fe - / li - / ce    [black ink]

Fiordiligi [later Dorabella]

io / son per il / mio per il / mi - / o    [brown ink]
io / so - no io / so- no fe - li - / ce    [black ink]

The result is a considerable improvement in clarity and elegance, However, in both the draft and the final versions of the libretto, it is Dorabella who sings 'Felice son io' and Fiordiligi 'Io sono felice'. Thus, although the text of the libretto takes account of the decision to switch the first two quatrains and pairs of lines between Fiordiligi and Dorabella, it does not do so for the mirror-image lines. It reflects the final order of precedence (in the sense that Fiordiligi's line is printed above Dorabella's), but the texts were not switched.

Mozart and Da Ponte rarely postponed their characterisations for long. Most of the figures in their operas enter and with a few deft touches start to act as complete and rounded human beings. The characterisation of the two sisters begins in their first recitative 'Mi par che stamattina', and it is rather surprising. Fiordiligi begins with a levity, far removed from the serious and reflective character who sings 'Per pietà'. Here she seems to be about to act as the *buffa* foil to Guglielmo. She feels in the mood for some mischief ('pazzarella'). She feels a certain tingling in her veins ('un certo pizzicor entra le vene') and she anticipates playing pranks on her lover ('che burla'). By contrast Dorabella seems quite pensive, thinking of possible marriage. It is certainly arguable that this characterisation goes back to a time when Dorabella was the serious character. The failure to change it perhaps stemmed from the dilemma caused by the crossing of the lovers. Fiordiligi now has to start off as the dramatic *buffa* foil to Guglielmo, and then change in Act II to become the musical *seria* partner of Ferrando.

At the start of Scene III, which occurs during the course of this recitative, accumulating suspicions over the characters of the two women become a reality, because Mozart and Da Ponte made a direct swap of text between the two sisters. The words sung by the two sisters in the libretto are reversed in the autograph score, as shown in Table 19.

In the libretto Fiordiligi answers her own remark ('Eccoli'), whereas in the autograph it is Dorabella who responds with the information that the new arrival is Don Alfonso. The change perhaps relates to the need to establish the

TABLE 19 The reversal of text between Fiordiligi and Dorabella in Act I, Scene III

| Libretto character | Autograph character | Text |
|---|---|---|
| Fiordiligi | Fiordiligi | Eccoli |
| Dorabella | Fiordiligi | Ben venga il signor Don Alfonso! |
| Don Alfonso | Don Alfonso | Riverisco! |
| Fiordiligi | Dorabella | Cos'è? Perché qui solo? Voi piangete? Parlate, per pietà! che cosa è nato? L'amante ... |
| Dorabella | Fiordiligi | L'idol mio ... |
| Don Alfonso | Don Alfonso | Barbara fato! |

characters of the two women. The slightly histrionic element in the first reaction to Don Alfonso's appearance ('Cos'è ...') needed to come from the sister who was to sing 'Smanie implacabili'. The implication therefore is that Fiordiligi preceded Dorabella in this character, and that Dorabella was indeed the more serious sister, as implied by her original position in the score above Fiordiligi. There will be many occasions during the following analysis in which a single alteration has the potential to be interpreted as evidence of two *or* three states. This discrepancy is one such case. Either Fiordiligi was originally intended to sing Dorabella's words and then did not (two states), or she was going to take over these words from Dorabella but in the event did not (three states). A further small reallocation of text perhaps occurred in 'Sento oddio' in bars 36–9, but here the characters of the two sisters are indistinguishable in their exaggerated and conventional posturing. The evidence lies not in the libretto but in some early manuscript copies.

Changing text between the two sisters would have had one other consequence: the few passages in which Fiordiligi or Dorabella name their lovers would have needed amendment. Among the possibly early red crayon cuts not in the end 'agreed' in **V1** are the only two occasions in Act I in which this happens: the start of 'Mi par che stamattina'; and a passage in 'Che silenzio'. The simple deletion of these passages would have the advantage that the text would work whatever was decided about the pairings. (The need to avoid text in which one or other of the sisters refers by name to her lover is apparently also seen in the Act II recitative 'Ei parte' where Fiordiligi's reference to the absent Guglielmo in the libretto was not set by Mozart.)

The idea that Mozart switched the character of the two sisters part way through the composition of Act I suggests a remarkable explanation for their apparent neutrality of characterisation. If the libretto text was insufficiently revised to take account of this change, then the two characters would appear as a+b and b+a, blurring any sense of individuality. Uncertainty over the pairings would in itself have encouraged neutrality until the question was finally resolved. Powerful evidence for the existence of this phenomenon in the first part of Act I is to be found in the early reception history of *Così fan tutte*. Many early arrangers and translators of this opera implicitly acknowledged what I term the 'Two Sisters Problem' by attempting to sort it out, sometimes with unfortunate results. Although this kind of evidence falls partly outside the chronological limits of this study, I include a brief account in Appendix 4.

It is not long before the two sisters learn of the imminent departure of their lovers for the battlefield. Mozart marked the moment of farewell with the quintetto 'Di scrivermi', which was added to the opera at quite a late stage. Widely admired for its expressiveness, the piece has also caused some puzzlement because of the apparent insincerity of three of the five characters. The idea that Mozart inserted this piece as a direct consequence of a move to the plot with lovers crossed deserves some consideration.

With uncrossed lovers, there would have been abundant musical communication between the 'real' couples, but with lovers crossed, there is hardly any such interaction. We are so used to listening to passionate musical declarations between real lovers, that it comes as something of a shock to discover how little there is in *Così*. In a three-hour opera, Ferrando and Guglielmo manage to address their real partners (individually) only for a few seconds. There is a brief moment at the start of the recitative 'Non pianger' when Guglielmo addresses Fiordiligi as 'idol mio' and Ferrando Dorabella as 'mia sposa'. In the further moment of parting in the recitative 'Non v'è più tempo', there is the following exchange, which is succinct if nothing else, and, incidentally, appears to herald the order of the switched couples:

> Fiordiligi:    Mio cor!
>
> Dorabella:    Idolo mio!
>
> Ferrando:    Mio ben!
>
> Guglielmo:    Mia vita!

And they are not yet even married! For the rest of the time, even this minimal level of personal dialogue is missing: the men address the women collectively in ensembles, or they sing about them in their absence, either in soliloquy or to a third person. When finally deciding upon a plot with lovers crossed, in which all the passionate seduction music would be between the 'wrong' couples, Mozart perhaps sensed the need for some musical expression of the feelings of the real couples for each other, to attempt to make some emotional sense of the restitution of the *status quo* at the end. Perhaps because they are about to trick their partners so cruelly, Ferrando and Guglielmo can empathise with their feelings of impending loss, leaving Don Alfonso to act the part of the cynic.

## *The Arrival of the Albanians*

The moment in Act I most likely to have needed revision following a change of plan over the pairing of the lovers is the first meeting between the officers disguised as Albanians and the two sisters. It was certainly the intention for the couples to be symbolically paired off at this point, even if not yet fully linked. Any change of mind over the pairings would have necessitated significant revisions. But if at this stage the two men were to continue to act as a pair, Mozart would be able to complete Act I before the resolution of this question. There is an abundance of evidence that the plot, from the time of the sisters' first encounter with the Albanians (part way through 'Alla bella Despinetta') to the exit planned for them (towards the end of 'Rivolgete'), underwent radical revision. It includes: the break in the composition of 'Alla bella Despinetta'; Ferrando's missing recall 'A voi s'inchina'; uncertainty over which sister should sing an aria where 'Come scoglio' is now located; change(s) of mind over which pairing Guglielmo should suggest at the start of 'Rivolgete'.

Analysis of the ink colours in this part of the opera reveals the strong likelihood of a break in composition at the start of the 3/4 section of 'Alla bella Despinetta' when the women enter. The fine black ink of the particella of the first section suggests that it might even have been done during the first layer of composition. There are a few bars at the start of the 3/4 section in a new ink, but from bar 20 the faded ink of the remainder appears to place its composition significantly later, around the time that the string instrumentation was being done for this part of the opera. Another tell-tale sign of a compositional break is the revision of the bass line in bars 54 and 58, where there was originally a crotchet F on the first beat. When he put in the string instrumentation of the middle section of the sestetto, Mozart deleted these two crotchets. This is an example of a characteristic type of revision. When completing a section, the composer naturally chose the ending most appropriate for it, but when returning later to continue the piece, Mozart often felt the need to change the length and articulation of the final note, or even delete it altogether as in this case, in order to characterise the start of the new section. Thus, although allocating a significant pile of the first of the two main paper types to this ensemble, only the first section of this movement seems to have been copied early. A break in composition does not necessarily imply a change of plan, but there are numerous other indications that the delay was a significant one, and that a major rethink was the cause. Here are only some of them. (1) There is a discrepancy between the libretto and the autograph as to where Scene XI should begin, either 'Ragazzaccia' at the entry of the two sisters, or at the start of 'Alla bella Despinetta'. (2) There is no indication either in the autograph or the libretto of the entry of the disguised Albanians. (3) There is no indication in the stage directions of the costumes to be worn by the Albanians, or of their names or nationality. Only from the reactions of the sisters and retrospectively from details given in the Act II finale do we learn their names and attire. (4) The word 'assai' was deleted from the original tempo designation 'Allegro assai' at the 3/4 section, presumably in response to the need for a revised sequence of tempo indications. (5) In the autograph the two sisters react with 'terror' to the antics of the Albanians rather than 'furor' as in the libretto. Depending on the manner of the introductions, different reactions would be possible: shock and fear, or anger. All these features point to a significant reorganisation of this part of Act I.[25]

One important clue as to what was to have happened at this point comes in Ferrando's celebrated 'missing' recall at the climax of Act II. 'Making extravagant compliments', he kneels before his 'bella damina' (Fiordiligi) in an apparent reference to the moment of his self-introduction, when at the very least he would have revealed his status and nationality as a 'Cavaliere d'Albania'. Opinion is divided as to the location of the original of this citation. Heartz's suggestion that it was to have come in the sestetto, gains force from the palaeographical evidence that only the first section of 'Alla bella Despinetta' was completed early on.[26] A change of pairing would not of itself have necessitated the removal of the passage, unless the woman had been identified by name as the object of Ferrando's compliments, but by cutting it Mozart effectively postponed the moment of symbolic pairing, as he did when he abandoned 'Rivolgete', and this allowed him to avoid for the moment any decision about the pairings.

One consequence of the loss of any proper introduction of the Albanians to the two sisters during the sestetto was that Mozart and Da Ponte had to insert an additional accompanied recitative, to allow Don Alfonso to identify the men as his friends and to engage in at least some banter with the sisters to make sense of the aria of rebuttal that follows. After the sestetto, Don Alfonso returns to find out what the pandemonium is all about in 'Che sussurro', but there was almost immediately a copying break in bar 7. Mozart apparently did not yet know how the scene was to continue, perhaps even which sister was to exclaim 'Oh ciel!' A notable feature of the *accompagnato* 'Stelle' is the number of significant textual variants between the autograph and **V1**. As usual in such cases, the explanation is probably that the copyist was working from a version that had become unusable, and that Mozart himself had to recopy subsequently for his own autograph, revising slightly as he went along.

If Mozart was unable for a while to continue with the writing of the recitative 'Che sussurro' beyond Don Alfonso's opening remarks, it could certainly have been because he was waiting for Da Ponte to compose or revise the following text, yet it is interesting that he came to a halt before Dorabella's very first exclamation 'Oh ciel', as though he had not finally decided which sister should proceed to sing an aria. The idea that he was uncertain about this is speculative, but it finds significant support in what happens in the autograph at the start of the recitative after Fiordiligi's aria ('Ah non partite!'). (Fig. 9.) At the head of the page is written: 'Dopo l'aria di fiordiligi', in itself a signal that some clarification was necessary. Considering that it was to have followed one of the major set-piece arias in the opera, its opening phrases betray a quite remarkable level of uncertainty on Mozart's part as to who should sing what. (Example 7.) The recitative originally began with the words 'Ah non partite' sung by Ferrando. Mozart immediately crossed this out, and started again with the same words

FIG. 9 The autograph of *Così fan tutte*, Act I, Biblioteka Jagiellońska, Kraków, fol. 104, 'Ah non partite' (bars 1–9), detail. Mozart had several changes of mind over which officer should begin with the words 'Ah non partite', and also which sister should sing first. Reproduced by kind permission of the Biblioteka Jagiellońska, Kraków.

sung by Guglielmo followed by Ferrando's response 'Ah barbara restate!' Very shortly after this, however, he went back and yet again reversed the singers of the opening phrases. He crossed out the notes and the names and substituted a new musical line (reusing the five notes originally sung by Ferrando at the start). Next, there was apparently a problem with the first woman's entry. Originally it was Fiordiligi who started 'con foco'; Mozart changed this to Dorabella. There is little to distinguish all these alterations in the ink colour; they seem to have been made at the same time. There were three, possibly four changes of mind. Mozart began with Ferrando at the start, then replaced him with Guglielmo, and then reverted to the tenor again. The change from Fiordiligi to Dorabella was either a fourth change, or more likely it was linked to the move back from Guglielmo to Ferrando. All this apparently happened before Mozart got as far as Fiordiligi's entry 'Come!', where the name has never been changed. Another

EX. 7 Successive revisions by Mozart allocated the opening of 'Ah non partite' (bars 1–3) first to Ferrando, then to Guglielmo and then to Ferrando again.

point to note is that Mozart omitted the libretto's stage instructions in these early bars. Guglielmo is supposed to address Dorabella ('à Dor.') and then Don Alfonso ('à D. Alf.'). Mozart usually entered this type of stage instruction in his autograph.

Short though it is, this recitative comes at an important symbolic moment in the opera. If Ferrando's self-introduction to one of the women had by then been cut, this would be the moment for one of the Albanians, by taking the lead in response to Fiordiligi's aria, to imply a potential pairing. The reallocation of the first response from Fiordiligi to Dorabella is also significant. At this point in the opera, the women are still acting as a pair. 'Come scoglio', which begins ostensibly as a personal reaction from Fiordiligi to her situation, broadens out to incorporate Dorabella. Whichever woman had not sung the aria would be the first to respond in the recitative, aligning herself with the sentiments expressed therein. The impression given by the autograph is of a series of stumbles by Mozart, briefly uncertain, perhaps because of the disordered state of a much revised libretto. Yet even though a momentary lapse, this series of changes points unequivocally to a much more substantive debate. Once again the question of the musical and dramatic character of the two sisters seems to be part of a series of ongoing choices to be made. If Dorabella was to have sung an aria here, that immediately raises the question as to the identity of this aria. Was it to be 'Smanie implacabili' in her present character, or was it to be 'Come scoglio' sung by the more serious character, but at that stage still called Dorabella rather than Fiordiligi?

On the folio following the recitative 'Ah non partite' comes the start of Guglielmo's abandoned aria 'Rivolgete', where uncertainty over the pairing of the lovers finally comes to a head. There are two firm signs that a change of pairing was under consideration: Mozart changed the stage directions so that the order in which Guglielmo addresses the two women is reversed; and the opening words of the text were changed from 'Rivolgete a me' (as in the *Verzeichnüss*) to 'Rivolgete a lui' (as in the libretto). The chronological relationship of these two changes is not at all clear. Indeed, taken together, the two reversals leave the original pairings unchanged, but it is likely that they were sequential, in other words, that a different pairing of lovers was under consideration. Perhaps the simplest of many possible permutations is as in Table 20. There are many other potential explanations of these features, which makes a firm conclusion problematic, but the level of uncertainty over the pronoun and the stage direction at the start of so significant a piece is certainly consistent with at least one change of mind over the pairings.

The structure of its text lends some support to the idea that 'Rivolgete a *me*' was the original opening line. In such a version, Da Ponte would have moved

TABLE 20 The pairings in 'Rivolgete a me / lui'

| STATE 1 | 'A Dor.' | Rivolgete a me |
| --- | --- | --- |
| | | Guglielmo imperiously claims Dorabella as his own, and directs Fiordiligi's gaze towards Ferrando, thereby effecting crossed pairings. |
| STATE 2 | 'A Dor.' | Rivolgete a lui |
| | | With the couples now to be uncrossed, Guglielmo addresses Dorabella but directs her attention instead to Ferrando. |
| STATE 3 | 'A Fior.' | Rivolgete a lui |
| | | With a reversion to a plot formulation with crossed pairings, Mozart needed either to return to the original text or make a change in the stage directions. The latter was much easier to do. |

systematically from first-person statements to third-person statements, skilfully building up the tension, as Guglielmo makes his comparisons in a quatrain, couplet, single line and half line. The original text might thus have read as follows, with the final version in parentheses:

*first-person quatrain*
Rivolgete a me [lui] lo sguardo
E vedrete come sta:
Tutte dice io gelo, io ardo;
Idol mio, pietà, pietà.

*third-person quatrain*
E voi cara un sol momento
Il bel ciglio a lui [me] volgete.
E nel suo [mio] ritroverete
Quel che il labbro dir non sa.

*first-person couplet*
Un Orlando innamorato
Non è niente in mio confronto

*third-person couplet*
Un Medoro il sen piagato
Verso lui per nulla il conto:

*first-person line*
Son di foco i miei sospiri

*third-person line*
Son di bronzo i suoi desiri.

*first- / third-person half-lines*
Se si parla poi di merto
Certo io sono, ed egli e certo,

*the two together for the climax*
Che gli ugali non si trovano
Dall' Sebeto al Canadá.

With the text structured in this manner, Guglielmo would have sorted out a woman for himself first, well in accordance with his swaggering character.

An examination of the inks used to copy the particella of this movement does not allow a conclusive view to be taken about the order of these changes. Of particular interest is a copying break on the third side of this aria. It occurs after a bar and a beat where (in bar 20) Mozart first entered a crotchet D in the bass part in line with the previous figuration. When he resumed, he crossed out the crotchet and entered a tied semibreve leading onwards into the new section. Significantly, the rather rich-looking brown ink used to cross out this crotchet appears to have been that used to write in the stage instruction in bar 22 ('à fiordiligi'). This indicates that the change in the names of the women in the stage instructions came after the text had been revised into the form we now know. Even more surprising is the aspect of the word 'lui' on the first side. After examining the photograph of this in the *NMA*, I wondered whether Mozart had changed 'me' to 'lui'. The original shows no sign of such a change, but it confirms that the word 'lui' is written in a different ink with a different pen by a different hand. (See Fig. 8 above.) It looks as though Mozart left a blank here to be filled in later. The upright 'l' with its triangular loop is unlike the composer's usual flowing looped 'l'. The explanation would appear to be that there was an earlier version of the text of 'Rivolgete a me' (as in the composer's catalogue) and that at the time that the autograph was started, it was in the process of being revised, so that Mozart could proceed no further than the opening measures of the piece, leaving a blank for the pronoun. Once the revised text was received, the copying continued from bar 20.

The uncertainty over the pairing invites an explanation. The coupling of lovers to have been suggested by Guglielmo was only a *proposed* pairing, nonetheless it would have been a symbolic moment of real significance: responsibility for the initiation of any pairing might be taken by the men, by the women or by Don Alfonso, but whatever the choice was it would have consequences for the denouement. One issue exercising composer and librettist could have been whether it was appropriate for Guglielmo to pre-empt the women's decision by proposing the pairings necessary for the Act II seductions. It could be that after several changes of mind on this point, Mozart eventually decided that any guidance at all from Guglielmo would be incompatible with the free choice to be made by the women in Act II, and for this reason cut the aria altogether. Yet this explanation has its difficulties. For one thing, it is hard to see why Mozart and Da Ponte should have gone to all the trouble of recasting the text of the first two stanzas to achieve this end, when all they needed to do was to revise the stage directions with the names of the women in the appropriate order as often as necessary. The fact that it was thought necessary to recast 'Rivolgete a me' as 'Rivolgete a lui' seems to imply that they wished to retain an order of precedence, with one woman being addressed before the other as of right.

As we have already seen, the concept of precedence is very murky in this opera. In a *dramma giocoso*, as this opera is described in the libretto, a well-known theoretical hierarchy existed, with the *seria* couple top, followed by the couple *di mezzo carattere*, and with the *buffa* couple lowest. That scheme might or might not be reflected in the social status of the characters, but in reality it was rarely as clear-cut as this. With lovers uncrossed, the essential categories of the *dramma giocoso* model remain intact, albeit hidden from some of the participants on stage. But with lovers crossed, any formulaic categories are challenged. Thus Dorabella might have notional precedence at the start of the opera as the partner of the *seria* tenor, but should she retain it in Act II, when Fiordiligi emerges as Ferrando's vocal partner?

To summarise this seemingly simple but actually very complex problem, the autograph suggests the following stages: (1) The first version of the text 'Rivolgete a me' was apparently still being revised when Mozart started work on the first page of the present autograph. (2) Mozart wrote the start of the particella, omitting the pronoun, either because he did not know to whom to direct the attention of the first woman to be addressed, or more likely because he was waiting for Da Ponte to come up with the revised text. (3) When he received the text, he completed the movement. (4) Some time before finally abandoning the aria, he switched the stage directions, reversing the pairings proposed by Guglielmo.

Another element of the problem is the timing of Mozart's work on the extant manuscript of 'Rivolgete', which is bound in with Act I of the opera in what would have been its correct position. The spelling 'Guillelmo' at the opening and the use of the earlier paper type throughout points to an early date, at least for the first few bars of the particella. Mozart is known on occasion to have drafted just the first melodic idea of an aria after allocating a batch of paper to it, as he did with 'La mano a me date'. 'Rivolgete' remained in the opera until shortly before the première, as shown by the printing of its text in the draft libretto, although by then the decision to remove it might well already have been taken in principle. The autograph confirms that the aria remained in the opera until late on: the wind instrumentation was completed (apart from the end of the horn parts); and the stage direction on the final page (which leads on 'attacca' to the following trio) uses the spelling of 'Guilelmo'. Indeed, the mere fact that there is a very full stage direction in the autograph is telling. There are usually relatively few, mainly references to off-stage sounds, instructions for one character to address another specifically, and the simple 'parte' ('he/she leaves') or 'partono' ('they leave').

One final question remains: the significance of the entry in Mozart's *Verzeichnüss*, in which 'Rivolgete' (K584) is the first entry for the month of December, followed by two sets of twelve dances, the music that Mozart had to compose to fulfil the requirements of his court position. The entry is as follows: '*Eine arie* welche in die Oper Così fan tutte bestimt war, für Benucci. *Rivolgete à me lo sguardo* etc: – 2 violini, viola, 2 oboe, 2 fagotti, 2 clarini e Timpany e Baßi' ('An aria, which was destined for *Così fan tutte*, for Benucci. *Turn your eyes upon me* etc: two violins, viola, two oboes, two bassoons, two trumpets and timpany and basses'). Similarly, the incipit reads: 'Rivol=gete à me lo sguardo'. There has always seemed a slight (though not necessarily insuperable) chronological difficulty about the date of 1790 on the first version of the printed libretto, which includes the text of 'Rivolgete a lui', because this entry in Mozart's catalogue appears to imply that the aria had already been put aside in December 1789. Mozart could have made the catalogue entry at an early stage, before the pronoun had been changed, or he could have catalogued the aria only after the piece had been finally abandoned, choosing to give it with its original (and preferred) first line. The use of the opera title *Così fan tutte* supports the latter interpretation, as does the absence of the horns from the instrumentation. Mozart copied out most of the horn part but late on crossed it out with the instruction 'corni tacciono'.

## *The Seduction Scenes*

The start of Act II would not have been greatly affected by changes of pairing. In the first recitative there is nothing to distinguish effectively the characters of the two sisters. Only in the second recitative does Dorabella finally take the lead in suggesting a little harmless fun. In the following duet when the sisters make their choices, no names are mentioned, and so the identity of their new lovers-to-be is still open to question. Only in the quartet are the new pairings finally formed.

The section of the opera that would have been most transformed by a change of mind over the pairing of the lovers would have been the seduction scenes. In a plot with lovers uncrossed each man would have to discover for himself the limits of his beloved's fidelity. The moment when Guglielmo reveals to

Ferrando the bad news of his lover's surrender would have been lost, as would the covert observation of his own woman's capitulation. This would have had the further effect of postponing any musical reaction from Ferrando (such as 'Tradito') until late in the Act.

The first seduction to take place is Guglielmo's successful assault on Dorabella's affections. In its final form the duet 'Il core vi dono' only makes sense in the plot with lovers crossed, because of Guglielmo's references to Ferrando's misfortune. There is no evidence of an earlier version without the aside 'Ferrando meschino', although there are clear signs of a break in composition here at the particella stage. This occurs in bar 48, the moment when the duet moves to individual utterances on the parts of the two lovers. Mozart originally ceased copying here after entering a crotchet in the brown ink of the particella in all parts. (The particella was unusually fully scored at this point in order to incorporate the special effect required for the beating heart.) When he restarted, he amended the score by adding hooks to the crotchets in the lines of Guglielmo and the wind instruments.

To judge by the number of changes that there are in the autograph score, the second seduction caused Mozart particular trouble. The short *accompagnato* 'Barbara! perché fuggi?' presents a conundrum. It is followed by a *segue* indication for Ferrando's aria, but below is written: 'dopo questo viene scena 7: [ma] – Recitativo Istromentato / di Fiordiligi e Rondò'. (Fig. 10.) It would have been very helpful if an examination of the ink colours of these indications had enabled a clear view to be taken as to whether one was put on before the other, but their appearance is too similar to make any firm conclusion possible. They may indeed have been written together. The 'Dopo' indication itself is untypical in several respects. It is unusual to find one at the end of a piece in the formulation 'dopo questo viene …' In *Così* all other such indications come at the head of the page and indicate what has come before not what is to follow. Also unusual is the way that it refers both the *accompagnato* and the rondò. The idea that this instruction implies the cutting of Ferrando's aria is quite wrong, because the numbers '24' and '25' were added to clarify the order. Moreover, the 'agreed' cut to the length of Ferrando's aria in **V1** is enough to demonstrate conclusively that it remained in the opera. A parallel situation in *Figaro* throws some light on the matter. Towards the end of Act III, Mozart was planning an arietta for Cherubino, to go before 'Dove sono' sung by the Countess.[27] At the end of the preceding recitative there are two instructions: 'segue l'arietta di cherubino'; and 'dopo l'arietta di cherubino, viene Scena 7:[ma] –ch'è un Recitativo istromentato, con aria della Contessa'. The parallel with the situation in *Così* is still more exact, because the numbers 20 and 21 were added after these two instructions. In the event the number 20 was crossed out as Mozart decided to abandon the idea of an arietta for Cherubino here, though this change of mind came too late to have the text removed from the libretto. It seems that the double instruction was intended to clarify the order of events for the copyist. Mozart wished to put this part of the opera in order but did not yet have a particella of the arietta ready (though its key had presumably been determined). By analogy, this suggests that the particella of 'Ah lo veggio' was not yet available to be placed in the final sequence, even though Mozart needed to make quite clear what the order was to be.

The character of 'Ah lo veggio' suggests a piece written for the plot formulation with lovers crossed. It has a somewhat impersonal, assumed ardour, and the instruction 'lietissimo' (added in late) encourages Ferrando to be convincing in his deception. (Perhaps subconsciously, Mozart was picking up his next stage instruction at the start of the following recitative which is also 'lietissimo'.) If 'Ah lo veggio' was inserted as late as seems to have been the case, then its key could to some extent have been determined by the existing recitative, although Mozart would certainly not have countenanced an unsuitable key on these

FIG. 10 The autograph of *Così fan tutte*, Act II (Mus. ms. Autogr. W. A. Mozart 588, vol. 2, fol. 209v), Staatsbibliothek zu Berlin, Preußischer Kulturbesitz, Musikabteilung mit Mendelssohn Archiv, 'Barbara! perché fuggi?' (bars 21–3), detail. Both the aria and the rondò are numbered, which suggests that Mozart was merely confirming the continuity of this part of the opera, without the particella of Ferrando's aria to hand. (Staatsbibliothek zu Berlin – Preußischer Kulturbesitz, Musikabteilung mit Mendelssohn-Archiv. Mus.ms.autogr. W. A. Mozart 588 vol. 2)

grounds alone. An interesting clue lies in the existence of a clarinet quintet fragment in A major (K581a) which begins with the melody of 'Ah lo veggio'. Scholars have debated which came first. On the whole it seems more likely that Mozart would have made use of the melodic start of an abandoned fragment, rather than the converse.[28] Had he not transposed it up a semitone, Ferrando would have had two A major arias and effectively a third within the duet 'Fra gli amplessi' ('Volgi a me').

A complicating factor when considering the changes made to this part of the opera is the idea that Fiordiligi's Act I aria 'Come scoglio' could have been intended to come here as a rebuttal of Ferrando's first attempt to seduce her and a powerful statement of her rock-like constancy prior to the shock of her 'fall'. Evidence of Mozart's uncertainty as to which of the men was supposed to reply to it, has been discussed above. At the head of its first page is written 'atto primo'. This note, also written on the score of the undoubtedly late 'Non siate ritrosi', was interpreted by Tyson as a possible indicator that the aria in question was being copied during work on Act II, yet it is the relationship between the autograph version and the copy in **V1** that throws up the most thought-provoking questions. A curious feature in the copyist's score (replicated in other early copies) is that several small musical variants are recorded. Tyson wondered whether these changes were authorised by Mozart, perhaps at a rehearsal.[29] They are virtually the only substantive differences (apart from the cuts and obvious errors) between the musical text of the opera in the autograph and the copy. Analysis of the texts of the preceding pair of accompanied recitatives shows an unusually high level of disagreement between the text of the autograph and **V1**, and in one notable instance this extends to the words of the aria. The second stanza in **V1** begins 'con voi', not 'con noi' as clearly written in the autograph. The explanation is probably that the copyist was working from a discarded but usable first section of the score, while Mozart revised or added the final section.

The idea that this aria was hastily revised for a very different location in the opera than the one originally intended suggests that its text should be examined for possible signs of this change. The three stanzas are as follows:

> Come scoglio immoto resta
> Contra i venti e la tempesta,
> Così ognor quest'alma è forte
> Nella fede e nell'amor.
>
> Con noi [voi in **V1**] nacque quella face
> Che ci piace, e ci consola,
> E potrà la morte sola
> Far che cangi affetto il cor.

Rispettate, anime ingrate,
Questo esempio di costanza,
E una barbara speranza
Non vi renda audaci ancor!

As so often in *Così*, a sense of ambivalence surrounds the use of pronouns. The first stanza appears to be an unambiguous statement on behalf of Fiordiligi as an individual. It is her spirit that is immoveable as a rock, standing against the tempests. In the second stanza, however, the unexpected appearance of the pronoun 'us' ('noi') raises a question as to whether this other person is her sister or her absent beloved. (If her lover, then presumably the original text ran 'Che mi piace, e mi consola'.) By the third stanza she is evidently addressing the Albanians, and is now in a sense speaking on behalf of Dorabella, although still referring to the example of her own constancy. The use of the pronoun 'voi' in **V1** suggests that 'noi' was a revision to allow Fiordiligi to speak on behalf of her sister as well. It is even possible that the piece started out with a conventional two-tempo structure, and acquired a third for the additional (or replacement) stanza beginning 'Rispettate anime ingrate'. The musical character of the third section, with its running triplet quavers in the violins, lightens perceptibly. Such a revision would, of course, have necessitated a substantial rethink of the overall structure. The location of the variant in the violin parts immediately before the final 'più allegro' could be simple coincidence, but it might represent ongoing work by Mozart, tidying up a transition to a new final section. It is also clear in the autograph that 'più' was a later addition to the original tempo indication.

The idea that this piece switched Acts has an obvious bearing on the interpretation of one of the most intensely contested aspects of its musical character: its status as a parody. This has been a long running debate, from which several key issues have emerged. A basic problem is how to identify what is parody. In her examination of *opera seria* elements in *opera buffa*, Hunter discussed the distinction between parody and assimilation. In her view, the more specific a reference to *opera seria*, the more likely it is to have been intended as a parody. Where the reference appears general in character – for example, the use of a Metastasian aria type, high diction or serious musical language – it may relate to the assimilation of a serious character into a comic plot.[30] Webster considered the possible mechanisms for producing parody, either purely musical excess or incongruity between the music and dramatic features.[31] As he pointed out, musical signs are themselves 'malleable' and can be used both 'authentically and parodistically'. Making this distinction on musical grounds alone can be problematic, especially if the styles to be parodied already have rather exaggerated characteristics.

In the case of 'Come scoglio', it is likely that in any Act II location it would have counted as an unambiguous piece of assimilation, a serious piece, in a serious context, for the *seria* soprano. If switched to its present location quite late on, the aria might then have acquired a gloss of parody almost by accident. Now the emotions expressed seem too extreme for the situation in which Fiordiligi finds herself. The two Albanians have only just appeared on the scene and there has been no individual attempt at even the beginnings of a seduction. The very different affect of the aria in Act II is illustrated in Table 21.

The failure of Fiordiligi to leave the stage after so obvious an exit aria has provoked comment. According to Goehring, the lack of an exit 'invokes a convention only to undermine it'.[32] There is also the question as to whether 'Come scoglio' would have been called a rondò in an Act II position. Mozart is known to have changed his mind over the use of this prestigious generic title on occasion. In the autograph of *Figaro*, the Act II aria for the Countess ('Dove sono') was originally to have been titled a rondò. Mozart scratched out this word and substituted 'aria'.[33] If this change of position did occur, it is very easy to see why 'Come scoglio' ended up a profoundly ambiguous aria.

There are no physical indications of a change of position for 'Come scoglio' in the autograph, but in **V1** there are clear signs of such a switch, notably the addition at its head of the cue 'E tradimento' which should lead into 'Per pietà'. By itself this stray cue, which could have been added in later, would not mean very much, but it also appears on the score **S** which stems from **V2**, and this implies that it was there at a very early date. In fact 'Come scoglio' was transferred to an Act II position in some early productions of the opera in Vienna, and again this raises the general question as to whether the early reception history of this

TABLE 21  'Come scoglio' in an Act II position

| Act II (serious assimilation) | Act I (hint of parody) |
| --- | --- |
| addressed by Fiordiligi to her would-be suitor | addressed by Fiordiligi to the two Albanians |
| a statement on behalf of herself | a statement on behalf of herself and then Dorabella as well |
| two-tempo? | three-tempo |
| unambiguously serious in musical style and dramatic context | suggestion of parody because of the mismatch between serious musical style and comic dramatic context |
| two serious sections? | two serious sections and a lighter third |
| singer exits | singer attempts to exit but is detained together with her sister |

opera was influenced by knowledge (which many must still have had) as to the circumstances leading up to the first production.

If 'Come scoglio' did switch Acts, there would have been consequences for its introductory *accompagnato*. Brown has drawn attention to the notable harmonic parallels between several of the accompanied recitatives in *Così*.[34] To some extent this is because they all use generic musical language – rushing scales, dotted interjections, quiet held chords. One could in theory envisage a situation in which the switching of an aria from one place to another could generate compositional activity that would contribute to this sense of familiarity. An *accompagnato* drafted for an aria in one position might well need to be cut altogether if the aria changed position, because its text would probably be appropriate only for the original location. The abandoned *accompagnato* might influence the composition of a new recitative for the moved aria, whilst at the same time be reinstated itself to introduce the replacement in the original location. This could lead to the situation where it would be seen to mimic its own offspring.

The *accompagnato* 'Barbara!' perché fuggi?' has some unusual features. Its final cadence is untypical. Mozart is basically very consistent in following convention when cadencing at the end of a recitative: the final vocal syllables (usually two quavers) with an implied I$^c$ harmonisation on the strong beat, followed by a V – I cadence (weak / strong beats), with the I starting the next piece in an *attacca*. At the end of this recitative, however, there is a V$^7$ chord for the words 'e poi so-' and Ferrando ends in the usual way with '-spiri' over an implied tonic, but there is no subsequent V – I cadence, merely an F major chord on the last beat. There is also the question of what might be thought a slight discontinuity of tone. As things stand, the typically exaggerated sentiments of the *accompagnato* appear to be about to lead into an aria of rebuttal from Fiordiligi, until the last moment when the breezily cheerful 'Ah lo veggio' intervenes. It is possible that Mozart first drafted it to lead into an aria from Fiordiligi, and that when he decided that an aria from Ferrando should come first, he recast the ending of the recitative, adding the double *segue / dopo* instructions to draw attention to the change of plan. It may be no coincidence that in **V1** this recitative is covered with a wholly exceptional quantity of the small number checks for the copyist. The late removal of 'Come scoglio' would have left Mozart with a minor problem: the need to indicate some resistance on Fiordiligi's part, otherwise only evident in the sigh observed by Ferrando at the end of the *accompagnato*. It is not impossible that an extra stanza ('Ma tu fuggi') was added to the end of Ferrando's aria in order to indicate this (even though it was he who was about to leave), and this in turn could have produced the big 'agreed' cut that precedes this section.

In 'Ei parte', the *accompagnato* which follows Ferrando's exit, there is a telling feature which suggests that the issue of the pairing was still the driving force behind the process of revision. In the libretto there are six lines of text which do not appear in the musical setting. In these omitted lines, Fiordiligi addresses by name her absent beloved, and imagines his reactions to her betrayal:

> Guglielmo, anima mia! Perché sei tanto
> Ora lungi da me? Solo potresti ...
> Ahimè! Tu mi detesti
> Mi rigetti, m'abborri ... io già ti veggio.
> Minaccioso, sdegnato; io sento io sento
> I rimproveri amari, e il tuo tormento.

These missing lines add powerfully to the sense of betrayal, hardly yet justified by her actions. The omitted passage is in fact the only substantial section of recitative text in the libretto not set by Mozart, and its loss could well relate to the re-pairing of the lovers. With lovers uncrossed, Dorabella would have been Ferrando's *seria* partner, and in this recitative she would have had to sing 'Ferrando, anima mia!'. The name change could have been made without difficulty, but the character of the unset lines points to a deeper problem. The existing text climaxes with a truly histrionic utterance, an exaggerated catalogue of woe – 'smania' ('madness'), 'affanno' ('grief'), 'rimorso' ('remorse'), 'pentimento' ('repentance'), 'leggerezza' ('fickleness'), 'perfidia' ('perfidy') and 'tradimento' ('betrayal'). This seems a rather strident introduction to the essentially calm remorse of 'Per pietà', since Fiordiligi's betrayal has so far been in her mind only. Steptoe noted its 'taxonomy of histrionic inflations' and the contrast with an 'authentic note of fragile honesty' at the start of the aria.[35] Brown commented that at this point, the singer and the music 'cross over into parody'.[36] In character, these lines would seem rather more appropriate to a piece like Dorabella's 'Smanie implacabili'. The six unset lines could thus have represented an alternative ending, encapsulating the reaction of the sincere character, a Donna Anna rather than a Donna Elvira.

Another way of looking at the possibility that 'Come scoglio' was originally intended for Act II, is to consider how the plot might have worked. As it stands, there are a number of small oddities in this section of the drama, notably a persistent sense of uncertainty as to who is about to leave. Ferrando is presumed to have made his initial approach offstage, and then in the *accompagnato*, he declines to accede to Fiordiligi's furious demands that he leave until she has given him a kindly glance. Despite apparently observing a tell-tale sigh, Ferrando remains to sing his aria. Towards its end, he indicates that it is now Fiordiligi who is trying to leave. Yet at the conclusion of the aria it is he who finally quits the stage. As an aria of rebuttal, 'Come scoglio' would most likely have come after an attempt at seduction, as in the following hypothetical order: seduction on-stage or a report of an off-stage attempt; *accompagnato*; aria of rebuttal followed by Fiordiligi's exit; recitative in which Ferrando reports Fiordiligi's fidelity.

The simple recitative following Fiordiligi's exit suits its present purpose well enough. Ferrando describes how his attempted seduction has gone. Fiordiligi's first response, he claims, had been to treat it as a joke ('Ella da prima / Ride scherza mi burla.'). She then made a pretence of feeling pity ('E poi / Finge d'impietosirsi.'), but quickly her mood changed: 'Alfin scoppia la bomba; / Pura come colomba / Al suo caro Guglielmo ella si serba: / Mi discaccia superba. / Mi maltratta, mi fugge, / Testimonio rendendomi e messaggio / Che una femmina ell'è senza paraggio.' ('At last the bomb exploded. She was preserving herself as pure as a dove for her love Guglielmo. Proudly she rejected me, ill-treated me, fled from me, giving me proof and the message that she is a woman without equal.') In the context of the opera as we know it, this must refer to events that have taken place off-stage, since it is Ferrando who exits after his aria, leaving Fiordiligi alone for her soliloquy. It seems curious that he should describe this unseen episode when his more recent exchanges with Fiordiligi are in the mind of the audience. As Ford noted, 'Ferrando's account departs significantly from our first-hand knowledge of the affair.'[37] But if this recitative was intended to follow 'Come scoglio', it would reflect on-stage events accurately. The aria could with justice be represented as a haughty rejection of his advances, even, with a touch of humour, as a 'bomb' going off, and it would have been followed by Fiordiligi's exit.

The most significant structural difference between a plot with lovers crossed and one with lovers uncrossed is the manner in which the men discover that their lovers have betrayed them. There is a rich asymmetry in the formulation of the plot as it now stands. Ferrando learns of his lover's betrayal and then has to pull himself together to continue with his part in the deception. Guglielmo's ego is flattered by his early success as a seducer, and he in turn is humiliated at the climax. With the pairings uncrossed, each man would find out for himself. In the plot as we have it, Ferrando's reaction comes in the short but passionate cavatina 'Tradito' in which he expresses the classic operatic dilemma of continuing love after betrayal. Steptoe points out that the way in which he reacts to the news of his betrayal, shows 'marks of confusion', since his fury at Dorabella's betrayal is 'duplicated' in two passages of accompanied recitative.[38] On first being told the news, he bursts out with 'Il mio ritratto', only to be interrupted by his friend's big aria 'Donne mie'. After Guglielmo's departure he begins again with 'In qual fiero contrasto', this time as a soliloquy. An explanation for this could be found in an earlier plot with uncrossed lovers. For this there would certainly have been a requirement for a soliloquy. 'Tradito', positioned rather later in Act II, could first have been envisaged as a response to its singer's unwelcome success in winning the affections of his own lover, a powerful and private expression of bewilderment at the unexpected turn of events. After the reformulation of the plot with lovers crossed, the cavatina would still work, but a new recitative would have been needed in which Guglielmo breaks the news.

A complicating factor in the order of this section of the opera is Mozart's late decision to insert Guglielmo's aria 'Donne mie'. The immediate result of this was that 'Il mio ritratto' had to be provided with a different ending, diverting the music away from its original cadence in C minor, which was presumably intended to lead into 'Tradito'. It is conceivable that 'In qual fiero contrasto' was originally intended as Ferrando's anguished soliloquy in a plot with lovers uncrossed, and that it was brought back into the opera when (as a direct result of the inclusion of 'Donne mie' and Guglielmo's subsequent departure) a soliloquy was after all needed. The cavatina itself could have been changed as a result of this. In its original form it could even have begun in E♭ with 'Io sento che ancora / quest'alma l'adora', lines which do in fact take up the final sentiment of the recitative 'Il mio ritratto', when Ferrando's thoughts appear already to be turning from revenge. This would have produced a direct match between the key of the final cadence and the cavatina. The form of the piece might thus have been a more conventional A–B–A, with 'Tradito' as a B section reverting to his earlier outrage. The autograph score contains no obvious signs of any such reconstruction, but there is one interesting feature in the cavatina. The brace (including the names and clefs of the strings and Ferrando's part) and the particella (upbeat, six bars and three crotchets) were written first. Then apparently there was a break. Next, in a warm brown ink (otherwise uncommon in this part of Act II) Mozart wrote the names '2 Clarinetti' and '2 Fagotti' and the two bars and an upbeat of this wind entry in bar 8, but not the original clefs and key signatures of these instruments and their intervening rests. The remaining two bars of this opening wind passage come overleaf, and seem to be in a different ink. (Directly comparing the ink colours at the end of a recto with those at the start of the verso of the same leaf is, of course, impossible.) It is interesting that the final crotchet rest in Ferrando's bar 7 was also written in the warm ink, showing that when originally drafting the first few bars, Mozart had not ruled out the possibility of Ferrando continuing directly with his new phrase (rather than the wind interjection in E♭). Perhaps there was a draft of another version beginning in E♭, the start of which was incorporated after the C minor introduction.

In a light interlude before the final climactic duet, the two sisters and Despina are discussing the merits of having some fun with their new lovers. By now, Dorabella is a whole-hearted convert to the maid's way of thinking, and she joins in the attempt to persuade Fiordiligi. There are signs that changes were made here as well, but it is far from clear what they signify. Below the heading Scena X, Mozart first wrote 'Dorabella, Fiordiligi' but immediately smudged out 'Fiordiligi' and added in 'Despina, poi Fiordiligi'. This was perhaps nothing more than a momentary lapse, as Fiordiligi is not present at the start of the score, though she quickly enters. On the other hand, the slip may relate to uncertainty over how the recitative was to start. In **V1** one of the 'agreed' cuts removed everything before Fiordiligi's entry with 'Sciagurate'. During the course of the recitative, which is elegantly copied out in a dark ink with a fine-tipped quill, Mozart made a tiny slip (or attempted a correction) which could have stemmed from uncertainty over the pairing. In the duet 'Prenderò quel brunettino', Dorabella has already gone for the darker-haired officer, leaving 'il biondino' to Fiordiligi. There is nothing in the plot up to this point, however, to identify which officer was meant, and if there was any question over whether the lovers should be crossed or uncrossed, this duet would work either way. In the recitative this motif is taken up again. Dorabella asks whether Fiordiligi has yet fallen in love with the 'galante biondino' and then proposes seventy thousand kisses from each of them: 'Tu il biondino, io'l brunetto'. At the word 'tu', some mistake, hesitation or correction affected the writing of the word. It would be nice to be able to report that Mozart started to write 'io', but it is not clear that this is what happened.

A significant change of plan at the end of this recitative led to a 'wrong' cadence into Dorabella's aria 'È amore'. The recitative cadences in E, but the aria is in B♭. The late copying of this aria is evident not only in this tonal disjunction, but also in the enlarged bass note-heads, a feature shared with two other undoubtedly late pieces, the overture and the replacement for the Act II finale canon. In the libretto, moreover, there is space after its end, usually a sign of an inserted text. The correct recitative ending appears in **V1**. Dorabella, by now a thorough-going convert to Despina's philosophy, lightly remarks: 'Credi, sorella, è meglio che tu ceda' ('Believe me sister you'd better give in'). A piece such as 'È amore' seems to be intended, and yet the key implied by the recitative cadence is A major or E major. One explanation is that Mozart was indeed intending this aria to be in A major, but for some reason, perhaps the proximity of the A major duet, decided to put it up a semitone after the recitative had been copied.

In the sequence of recitatives following 'È amore' which are not extant in Mozart's hand, the idea of the women dressing in the officers' uniforms and going off to confess to them enters the plot. As yet, Fiordiligi has not fully succumbed to Ferrando's advances, and her betrayal, although deeply felt, is still in the mind only. In Scene XI, the two officers overhear Fiordiligi resolving to remain constant, and she then summons Despina to go and find the disguises. In Scene XII, Fiordiligi is again alone, but Ferrando enters (there is no direct indication where) and the other men again listen in, this time with a less happy outcome for Guglielmo. However, there is some confusion here, because Guglielmo is apparently already listening in, even before Ferrando enters. In Scene XI, he had proudly called on the others to take note of Fiordiligi's resistance ('Bravissima! La mia casta Artemisia! La sentite?'). In Scene XII, he also has a question ('Si può dar un amor simile a questo?'). There is thus a small element of repetition in the way that the idea of Guglielmo's offstage observation of Fiordiligi is treated. Perhaps the recitative of Scene XI was written specifically for where it now stands, with the second recitative being imperfectly revised from an earlier version, leaving in the stray line.

A physical sign of the late revision of this part of Act II could lie in the fact that neither of these two recitatives exists in Mozart's hand. There are two versions: one is in **V1** and is therefore to be found in other early copies; the other is bound in with the autograph but was rightly relegated by the editors of the *NMA* to an appendix. Although by virtue of its incorporation into **V1**, the former is to be preferred, it begins with a root-position chord, the only such occurrence in a recitative in *Così*, a clear divergence from Mozart's normal practice and a sign that an assistant may have been responsible for it. Another surprising feature is that the two versions embody radically different harmonic schemes, with different final cadences, as shown in Table 22. One reason for such a divergence in the tonal direction of the two recitatives could be that a different sequence was under consideration, in which the two recitatives were to be separated by an aria.

A sign of confusion possibly related to the pairings is the question of the choice of the uniforms. Whose clothing Fiordiligi chose to wear had potential symbolic significance, a point often noted. Surprisingly, in 'L'abito di Ferrando' she selects the uniform of her sister's lover and (unbeknown to her) her own would-be seducer, whereas in the previous recitative, she had quite naturally thought of Guglielmo's uniform first. It is arguable that this was an oversight

TABLE 22 Contrasting harmonic schemes in 'Come tutto' and 'L'abito di Ferrando'

| Version | Come tutto congiura | L'abito di Ferrando |
| --- | --- | --- |
| **V1** | C major → D major | A major → A major |
| later version bound in with the autograph | C major → B♭ major | G major → E major |

and that someone forgot to make the switch, so that Fiordiligi ended up making an inappropriate choice.

'No theory of *Così fan tutte* will do', wrote Kerman, that does not take full measure of the wonderful seduction duet 'Fra gli amplessi' in which Ferrando finally ensnares Fiordiligi.[39] It is hard indeed to avoid the conclusion that the secret of the opera lies in this dramatic and passionate scene, in which Mozart leaves behind altogether the opera world he had inherited with its closed forms, to embrace the free-flowing procedures of a later age. This duet is the point at which Steptoe's theory of the tonal representation of sincerity / insincerity seems to break down. The 'sincere' key of A major has to be explained away: 'Here the intensity of Ferrando's assault transcends duplicity, creating an episode of profound ambivalence. The duet taxes the link between meaning and key to its limits, paradoxically confirming the importance of tonality while undermining its force'.[40]

Palaeographic features in the autograph hint at the large scale of the changes made by Mozart as he worked. Ink colours allow the tentative identification of several copying breaks in the particella. The first occurs early on in bar 11, when a light brown ink with occasional dark note-heads copied with a fine-tipped quill gives way to a more even light brown, sometimes darkening, copied in a slightly broader-tipped quill. Although the change is not very noticeable, the impression is of slightly bolder writing. The next copying break is slightly more obvious. It occurs at the C major signature in bar 40, from which point the particella is copied in a more intense, chocolate-brown ink. It is evident that Mozart wrote Fiordiligi's minim C (of '[Ohi]mè') before putting in the new key signature, as it had to be squeezed in just before the staff, whereas the key signatures in the parts of Ferrando and the bass are positioned normally. It seems likely therefore that the decision to extend the C major section coincided with this copying break. The final one (much clearer than the others) occurred when Mozart decided against a prolongation of a German sixth chord in bar 96. After the deleted bar, the particella continues in a dark, blackish-looking ink.

Another telling clue about the scale of the changes which Mozart made to the first part of 'Fra gli amplessi' comes in the bifoliation numbers. Throughout the opera, these were added to the sheets on which a piece was to be copied before the writing began. Sometimes an additional folio became necessary because the piece was turning out to be longer than anticipated, and then it had its number added, often in a manifestly different ink. At the start of 'Fra gli amplessi', numbered as though it were an aria, the bifoliation numbers reflect a significant upheaval. The first folio (a single leaf) is numbered '1' in brown; the second (again a single leaf) is numbered '2' in a much lighter brown; the third bifolium (a pair of obviously conjoined leaves cut quite short at the bottom) is numbered with a '2' in brown which matches the number '1', but at some point this had been numbered with a '3' in the lighter brown ink. Thereafter, the bifoliation numbers continue normally but in a different ink. The first copying break occurs half-way across the verso of the first single folio, the second (at the C major key signature) at the start of the verso of the first leaf of the conjugate pair. The section of the duet covered by this unusual bifoliation thus extends up to the end of the C major recall of material from 'Una bella serenata' and the new key signature. Because there is a strikingly exact match between the unexpected appearance of the single folio with the light brown '2' and the equally unheralded appearance of Ferrando on stage, there is the distant possibility that contrary to his normal working practice Mozart creatively 'merged' two existing particellas. This would imply that at least a few bars of Ferrando's entry 'ed intanto' had already been written out, and that Mozart composed the start of the duet (after the first ink break) to lead into this continuation. The ink colours provide no real support for this unlikely scenario. A preferable hypothesis takes into account the fact that there is an ink smudge at the start of the first bar of Ferrando's entry. There is no sign of text, note-stem, or even note-head, and so the original is likely to have been a rest, probably a crotchet rest.[41] While there is a simple explanation, that Mozart briefly thought of having Ferrando respond even more hastily to Fiordiligi than he now does, it is also possible that this smudged out rest was as far as Mozart had got with a particella with a light-brown foliation number series, consisting of bifolium 1 (missing), bifolium 2 (one sheet used in the final score), and bifolium 3 (renumbered 2). It is not possible to say what this hypothetical earlier version might have contained, but there would have been enough space for a more conventional start to a seduction duet: a stanza from the man; followed by a stanza from the woman in reply. Ferrando's 'Ed intanto' which certainly seems like a response to Fiordiligi, would have been his next try.

The bifolium numbered '1' in brown in the autograph almost certainly had its second leaf removed. The mere fact that it was numbered '1' at all is of interest. Mozart normally included all the ensembles in his long bifoliation number series, 'La mano a me date' being an exception because it was originally intended as an aria. Although there are musical and textual grounds for supposing that Fiordiligi's first quatrain could have been conceived originally as the start of an aria for her, this was not the case by the time that Mozart ruled out the brace of the particella, which has space for a line for Ferrando. The particella with the light brown number sequence could also have been derived from paper allocated to something else. The loss of the other sheet of the second bifolium might indicate that it had already been written on. Little can be said for certain about the circumstances that led to the bifoliation sequence as we have it, except that at least one change of mind very much more drastic than usual seems to have taken place. (One other unusual feature marks the moment in the autograph when the wind parts enter. An assistant added in twice the instruction 'con più moto', already given by Mozart at the foot of the page.)

As to how an earlier draft might have differed from the final version, our only source of evidence is **V1**. The copyist wrote out the text of Fiordiligi's opening quatrain with a different final word, repeated twice: 'in quest'abito morrò'. This is a more extreme sentiment than in the autograph, where she merely proposes to appear before her lover in the uniform rather than to die. The repeated discrepancy is unlikely to have been a slip. Mozart's Italian hand was not usually that bad! The copyist was perhaps instructed to start copying as a duet the discarded and amended particella of an aria opening. The word 'verrò' appears correctly in the libretto. An interesting consequence of this change is possibly to be seen four bars later in Ferrando's part in bar 18. As the editors of *NMA: KB* point out, Mozart scraped out a word, replacing it with 'mi m[or]rò'.[42] Perhaps there was a different word here that was changed once 'morrò' was removed from Fiordiligi's quatrain. No correction is noted at the next occurrence in bar 20, so it seems this was a momentary slip on Mozart's part, misreading an unclear or corrected original, rather than a deliberate later amendment.

At this point it will be useful to present a reconstruction of how the various elements of this duet might have been structured in an earlier version. This is given in Table 23. It is a speculative undertaking, but the state of the autograph encourages bold thinking.[43] Reasons for assuming this particular structure (which tries to take into account various palaeographical features of the duet in the autograph) will be discussed below.

This basic structure assumes balancing quatrains ('Volgi a me' and a response), then a more urgent plea from Ferrando and a further rebuttal from Fiordiligi, followed by a mutual recognition of her approaching surrender, and rapid exchanges as the moment approaches. A final duet would seal the new musical union. This would perhaps have generated a more straightforward tonal plan: A major for the opening quatrains; a modulation via A minor to C major for Fiordiligi's 'Taci' (which is where the C major key signature now is); A and D minor for the approaching capitulation, heralded by a prolonged German sixth chord on 'Dei consiglio', leading to the final duet in A major. Missing from this hypothetical scheme completely are Fiordiligi's 'Fra gli amplessi' (already identified as perhaps having been conceived as the start of an aria) and the whole of the C major section recalling 'Una bella serenata', which so dramatically interrupts the duet as we know it, pre-empting the move to C major at 'Taci'. This hypothetical original would have been much more conventional in structure, not unlike 'Il core vi dono'.

TABLE 23  Hypothetical original structure of 'Fra gli amplessi'

| Ferrando | Together | Fiordiligi |
|---|---|---|
| Volgi a me pietoso il ciglio, In me sol trovar tu puoi Sposo, amante, e più se vuoi, Idol mio, più non tardar. | | |
| | | [quatrain in response] |
| Ed intanto di dolore, Meschinello io mi morrò. | | |
| | | Taci ... ahimè! Son abbastanza Tormentata, ed infelice! |
| | Ah che omai la mia/sua costanza A quei sguardi, a quell che dice Incomincia a vaccilar. | |
| | | Sorgi, sorgi ... |
| In van lo credi. | | |
| | | Per pietà, da me che chiedi? |
| Il tuo cor, o la mia morte. | | |
| | | Ah, non son, non son più forte |
| Cedi, cara! | | |
| | | Dei consiglio! |
| | Abbracciamci, o caro bene, E un conforto a tante pene Sia languir di dolce affetto Di diletto sospirar. | |

Before discussing whether a duet structured like this would have been appropriate for the plot with lovers uncrossed and the significance of the C major recall of music from 'Una bella serenata', there are a number of other musical features which could be a legacy of such a structure. First is the opening orchestral A major arpeggio, close enough to the flourish at the start of 'Un'aura amorosa' to suggest an intentional reference, and yet an inexact one. If a recall was intended, it is a puzzling one. In Act I, the arpeggio introduces Ferrando dreaming of Dorabella and true love. At the start of 'Fra gli amplessi', it introduces Fiordiligi. However, if the arpeggio had first been intended to introduce 'Volgi a me' in the plot with lovers uncrossed, it would have been entirely appropriate, and it might well then have been an exact recall, as 'Volgi a me' is in 3/4. (In considering whether or not a recall was intended, it is worth bearing in mind that the arpeggio at the start of 'Un'aura amorosa' might itself have been a late addition to the particella. Originally the intention seems to have been to end the previous recitative with a perfect cadence and a *segue* to an aria beginning softly with muted strings.)

In musical character, the quatrain 'Fra gli amplessi' is certainly aria-like. Fiordiligi, either regretting her fall or fearing it, decides to go to her own lover in disguise. Its appearance at the start of the seduction duet results in some unusual features. The failure of Ferrando to begin the piece is in itself surprising, as is the uninvolved tone of Fiordiligi's opening words – her first lines read much more like the text of a soliloquy than the opening of a passionate encounter. When he does enter, Ferrando seems to materialise out of nowhere, responding to Fiordiligi's remarks without an opening statement of his own.

A feature which distinguishes the start of 'Volgi a me' is that its opening melodic phrase was revised more substantially than any other in the opera. This might well have been done for purely musical reasons, but a change of position would at least have given Mozart occasion to reconsider. There is another clue in **V1**. At the start of 'Fra gli amplessi' is written 'No. 29', but over the section 'Volgi a me' there also appears 'No. 29', later crossed out in red crayon. The copyist was apparently working from a draft in which 'Volgi a me' had once been the start of No. 29.

An important clue to the possible restructuring of this duet comes after the word 'Crudel' in bar 95, at which point in the autograph score Mozart crossed out a bar. (Fig. 11.) When he resumed copying the particella, it was in a different ink. The deleted bar would have contained a prolonged German sixth chord, which now only appears on the first crotchet of bar 96. In the hypothetical plan of the original duet, it was suggested that the lead into the final section ('Abracciamci') was the series of exchanges culminating in Fiordiligi's 'Dei consiglio' with its dramatic pause on an augmented sixth chord. By restructuring and expanding the duet so that this first German sixth chord no longer expresses the actual moment of Fiordiligi's fall, Mozart now had the problem of whether to repeat the chord at the real moment of surrender. He was obviously intending a prolongation of the chord, but apparently stopped to consider the matter further, finally deciding to remove the bar. But there was another possible reason for a hiatus – a potential lacuna in the text. In the hypothetical earlier structure, Fiordiligi would have indicated her surrender in the exchange: 'Ah non son, non son più forte' / 'Cedi cara' / 'Dei consiglio'. With this passage placed earlier in the duet, there was now the need for Fiordiligi to express her submission to Ferrando. She has not done so by the time of the word 'Crudel!' at the second augmented sixth chord. Mozart had the inspired idea of adding a few bars (over a $I^c - V$ progression) with the words 'hai vinto' ('You've won') and 'Fa' di me quel che ti par' ('Do with me what you will.'). A short but piercingly beautiful oboe melody signifies the actual surrender. The final layer of additions to this passage

FIG. 11 The autograph of *Così fan tutte*, Act II (Mus. ms. Autogr. W. A. Mozart 588, vol. 2, fol. 267v), Staatsbibliothek zu Berlin, Preußischer Kulturbesitz, Musikabteilung mit Mendelssohn Archiv, 'Fra gli amplessi' (bars 94–6), detail. An additional bar containing a prolongation of the augmented sixth chord heard on the first beat of bar 96 was crossed out. (Staatsbibliothek zu Berlin – Preußischer Kulturbesitz, Musikabteilung mit Mendelssohn-Archiv. Mus.ms.autogr. W. A. Mozart 588 vol. 2)

was done in an identifiable 'fuzzy' warm brown ink. Mozart added a beautiful chromatic touch to the oboe melody in bar 97, a musical acknowledgement of Ferrando's previous plea.

The question of whether the suggested recomposition of 'Fra gli amplessi' could have stemmed from a change of mind over the pairings brings to the fore the central enigma of this duet: the fact that in the C major section, which according to my theory was inserted into the recast structure, there appears to be a deliberate reference to Ferrando's music in 'Una bella serenata'. The meaning of this unmistakeable but inexact recall has been much discussed.[44] In 'Una bella serenata', Ferrando sings his intensely lyrical, soaring phrase, to express confidence in Dorabella's fidelity. When it resurfaces in 'Fra gli amplessi', he is now acting a part to undermine Fiordiligi. The problem with the citation (if such it is) is not so much that the melody reappears in a context in which true love is about to be shown to be an illusion, but that true love (on the part of the man singing the melody) should not be at issue at all. Perhaps the idea of making this recall emerged during the time when Mozart and Da Ponte were attempting a structure with lovers uncrossed. In this context, there would have been absolutely no ambivalence about its meaning, as the melody would encapsulate a terrible and salutary lesson for Ferrando in the 'School for Lovers'. Having confidently resorted to this melody for the final assault on his own beloved's integrity, to his horror he would have witnessed her succumbing to the very music with which he had predicted her undying fidelity.

The message of the C major recall in the plot with lovers uncrossed would have been unambiguous, but in the plot with lovers crossed its meaning is obscure. The first surprise is that it is Fiordiligi who introduces a very recognisable and characteristic fragment of the melody, even though she has never heard it. (This alone might be enough to show that Mozart was adapting material envisaged for another purpose.) Her introduction of the phrase results in a very sharp rise in dramatic temperature. It seems indeed a rather extreme response to Ferrando, who so far has only sung the miserable 'Ed intanto di dolore, meschinello io mi morrò'. The essential point is that whatever use Mozart may have been intending to make of the C major recall material in a plot with lovers uncrossed, it would have been expressing Ferrando's real emotions about his own lover. This brings us back to the crux of the dilemma.

By choosing the plot with lovers crossed, Mozart ensured that Ferrando's attitude in the seduction duet would be profoundly ambiguous. Throughout the opera he has acted the part of the stereotypical *seria* lover, ardent and sincere, but now he must seek to entrap his friend's lover. His glorious tones are to be deployed in a devious and unkind deception. Some have wondered (perhaps even hoped) that in response to the seemingly insoluble problem facing him, Mozart decided that the tenor should begin genuinely to fall in love with Fiordiligi, as the natural musical pairing of the *seria* lovers begins to override the original mismatches. Whereas Guglielmo, through asides such as 'Infelice Ferrando' and 'Ferrando meschino!' clearly indicates that he is acting a part, Ferrando, by contrast, seems totally absorbed in his task, never once referring to his fellow officer, although this may simply reflect the different conventions of writing for a *buffo* bass and a lyrical tenor. The only hint that Ferrando's own emotions might be changing comes in a remarkable example of indecision on Mozart's part. In the passage in which Fiordiligi and Ferrando sing of the threat to their constancy, Mozart first wrote for Ferrando a line suggesting that his own constancy was wavering. He crossed out 'mia' and substituted 'sua' (as in the libretto), but then he reverted to 'mia'. (Fig. 12.) Both the original and the two changes seem to be in the same ink. It is always possible that the draft of a much revised libretto was seriously unclear at this point. It may be significant that shortly after this point, the composer himself made two further slips in the verbal text, which he quickly corrected, writing 'Invan lo chiedi' (instead of 'Invan lo credi') and 'Oh non son' (instead of 'Ah non son'). Such errors do occur, but are not at all common in the autograph of the opera as a whole.

A pragmatic explanation for the rejection of the pronoun 'sua' for Ferrando might be that in the hypothetical original structure this phrase would have immediately preceded Fiordiligi's surrender. Ferrando's observation that 'her' constancy was wavering would signal this. In the final version, such an unambiguous statement might have seemed premature, as we have yet to hear Ferrando's passionate plea 'Volgi a me'. But this still leaves open the question as to why Ferrando should be worried about 'his' constancy at all, unless it is simply a tactic in the ongoing seduction. While he might with equally good reason comment on Fiordiligi's wavering state (in alarm, if she is his own woman, in anticipation of success, if she is Guglielmo's), to imply that his own emotions are changing must either be an outright deception or else an indication that he is starting to realise the strength of Fiordiligi's charms, making sense of the ardour of the music for the time being, but adding to the emotional let-down of the opera's final resolution. The copyist of **V1**, either through error or perhaps because he too was working from a very unclear original, managed to get the

FIG. 12 The autograph of *Così fan tutte*, Act II (Mus. ms. Autogr. W. A. Mozart 588, vol. 2, fol. 264), Staatsbibliothek zu Berlin, Preußischer Kulturbesitz, Musikabteilung mit Mendelssohn Archiv, 'Fra gli amplessi' (bars 43–7), detail. Mozart had several changes of mind over the pronoun Ferrando was to sing, changing from 'mia' to 'sua' and then back to 'mia'. (Staatsbibliothek zu Berlin – Preußischer Kulturbesitz, Musikabteilung mit Mendelssohn-Archiv. Mus.ms.autogr. W. A. Mozart 588 vol. 2)

pronouns wrong for both Fiordiligi and Ferrando, thereby placing the spotlight firmly on the latter's changing emotions.

If the transition from a conventionally structured duet to the remarkable piece we know today occurred as the result of the circumstances suggested above, it would have to count as a supreme example of 'making a virtue out of necessity' a phrase that Mozart himself once used. As it now stands, 'Fra gli amplessi' provides a fluid, dynamic and potentially even unpredictable climax to Fiordiligi's seduction.

## *The Denouement*

Signs of late reorganisation are evident in the short recitatives before the finale, in which the deception is finally revealed. Uncertainty over which women the two officers should marry seems to have contributed to several gaps and inconsistencies in the plot at this critical juncture. Despina's doings seem particularly obscure. She was last seen leaving the stage at the end of Scene XI, to carry out Fiordiligi's instructions to have a servant fit out post-horses for their journey to the battlefront. Now she suddenly reappears, apparently knowing all about the plans for a double wedding and reporting that the sisters will sign a contract. In both the autograph and the libretto, an incorrect stage direction at the start of Scene XIII seems to show that she was to have come back on stage sooner: 'Guil. Don Alf. poi Ferrando indi Despina'.[45] The maid was thus to have entered, presumably to hear about the new plan. But there was an obvious difficulty: she is not supposed to know the secret identities of the two Albanians and could therefore only have come back after all dealings between Don Alfonso and the two officers in their 'real' characters were over. Don Alfonso begins by asking whether the two officers still love their 'plucked crows' ('cornacchio spenacchiale'), an undoubted reference to their original lovers, and he then suggests a double wedding to settle matters. In a plot with lovers uncrossed, all this would have been unproblematic. Despina would have entered, and although in ignorance of who the Albanians really were, she would make arrangements for the betrothal of the right couples. As for the assumed names adopted by the officers 'Sempronio' and 'Tizio', the libretto does not identify who takes which name, so that this aspect of the plot would have worked either way.

There is, of course, another reason why this recitative might have been amended to end with 'Tutti accusan le donne', as this short trio was now to proclaim the motto of the opera. It is widely believed to have been composed late on, after the decision was taken to change the opera's title. While there may have been a wish not to offend Salieri who had begun work on the libretto and with whose earlier 'school' opera Mozart's new work was certain to be compared, the change could also have been precipitated by the abandonment of the plot with lovers uncrossed, in which both the men and the women would have been 'schooled', in favour of one in which the behaviour of the women is firmly under the spotlight.

The question of whether or not the lovers should be crossed reaches a climax in the Act II finale. Although its structure could remain unchanged, the emotional consequences of the officers' revelation of themselves to their own partners would be quite different. There are in fact nine features that might relate to a possible switch in the pairings:

1    As they leave the wedding preparations, Don Alfonso and Despina were originally to have commented that 'a more pleasing scene' ('Una scena più piacevole') had never, and would never again be seen. In his score, Mozart changed this to 'la più bella commediola'. The new phrase 'a very pretty little comedy' implies a theatrical 'crisis'.

2    A seemingly trivial matter is whether the men should join in raising their glasses at the end of the canon quartet. In the preceding bars both couples are apparently preparing to drink – they sing in pairs 'Tocca e bevi / bevi e tocca' – but there seems to have been a question as to whether the men should actually drink this toast to oblivion. In the autograph Mozart wrote 'bevono' (and placed the instruction so that it would include the men), but in the libretto only the women drink ('le donne bevono') and Guglielmo's outburst 'Ah bevessero del tossico / Queste volpi senza onor!' ('Would they were drinking poison, these shameless vixens') gains point. A significant stage direction for Guglielmo ('da se sotto voce') is missing in the libretto.

3    At the end of the canon quartet, there is a crossed-out bar in which Dorabella was to have begun the last phrase of her full statement of the canon. Guglielmo, having by now vented his anger, was apparently to address her individually, to judge by the stage direction '/à Dor:/'. Throughout both finales, individual communication between the two couples is kept to an absolute minimum, until the point at which the men address the women separately at the denouement. What Guglielmo would have sung in the continuation of the canon is uncertain, but as he was about to address his new lover Dorabella, he must have been about to temper his anger. The sketches for this passage do not shed any light on the question: they merely contain the first phrase and a few notes of the second phrase of Guglielmo's previous interjections.

4    Mozart composed a short replacement for the entire canon quartet, extending the music of the previous passage to the new text. It is not known whether this new section was in use around the time of the première, but it was incorporated into Guardasoni's 1791 Prague version, and, following his discovery of the

autograph, Treitschke included it in the Vienna *Mädchentreue* version in 1804. It was not otherwise widely adopted.

5 When Ferrando and Guglielmo return safe and well, it is to the loving embraces of their 'most faithful lovers' ('Delle nostre fidissime amanti'). In his autograph, Mozart substituted 'spose' ('promised ones') for 'amanti', a distinctly more cutting observation in the light of the newly signed contracts.

6 When Ferrando finally reveals his true identity to his lover, he does so through the device of musical and dramatic recall. He recalls the moment when he was to have introduced himself to one of the women as an Albanian nobleman ('A voi s'inchina'). The suggestion that this was an intentional 'non-recall' seems out of character for such a theatrical composer as Mozart, and it is usually assumed that this was an oversight.[46] If so, then it is a sign that after the Act II finale had been drafted in particella, Mozart went back to Act I and revised the section in which the introductions were to have been made.

7 When it is Guglielmo's turn, he confronts Dorabella with the opening bars of their duet. Palaeographic features of 'Il core vi dono' and its recall here in the Act II finale raise interesting questions about the relationship between the two pieces of music. Some compositional interplay between the two seems very likely. Three features of the recall catch the eye: the text has five- rather than six-syllable lines; the orchestration is different; and there is a small vocal flourish on the word 'coricino'. The change in the number of syllables could simply indicate that Mozart and Da Ponte wished to fit this brief recall into the prevailing metre. The variants in the string instrumentation suggest that the recall was worked out at the particella stage (as indeed demonstrated by the later addition of slurs in the string parts at both locations). The vocal flourish is a nice ironic touch. There is insufficient evidence here to demonstrate the existence of an earlier version of 'Il core', although that must remain at least a possibility. Other features of the recall deserve further comment. At the start there is an unusual phenomenon. Mozart normally wrote in the text with an elegant, essentially level, horizontal flow. Here, however, 'ritrattino' and what follows is much lower than 'Il'. It is as though Mozart was suddenly struck by a thought and paused before continuing. Very likely he was worried by the contrasting accentuation of the word 'Il', which comes on the anacrusis in 'Il core' but here is on the stressed first beat. In bar 502 the first violin originally had a pause over the note D. It was later repositioned over the following rest to allow a contrast with bars 502 and 506, where the note is sustained. In bar 2 of the bass part in the particella of 'Il core vi dono' there is a similar change. Mozart originally wrote a quaver rest on beat 3. When putting in the string instrumentation, he decided that there should be a pause

on beat three, so he turned the quaver rest into a semiquaver rest with a pause and added the extra semiquaver rest. In both the original location and the recall a pause was first placed on the second quaver. It is evident that at the stage of the string instrumentation of 'Il core vi dono' when the articulation, dynamics and other performance marks would usually be established, Mozart worked on both the original and the recall. Mozart's initial choice of a 3/4 signature at the start of the duet might also indicate that there was an earlier particella in that time signature. It is not clear whether the change to 3/8 would then have preceded the composition of the recall or have been provoked by it.

8  Perhaps the most surprising feature of all in the libretto of this opera is the complete absence of any reference to the repairing of the couples. In fact the two officers do not address their original partners individually again, nor are there indications in the stage instructions of any reversion to the *status quo*. The realignment is assumed to take place: because of what is said in 'Tutti accusan le donne'; because of the apologies given at the end; and because it was the accepted convention in *opera buffa*.

9  After the Act II finale had been copied in **V1**, Mozart apparently suggested a small cut, the effect of which would have been to remove a line sung by the two sisters: 'Idol mio se questo è vero'. This section also exists in a sketch, which Tyson suggested could even postdate the composition of the main opera.[47]

If there is one certainty about the state of the plot immediately prior to its final revision, it is that one or other of the disguised officers was to take the all-important symbolic initiative in setting up the new couples for the following seductions, either Ferrando in 'A voi s'inchina', or Guglielmo in 'Rivolgete'. Very late on in a major rethink, Mozart and Da Ponte decided that the officers should not influence the pairings – in this respect Guglielmo's replacement aria is strictly neutral. By doing so, they allowed the sisters to express their own preference in 'Prenderò quel brunettino', and it was then left to Don Alfonso to give effect to these choices in the quartet 'La mano a me date'. In the tiny recitative leading into this piece, Guglielmo hastily interrupts Ferrando who is about to address Dorabella as an individual: Ferrando: 'Madama ...'; Guglielmo: 'Anzi, madame'.

A late switch in the pairings could itself have been the reason why Mozart and Da Ponte abandoned pieces in which the two officers take the lead, in favour of allowing the women a free choice. If the lovers had been uncrossed, it would hardly have done for the women to choose their own partners. A much sharper lesson is learnt if their affections are transferred, and they make the 'wrong' choices. The balance of culpability in a plot in which the disguised men presented themselves to their own women in order to test their fidelity would be very different. The message would be not the faithlessness of women but the stupidity of men who seek to put to the test what should be taken on trust. In such a plot, the women could have resorted to a ready explanation of their seemingly fickle conduct: of course they had recognised the officers instantly, but had played along with the deception, angry at the lack of trust, or simply to humour an immature escapade. As Steptoe points out, 'if the men seduced their own beloved, it could be argued that the women did not succumb but unconsciously detected the fundamental qualities of their admirers.'[48]

In considering whether any of the other small changes relate to the question of the pairings, it would be possible to assume, for the sake of argument, that the Act II finale (much as it stands) was written for the plot with uncrossed lovers and then through pressure of time left virtually unchanged, but it would probably be rather difficult to distinguish this from the alternative, which is that the end of the libretto was hastily revised for the plot with lovers crossed, albeit retaining some signs of its earlier purpose. In reality, the finale almost works for either ending. The only firm indication of the plot with switched lovers is the pair of stage directions 'à Fiord:' and 'à Dor:' above the start of the recall passages. The impact of the musical recalls would have been even more dramatic if sung by their real lovers. Ferrando would reveal himself theatrically to his own 'bella damina' in a repetition of his original self-introduction, while Guglielmo would have the appropriately embarrassing task for a braggart of returning the miniature of his own likeness to his 'signora'.

As Link has shown, Mozart's decision to compose a canon for the lovers' toast ('E nel tuo nel mio bicchiero') relates to a well-established tradition of operatic canons in Vienna, notably by Martín y Soler and Salieri. Mozart's celebrated example may legitimately be seen as an 'episode of professional rivalry'.[49] Surprisingly, however, Mozart composed a simple substitute on the same text. Although this seems to have been performed in Prague in 1791, as seen in **C1**, it has not been possible to establish that it was written specifically for Guardasoni, although this cannot be ruled out entirely. More likely it was part of a revision of *Così fan tutte* undertaken in Vienna, the version **V2** as represented by **Ca**. Practical explanations for the replacement – that there were worries about the length of the scene or its difficulty for the singers – are always possible.[50] Less convincing, however, is the idea that Mozart regarded it as an avowed 'competition piece', which he was happy to sacrifice for the sake of the finale's momentum, 'once he had publicly proved his superior contrapuntal skills'.[51] Another explanation lies in the character of the music, one of the most beautiful passages in the whole opera. In a plot with uncrossed lovers, the scene would have been richly asymmetrical and full of irony. The women, confident in their new

love, would drink to the oblivion of the old. The men, knowing that their vic-
tims were actually doing no such thing, would anticipate the imminent consignment of the whole unfortunate experiment to history: or so they would
be hoping. The warm glow and exalted music of the canon would anticipate
the 'bella calma' of the coming reconciliation between true couples, who had
never in fact been parted. When the plot with crossed lovers was finally chosen,
Mozart perhaps began to worry about the effect of this music. It would now act
as a powerful affirmation of the musical union of the wrong couples, and there
would be little opportunity to counteract its sublime power. The replacement
passage, routine in character, would allow this moment to pass by quickly without adding further to the musical bonding between Fiordiligi and Ferrando. In
one sense, the contemplated loss of the canon could be seen as the converse of
the late decision to insert 'Di scrivermi' into Act I. This piece is also exalted in
tone and (notwithstanding the deception) expresses the musical reality of the
love of the original couples, a relationship in danger of being lost altogether in
the plot with lovers crossed. I agree with Hunter's view that: 'What Mozart has
done in these three numbers [she is also considering 'Soave sia il vento'] is to
deploy his genius for absolute beauty precisely at the crucial joints in the drama,
as the experiment begins and ends.'[52]

But, of course, the feature of the finale most suggestive of a plot with uncrossed
lovers is the failure to make clear that the original couples are restored. This
is quite remarkable in so symmetrical a plot, one moreover in which Mozart
and Da Ponte had considered at great length how the original switch should be
made. Dent went so far as to say that it was not clear in the libretto whether the
women pair off with their original lovers or their new ones.[53] However, as many
scholars have since pointed out, the conventions of eighteenth-century opera
dictated a return to the original couples. Steptoe makes a further valid point
against the ending seen in some modern productions, in which the original couples are not restored: 'It is misleading to suppose that Fiordiligi comes to love
Ferrando (or Dorabella to love Guglielmo); rather the women are overcome by
the disguised forms of these men.'[54] The denouement as we have it would have
worked perfectly in the plot formulation with lovers unswitched. Ferrando and
Guglielmo would reveal themselves to their own women with embarrassment all
round. Fiordiligi and Dorabella would ask for forgiveness, and so too would the
two men, promising never again to indulge in the folly of putting their love to
the test. The marriage contracts would pose no problem; they would unite the
'right' lovers after all. The 'bella calma' restored at the end would seem appropriate. Above all, it would explain the aspect of the ending that has disturbed so
many critics and producers: the obvious incompatibility of the restored couples.
We return to an eloquent passage in Heartz:

Critics have been understandably loath to see the high-spirited Fiordiligi go back to the grumbling Guglielmo. Leaving aside the question of
matching temperaments, we arrive on musical grounds alone at the ver-
dict that the new pairing is better than the old. Fiordiligi belongs with
the tenor Ferrando because by all the laws of opera, if not of Heaven,
high voices should be paired together. In some other type of opera this
argument might weigh less. In an opera about opera, the prima donna
surely deserves to contemplate going through life into eternity singing
love duets with the tenor, not the bass.[55]

In the alternative formulation, the 'right' pairings could continue, albeit with
both couples in a chastened frame of mind. In this 'scuola', it would have been
the men who received the sharper lesson, Ferrando, in particular, learning the
unwarranted risk of putting to the test what best exists on trust.

The severity of the lesson learned by the women in the final version of the
opera depends on one other factor: the status of their original relationship with
the men. Are Ferrando and Guglielmo presumed to be 'amanti' or 'sposi'? In
the case of the former, the switch in the women's affections would constitute a
personal betrayal; in the latter case, their action might also involve the breaking
of a more formal promise. Without exaggerating the distinction between the
two terms, it is interesting to follow their usage throughout the opera. In Act I,
except for a few (probably late) recitatives around the farewell scenes, both the
men and the women, and, indeed, Don Alfonso and Despina, refer to 'amanti'.
Throughout Act II, however, the preference is for 'sposi'. This is made especially
clear in 'Sorella, cosa dici?', when Fiordiligi refers to Dorabella and herself as
'already promised ones' ('omai promesse spose'). The reason for thinking that
Mozart and Da Ponte actively considered this issue is that at the start of the
Act II finale, Ferrando and Guglielmo refer in the libretto to 'our faithful lovers'
('nostre fidissime amanti'), whereas in his score Mozart crossed out 'amanti' and
substituted 'spose'. Close to the end of the Act II finale, Don Alfonso makes his
final pronouncement. His excuse for deceiving the women is that by doing so
he has undeceived their 'lovers' ('amanti'). In the autograph, the word 'amanti'
(bars 534–5) was written above something else, smudged out. It is not possible
to read what was there, but 'sposi' seems a likely possibility. The reason for such
a change here is that a few lines later Don Alfonso commands the couples 'be
promised ones!': 'siete sposi'. The implication of this remark would have been
slightly different in a plot with lovers uncrossed. In this context, Don Alfonso
would be urging all four to accept their change in status from 'amanti' to 'sposi',
even though the correct documentation (albeit with bogus names) had been
achieved in a far from desirable fashion. In the final version of the opera, Don

Alfonso is encouraging the lovers to set aside the (invalid) contracts with the wrong lovers and act as 'sposi'. In view of Da Ponte's original title for the opera, 'La scuola degli amanti', it is perhaps not surprising to find that in the stage directions the two couples are consistently designated as 'amanti'. Curiously, the only exception is in the Act II finale, when it is 'gli sposi' who prepare to drink the toast, even though Despina has not yet appeared with the contracts. The alternative plot perhaps would have concerned two pairs of 'amanti' who accidentally (from the point of view of the sisters) become 'sposi' and could therefore remain 'sposi' at the end since they are paired correctly. With the women choosing the wrong lovers, it was necessary for them to be already spoken-for spouses to add to their shame.

The central dilemma facing Mozart and Da Ponte was not a technical one: the symmetrical structure of this elegant demonstration comedy would allow it to be adapted readily to either ending with a minimum of recomposition. But it was a choice that would wreck a spectacular emotional transformation on the whole opera, at least insofar as its subsequent reception was concerned. With lovers uncrossed, the music of love (unbeknown to the sisters) would have been directed towards the appropriate beloved, its force held in check only by the need to preserve dramatic credibility. With lovers crossed, a massive dose of ambiguity was injected into the opera libretto. Deeply felt musical expressions of love are now best realised in soliloquy, the seduction scenes are uneasily balanced between the need for the music to represent passion and the dramatic charade, and the ending, to many in posterity, began to seem unworthy. The ambiguity pervades even the soliloquy. Ford was unconvinced by the 'triumphant strength and beauty' of Ferrando's final reaffirmation of his love for Dorabella in 'Tradito', and argued that his 'typically abstract *voci d'amor* are speaking to him of Fiordiligi rather than Dorabella'.[56] Yet there was no choice but to follow convention. In removing the line in which the women refer to their original lovers with the words 'idol mio', Mozart was perhaps registering a small objection to the decision he had had to take. With lovers uncrossed, these words were perhaps appropriate, but the composer perhaps could not stomach such an easy reversion to the original affections, the essential distinction being that in the meantime the music has taken over and aroused new feelings of love which the plot will not allow to be requited.

The idea of an opera overture as a piece that foreshadows or perhaps even encapsulates the coming drama is of obvious relevance to *Così fan tutte*, as its overture opens with two important musical elements from the opera itself: a soaring oboe statement of Ferrando's C major melody; and the chords of the motto 'Così fan tutte'. Ferrando's C major melodic complex is always in ¢ or ₵. In probable order of composition, the occurrences are 'Una bella serenata',

'Tradito', 'Fra gli amplessi', and the overture. As many commentators have pointed out, Fiordiligi's music includes very similar melodic elements. Heartz wrote aptly of the growing 'melodic symbiosis' between her and Ferrando.[57] The underlying musical ideas of this melody are all the more powerful for their simplicity. Ferrando's opening phrase in 'Una bella serenata' consists of two elements: an ascending triad in C major; a held top note, falling quickly through a semiquaver run down to the tonic, with an upper auxiliary note. The other element is a simple ascending crotchet scale. In Act II, as the drama reaches its climax and Ferrando's emotions intensify, the opening C major melody returns. In 'Tradito', the use of the falling theme with the upper auxiliary note is best described as a resemblance rather than an actual recall. It occurs three times, twice with the top note prolonged to increase the intensity, once with a striking continuation, of a rising sixth (C to A) over a subdominant chord. Most commentators agree that in 'Fra gli amplessi' the melodic similarity with 'Una bella serenata' amounts to an actual reference. When Ferrando sings 'e se forza, oh Dio, non hai' ('and if, oh God, you do not have the strength') he uses the passionate ascending sixth continuation, but, that apart, this was the melodic statement that Mozart chose to use for the oboe melody at the start of the opera. It would not be justifiable to seek significance in the precise words that Ferrando is singing at this moment, but it is interesting that the overture recall is closer to the melody as sung to Fiordiligi than that in 'Una bella serenata' which refers to Dorabella. This raises the question as to whether, when writing the oboe melody at the start of the overture, Mozart had yet finally resolved the question of the pairings. In this sense, the opening bars of the opera encapsulate the central ambiguity of the opera as a whole. With the lovers uncrossed, the melody of Ferrando's serenade follows him through all the stages of his lost innocence, from blissful ignorance, to alarm at the prospect of betrayal, to a passionate reaffirmation of love after betrayal. But the moment that Ferrando addresses this melody to Guglielmo's woman, the signals become very mixed indeed.

In view of the hypothesis that a major problem with the plot occupied the attention of Mozart and Da Ponte during work on *Così fan tutte*, it would be interesting to know whether the two men co-operated in trying to find a resolution of the difficulty, or whether they were at odds with each other, arguing for opposing solutions. Whether composer and librettist held different views on the question of the pairings is impossible to say. Kerman certainly believed that Mozart and Da Ponte had 'unresolved differences' about [the plot]. He concluded: 'the confusion is in the piece as well as in the minds of the audience'.[58] A passing reference in the satire *Anti-da Ponte* to the effect that Mozart had no wish ever to set another 'dapontischen' text, together with the librettist's own silence over his role and his pointed insistence on calling his work 'La scola degli amanti', may point to a difficult conclusion to their successful partnership. The idea that a composer (with or without the consent of a librettist) could contemplate such a major change of emphasis part way through the composition of a work, might seem shocking, but one well-established (though often challenged) school of thought about *Die Zauberflöte* assumes an equally abrupt gear-change, which turned Sarastro from an evil to a benevolent figure.

This lengthy discussion of the theory that a plot with lovers uncrossed was under consideration has focused on the questions of dramatic credibility that such a revision would have raised, as this is the incarnation of Mozart as creative artist that we now like to imagine. Yet implausibility in general was certainly no bar to the success of an eighteenth-century *opera buffa*, and there are other possible motivations. Some have wondered whether Mozart's personal circumstances had any influence on his composition of this opera. Apparent worries over Constanze's behaviour during his absence from Vienna in the spring of 1789 have some resonances in the plot of *Così*, but it is unlikely that such considerations would have unduly influenced a professional composer. Another possibility is that it was the underlying moral question that was driving the issue. A drama in which the women never fell for men other than their own would be significantly less scandalous than one in which the unthinkable betrayal happened. Although the general implausibility of the drama did not escape early critics, by far the main focus of their discontent was its supposed immorality. In the nineteenth century, the idea of a plot with lovers uncrossed was merely one of many attempts to cope with the unacceptable actions of the sisters.

But perhaps the search for an underlying motive for this hypothetical plot change is in itself anachronistic. There is very little in the original sources to suggest that the issue was considered at length, and, given the extreme haste with which preparations for the first performance were made, there would have been no time for prolonged thought. Faced with such a dilemma, Mozart and Da Ponte would have had to take a decision quickly, one way or another, and then implement it with pragmatism. They are more likely to have been preoccupied by what would make an effective drama and what would best show off the talents of the singers, than by the wider cultural and moral issues that came to obsess posterity.

# PART III

*Mozart's Revisions for Vienna and Prague*

# The Vienna Court Theatre Score

THROUGHOUT the foregoing discussion of hypotheses relating to the composition of *Così fan tutte*, the autograph has remained our central source, yet there have also been repeated references to the Vienna Court Theatre score (**V1**) because of the light that it can shed on the later stages of the compositional process. It is now time to consider in more detail the nature of this source (and of subsequent copies). The justification for so doing is that our modern understanding of what a compositional history should entail, extends well beyond what exists in the composer's autograph, and, indeed, beyond what can be shown to have been performed at the première itself; it must also embrace subsequent changes made to the opera by, or directly on behalf of the composer, during his lifetime. In this endeavour, the Court Theatre copies come into their own as documents of equal significance to the autograph.

One of Tyson's landmark contributions to the study of Mozart's operas was the discovery of the importance of the early manuscript copies.[1] Once an opera had been accepted for performance in Vienna, at least two copies were produced almost simultaneously. I have labelled them **V1** (the reference copy) and **V2** (the conductor's copy). The firm regularly employed for this task during Mozart's later Vienna years was headed by the Moravian Wenzel Sukowaty, an analysis of the activities of whose 'copy shop' forms a major part of Edge's thesis.[2] After the end of the first production run, the reference copy was retained, and if further scores were required for productions elsewhere, they were almost always purchased from this source. The autograph remained in the composer's possession, but the fate of the conductor's copy was altogether less certain. Tyson demonstrated convincingly that small changes made during the rehearsal period were entered in a theatre copy rather than the autograph. In the case of *Così fan tutte* the composer himself seems to have marked up the conductor's copy **V2**, and then the changes were quickly transferred to the reference copy **V1** by an assistant. Mozart himself could have used the autograph to direct his opera, but had he done so, he would have needed to remember where all the 'agreed' cuts were, as these were not fully marked in his own manuscript. A duplicate of the court theatre score would have been much more practical, and would have been needed by any other musician taking the role of conductor.

The discovery that after a certain point Mozart ceased to incorporate changes in his own manuscript has weakened the primacy of the autograph in textual matters. As Tyson rightly observed, we can only ever guess at his attitude to the alterations which he made. They might equally well represent what he regarded as conceptual improvements or changes that he had to agree to reluctantly for any number of practical reasons. The distinction indeed no longer seems a particularly significant one.

The copy of *Così fan tutte* produced for the Vienna Court Theatre as a reference score **V1** is in the Musiksammlung of the Österreichische Nationalbibliothek in Vienna under the pressmark O.A.146. This manuscript was described by Edge in his thesis.[3] My own examinations of it were made before I consulted his work. The title-page of the first volume is in a conventional format. It reads: 'Così fan tutte / osia / La / Scuola degli Amanti / Dramma giocoso / in due Atti / Rappresentato nel Teatro di Corte a Vienna L'Anno 1790 / La Musica è del Sig^re Wolfgango Mozart.' The words 'La Scuola degli Amanti' appear to have been written first and this remains the sole title of the second volume to this day. The use of the original title is a significant pointer to how soon work on this copy was begun. In Edge's view, its copyists and paper types are consistent with a date around January 1790, although a small number of items perhaps date from the first major revival in Vienna in 1804.[4]

Although it came to act as the 'official' reference score, **V1** is no longer complete. By the time that it was bound, it had lost Ferrando's aria 'Un'aura amorosa' and the following recitative. Also missing is 'Amico abbiamo vinto' and Guglielmo's aria 'Donne mie'. The Act I duet 'Al fato' ended up oddly disordered, and Ferrando's 'Tradito' with its preceding *accompagnato* was placed too late, though not wrongly numbered. As Edge points out, **V1** is the primary source for elements missing from the autograph, except perhaps for the wind parts written on extra sheets which are of later date.[5]

The most visually striking feature of **V1** is that it contains a series of cuts. The original material was not physically removed but covered up with pasted slips which were themselves lifted off at a much later date. It is common to see crossing out in red crayon, a method of erasure that almost always left the original version still visible. Red crayon is a relatively ambiguous source of physical evidence. After numerous periods of studying **V1**, I have begun to be able to discern some of their distinguishing features: a few are essentially a darkish red (described by Edge as brick-red), others have an orange tinge; some had a sharpened tip, others were quite blunt; some were applied heavily, others sketchily.[6] Yet the markings are predominantly rather nondescript in character, features such as crossing and scribbling out, erasure through the application of hatching lines, and the use of simple location signs such as 'x', '+' or 'xx'. The absence of any significant amounts of verbal or musical text makes any attempt to date by red crayon alone hazardous. I reached the same general conclusion as Edge that some of the brick-red markings are earlier than some of the orange-red ones. But however uncertain their dating may be, these ubiquitous marks do at least enable us to define the complete corpus of passages revised during the history of **V1**.

The cuts and alterations are listed systematically in Edge's thesis.[7] Many of them were made in conjunction with the 1790 performances, but others are undoubtedly of later date. Radical changes such as instructions to move arias to different positions or assign them to different characters relate to the Viennese performance history of the opera in the nineteenth century. Distinguishing the 1790 layer from the subsequent additions is a matter of considerable importance, although a completely clear-cut division is unlikely ever to be possible.

The first question to be considered is when work on **V1** was begun. The copyists did not start the moment that Mozart completed the earliest ensembles, because (with a few lapses) the name 'Guglielmo' is given in the form 'Guilelmo', rather than as 'Guillelmo', the spelling used by Mozart in the first part of Act I. This confirms what we would expect: that the composer's first phase of composition pre-dates the start of work on the copy. But Wenzel Sukowaty did not wait until he had received the complete score before handing out assignments to his assistants. This is evident both from the exclusive use of the title 'La scuola degli amanti' on the original title-page and from a few occasions when a significant change was made with Mozart's sanction after a piece had been copied. The repeat of the 'magnetic' music for wind, for example, was not in the autograph when the copyist did the Act I finale. Another factor to be borne in mind is the schedule for the production of performance materials. Although now all seemingly lost, these would have included vocal role books for the singers, cheaply produced string parts for the early rehearsals, better-quality duplicate parts for the full string band, and parts for the wind instruments. Edge's work on the extant original parts for the other two Da Ponte operas suggests that the first-desk string parts and the wind parts were sometimes generated directly from the autograph itself rather than the theatre copy, and unless information comes to light to suggest the contrary, we might do well to assume that the same was true for *Così fan tutte*.[8]

Analysis of the ink colours in **V1** casts some light upon the relationship between the composing and copying processes. There are two sequences of ensembles in which the wind instrumentation appears in a slightly different coloured ink from that of the other parts: the Act I sequence includes 'Sento oddio' (after the first few pages), 'Al fato', (but not 'Bella vita militar'), 'Di scrivermi', 'Soave sia il vento' and 'Alla bella Despinetta', in all of which the wind parts appear slightly lighter on the page; the Act II sequence includes 'Prenderò quel brunettino', 'Secondate' (except for the first clarinet which was used to generate the particella), 'La mano a me date' and 'Il core vi dono', in all of which the wind parts are written in an ink with a slightly greyish tinge. In both cases this matches closely the patterns of ink usage seen in the autograph. It therefore seems probable that Mozart gave these sequences of ensembles to the copyists to start work and then reclaimed them to complete the wind scoring.

Further signs of this working relationship appear in a few pieces in which the first layer in **V1** was taken from a particella into which some wind fragments had already been entered. This is especially clear in the final section of the Act I sestetto and in 'Il core vi dono', in which the clarinet figure starting in bar 86 and again in bar 102 was first copied with a semiquaver rest at the start, as it had appeared in Mozart's particella. When the wind instrumentation was completed, this rest was replaced with a semiquaver, and the copyist then had to make the same change.

Of all the places in **V1** where there is evidence that work on the autograph and the copy went on in parallel, of most interest are naturally those that reflect the continuing process of composition and revision. We shall consider six examples.

1 **Overture** An important sign of the proximity of the copyist of **V1** to Mozart lies in three *piano* marks added by an assistant to the bass part in the autograph in bars 80, 149 and 194. I failed to spot these additions, and this information comes from *NMA: KB*, which suggests that the first of them could be in the hand of the **V1** copyist himself.[9] The location of these three added dynamic marks is certainly no coincidence: each comes at the start of one of the 'agreed' cuts, as entered in **V1**. This indicates that these *piano* marks belong to the period of composition prior to the première. They could indeed have been entered in both sources at the one time.

2 **'Di scrivermi'** In the autograph, Mozart first scored this piece for strings. He then added the bassoon parts on the blank staves below the score and the clarinets on the blank staff above. The copyist wrote out the basic string score before Mozart added in the wind instruments. He then added the bassoon parts on the blank staff above the score, after scraping out the title 'recitativo', but for some reason he put the clarinet parts on a separate sheet rather than use the two blank staves below, and this led to their loss from quite a few early copies. The order in which this happened could indicate that Mozart decided to put in the bassoon parts first, and only then the clarinets.

3 **'Alla bella Despinetta'** In **V1** the tempo designations form a clear counterpart to what was happening in the autograph. In bar 53 'Allegro assai' is written in red crayon and half smudged out, and in bar 54 the same instruction is added

in three different hands. In bar 127 'Allegro molto' appears three times in similar positions. In the autograph Mozart first had the unmodified term 'Allegro' here; only later did he add in the word 'molto'. It was this decision that apparently prompted him to remove the word 'assai' from the previous tempo designation. The copy thus appears to demonstrate that the final tempo sequence was under consideration at a late stage.

4 **'Come scoglio'** This is the only piece in the opera in which the basic text of **V1** differs slightly from that of the autograph, if obvious errors are excluded. Establishing what Mozart wanted is no easy matter. In the copy there is red crayon smudging around the first bassoon part in bars 16, 18, 67, 69 and 71, all of which contain an ascending arpeggio which is not in the autograph. The copyist of **V1** apparently first noted these arpeggios in red crayon and then went over them in a warm brown ink, unlike that used in the rest of the score. In each case the original phrase ending had to be scratched out. There are signs of this in the clarinet parts as well. It is hard to reconcile these changes with what is in the autograph, in which Mozart wrote out the first bassoon arpeggio in bar 16, but then crossed it out, and omitted it in the subsequent repetitions. This leaves the status of this bassoon figure rather uncertain, as its exclusion from the autograph might represent the composer's final decision.

In bar 76 in **V1** there is further heavy red crayon smudging around the last two beats of the first and second violin parts, an extension of the cadential figure which is not in the autograph. The shorter version given in the autograph was originally copied in **V1**. Some time later, the longer version was notated lightly in red crayon, and this was gone over in the same brown ink used to amend the clarinet and bassoon parts. This version was transmitted in later copies.

5 **'Per pietà'** In bar 114 in **V1** what appears to be a minim B and perhaps a minim E was scratched out in Fiordiligi's line. This is another important sign of the proximity of the copyist to Mozart. He started to write out the first bar of something apparently resembling the three-bar version of Fiordiligi's cadence, which Mozart soon abandoned and crossed out in the autograph.

6 **Act II finale** In bars 234–5 in **V1** the bass line was originally written as F♯ but later changed to A. Then in bars 236–7 it was written B but later amended to A. In the autograph this passage was also revised, but apparently in the other direction. In bars 234–5 Mozart lowered the pitch of the bass line by a minor third (from A to F♯). In the first part of bar 236 there is a large black mark at the start of the bass line, though it is far from clear what (if anything) was being crossed out. The uncertainty over this reading caused tremendous confusion in subsequent sources, but it was a significant decision. With the bass line as in

the autograph, Mozart had two bars of II$^7$ harmony followed by a powerful dissonance when this chord is suspended over a V in the bass. Landon ingeniously suggested that this 'huge dissonance' in the wind parts and the following resolution in 'an antiquated manner' was an attempt by Mozart to depict the words 'colle regole ordinarie', that is, 'according to the prescribed rules'.[10] The amended version in **V1** has all four bars as a II$^{7b}$ chord, and the effect of the dissonance is greatly reduced.

Taken together, these six examples confirm that the copying process got under way while Mozart was still working on his score. The late changes of mind included aspects of the scoring, dynamics and even harmony. There is thus every reason to view **V1** as a working compositional document, and no particular reason to assume that work on it ceased at the moment of the première.

## *The 'Agreed' Aria and Ensemble Cuts*

The term 'agreed' here has a clear meaning: it refers to a series of cuts that were probably entered by Mozart in **V2** (the conducting score) and then transferred to **V1** (the reference score) by an assistant. These minor abbreviations were then routinely transmitted. Often all that was required after a cut had been agreed was a little remedial action to smooth the new joins. The probable procedure for making last-minute cuts to passages in arias and ensembles may be summarised as follows. After they had been noted by Mozart, an assistant was given the responsibility for making sure that the reference copy **V1** incorporated them. First, the location of a cut was marked in red crayon, sometimes with an '+' or 'x', and any problematic join smoothed over. This was only a temporary measure, perhaps pending a final decision on whether the proposed change was really an improvement. A sealing process took place some time later, once it had been decided to accord these changes a more permanent status. This was done through the pasting of slips of paper and if necessary by stitching up pages. Additional red crayon marks sometimes clarified the cut with instructions such as 'volti'. The pasted slips used to seal cuts in **V1** are of two types. An earlier layer consisted of white paper slips pasted onto small square patches of paper, which were themselves usually stuck onto the page all round the area to be obliterated (top, sides and bottom). The later layer is slightly bluish in colour. Slips of this kind appear to have been attached directly to the page (without patches), usually at the top and bottom. In a few cases, it is evident that a bluish slip was a replacement for an earlier (probably white) slip, because the patch paste marks on the original page are not replicated on the under side of the later slip. Occasionally, all that remains are the paste marks themselves, but it may still be possible to make an educated guess at the type of the original slip from the presence or absence of these patches. Even if sealed with a replacement slip, the cuts were nearly all revealed again at a later date.

This process allowed cuts to be identified quickly on a purely provisional basis: the red crayon marks did not obliterate any of the original text, and if it was then decided that the cut did not work or was in the wrong place, the marks themselves could be scrawled out. Only when the cuts were 'sealed' did they become part of the 'agreed' text. As we shall see, there is at least one significant cut in **V1** that may well have been entered in the score at a very early stage, but which was not sealed and thus did not become part of the 'agreed' text.

Changes to arias and ensembles that were apparently sanctioned by Mozart in **V2** and then accepted as part of the opera's 'agreed' text in **V1** are listed in Table 24. Apart from the straightforward abbreviations of the overture and the Act I chorus, two cuts reduced the demands placed on the singer cast as Ferrando. Perhaps Calvesi was struggling, not with any individual passage as such, but with the demands of his role as a whole. Much the most interesting cut is the fourteen bars lost from the Act I finale, because that is the only place where there is a loss of text. As we shall see, Mozart may well have made this cut in order to facilitate another larger cut that was in the end revoked.

Additional confirmation that these 'agreed' cuts represent the core text of the opera is provided by numbering series and bar counts. Series of tiny numbers (probably reference points for copyists) appear in **V1** and occasionally in the autograph. They are placed above or below the brace at roughly four- to six-bar intervals, no doubt representing the start of each new staff in the copy. Sometimes they are not numbers but '+' or 'x' signs or simple dash marks. They may be written in pencil or red crayon but are always unobtrusive. Sometimes there are several series (indicating repeated copying) and these will usually diverge after a point, as different copyists did not always incorporate the same number of bars on the page. The appearance of several sets of these marks in the autograph of

TABLE 24 'Agreed' cuts in the arias and ensembles

|        | Item              | Bars    |
|--------|-------------------|---------|
| Act I  | Overture          | 81–8    |
|        |                   | 149–56  |
|        |                   | 194–201 |
|        | Bella vita militar | 1–24    |
|        | Un' aura amorosa  | 5–57    |
|        |                   | 63–6    |
|        | Finale            | 461–75  |
| Act II | Ah lo veggio      | 57–91   |

Act II confirms that Mozart's own score was sometimes used, when the pressure of time meant that rehearsal parts had to be copied before the score in **V1** was available. The most useful feature of the number series is that they confirm the status of the 'agreed' cuts in **V1**. Only the passages listed above remained unnumbered; all other cuts have the numbers.

Also sometimes useful in establishing the pedigree of the 'agreed' cuts are the bar totals, written either at the end of a movement or after significant subsections. There are two series in **V1**. Those written in ink appear to date from when this manuscript was first copied, while those in pencil or red crayon are probably later. The usual pattern therefore is for the original ink number to reflect the total before the cut was made, and the pencil or red crayon total to incorporate the cut. Occasionally an addition may be identified by this method. In the Act I finale, the ink bar count 132 does not include the extra five bars of magnetic music, clear proof that this number was put in before the insertion of this sheet. The pencil [1]37 is in fact a correction of this.

Although the cuts made during the rehearsal period were probably first entered in the copy **V2**, there are occasional signs of them in the autograph as well, suggesting that it was in the vicinity. These markings are usually discreet and seem not to be in the composer's own hand. In the overture, as we have already seen, dynamic markings were added by one or more copyists at the location of the three cuts. The Act I finale cut is clearly marked with a hand-NB sign and a circle with an 'x' in it, written in red crayon. The end of the cut is indicated again in red crayon) with a London tube sign with a diagonal slash (upper left to lower right). These marks are not thought to have been made by Mozart himself, though it is difficult to be certain.[11] There are any number of practical reasons why copyists involved in the preparation of performance materials might have noted in the autograph the location of a discrepancy caused by an unmarked cut.

When the original sources of *Così fan tutte* were first studied, the existence of the early copy **V2** in which Mozart seems to have entered the 'agreed' cuts was not suspected, and so it was very natural to look for examples of his hand in the extant score. Opinion remained divided as to whether the very minor revisions in **V1** needed to facilitate the 'agreed' cuts are in Mozart's hand. In some cases Tyson thought that this was possible, but the editors of *NMA: KB* disagreed. The added material is so slight that it is hard to come to any firm judgement. Edge also noticed a minor rewrite in bar 156 of the overture following the second of the 'agreed' cuts, where the original note was scratched out in the violins and in the second clarinet part and replaced with a crotchet F, first in red crayon and then in ink. He considered that Mozart's hand ought not to be 'ruled out'.[12] Another piece of tidying up was occasioned by the 'agreed' cut in

Ferrando's Act II aria, where the syllable '-tà' (of 'pietà') had to be added in after the deleted passage. Tyson thought that the syllable was 'probably by Mozart', although this was again rejected in the *NMA*.[13] A further small revision necessitated by an 'agreed' cut seems never to have been made. In 'Un'aura amorosa', Ferrando's semiquaver B at the end of bar 49 should have been replaced by an E, so that it joins on to bar 58. This aria is missing in **V1**, but as the note is given wrongly in virtually all subsequent copies, it appears that it was not amended.

A slightly more substantive revision with which Mozart's hand might be associated is seen at the end of the 'agreed' cut in the Act I finale. The difficulty in interpreting the evidence here is that there appear to be two layers of change. In order to tidy up this join, it was necessary to delete the redundant 'io' at the start of bar 476 in the parts of Fiordiligi and Dorabella, and to add in the word 'tosco' in the parts of Despina and Don Alfonso. This was done, but later someone else noticed that 'tosco' was incorrect and changed the word for the three-syllable 'tossico', at the same time amending the musical text, both at the join and on other occurrences of the word in this passage. Some subsequent copies confirm this chronology by making the 'agreed' cut but without changing the word 'tosco'. Tyson appeared ambivalent as to whether any of these changes were in Mozart's hand, first describing it as 'likely' then as merely a possibility.[14] In the *NMA* the idea was rejected, even though Mozart's connection with this cut is firmly established in the autograph where its location is noted.[15] Now that the existence of the second copy **V2** has been established, there is no longer any need to strive to identify Mozart's hand at these locations in **V1**.

It is clear that the whole process of considering and implementing the cuts 'agreed' during the rehearsal period took place primarily in **V2**, and this is enough to cast a shadow over the older idea of the autograph as embodying a sacrosanct 'ideal' version of the opera, with the copy containing the compromises necessary for the particular production of 1790. Yet it would be an even more serious fallacy to assume that the continuous process of revision was necessarily 'improving' the opera, either in an objective sense or in the eyes of the composer. All theatrical works require numerous compromises, and without doubt Mozart had to make decisions in the light of the particular circumstances in Vienna in January 1790 that he might not otherwise have found acceptable. That neither invalidates such features nor makes them in any sense 'inauthentic': indeed, compromises have their own peculiar 'authenticity'. At this distance in time, our real problem is that there are no solid grounds upon which to distinguish changes made for pragmatic never-to-be-repeated reasons relating specifically to the première, from others decided upon as conceptual improvements. However, it is at least clear that the 'agreed' cuts represent the state of the opera as it was in the final days before the première. No one was subsequently in any doubt of their necessity, because they were invariably disseminated in both lines of transmission.

## The 'Agreed' Recitative Cuts

A series of five 'agreed' recitative cuts is also very early in date, and Mozart's involvement in making them appears highly likely. Whereas abbreviations to arias and ensembles were usually considered on musical grounds such as overall length or degree of repetition, those made to recitatives are more likely to relate to the need for dramatic effectiveness. Invaluable background information on why recitative cuts were often considered in the run-up to an opera première comes from Mozart's correspondence during the months before the first performance of *Idomeneo*. It is clear that for the composer this was one of the major issues to be resolved. In a letter to his father dated 19 December 1780, he was adamant that two scenes should be drastically abbreviated:

> The scene between father and son in Act I and the first scene in Act II between Idomeneo and Arbace are both too long. They would certainly bore the audience, particularly as in the first scene both the actors are bad, and in the second, one of them is; besides, they only contain a narrative of what the spectators have already seen with their own eyes. These scenes are being printed as they stand. But I should like the Abbate to indicate how they may be shortened – and as drastically as possible, – for otherwise I shall have to shorten them myself. These two scenes cannot remain as they are – I mean, when set to music.[16]

Mozart was happy enough for the published libretto to remain as it was, asking only that Varesco indicate what could be lost in performance. His concern that the audience might become bored seems paramount. When Leopold responded with Varesco's strong objections (which he supported) to the abbreviation of the first recitative of Act II on the grounds that it would result in too rapid a recognition between father and son, Mozart came clean as to his real reason for the request. It was because of the hopelessly inadequate acting skills of the singers who spoilt the recitative 'by singing it without any spirit or fire, and *so* monotonously'.[17] In near despair, he commented: 'They are the most wretched actors that ever walked a stage.' It seems that the experience of the rehearsal process itself often generated the ideas for cuts.

The five 'agreed' recitative cuts in *Così* transferred to **V1** are listed in Table 25. Careful scrutiny reveals that these cuts are linked palaeographically. As usual, red crayon marks were put in to indicate their provisional location, usually in the form of neat crosses written above the staff. Red crayon was also used to indicate the (fairly minor) musical changes required to produce the new joins.

TABLE 25  'Agreed' cuts in the recitatives

|  | Item | Start of cut | Bar | Text restarts | Bar |
|---|---|---|---|---|---|
| Act I | Che silenzio | Ti vo fare del ben | 28 | Prendi ed ascolta | 38 |
|  | [Oh la saria] | [È buon] | 35 | [Ite] | 57 |
| Act II | Andate là | Che diavolo | 20 | per Bacco ci fa | 46 |
|  | Sorella, cosa dici? | è mal che basta | 15 | sorella mia | 30 |
|  | Ora vedo | Ora vedo | 1 | Sciagurate! | 15 |

Edge identifies the colour of the crayon used as the probably earlier 'brick-red' variety. As with the 'agreed' aria and ensemble cuts, it is likely that Mozart himself entered them in **V2**, while an assistant was entrusted with the job of transferring them to **V1**. The remedial work is so small in scale and straightforward in character that it is not difficult to imagine Mozart standing at his helper's shoulder checking that he had it right.[18]

Once it had been decided to make the cuts permanent, redundant pages were hidden through the stitching of leaves and the pasting of small blank slips to block out any remaining material. For those passages requiring a new join, an extra leaf was inserted on which the new version was copied. It seems highly likely that all five recitative cuts were done at the same time. The hand which did the new copying has a very distinct way of ruling the recitative brace so that (claw-like) it exactly meets the highest line of the top staff and the lowest line of the bottom staff, and it has a tight loop in the middle (with no blank space). The original recitatives remained 'sealed' in this way for some considerable time. In one case a later cut made with a different red crayon runs directly across the paste-on slips, which were subsequently lifted. When eventually it was decided to recover the original text, the stitching was undone, the paste-on slips were lifted, and some of the extra sheets removed completely, leaving only the evidence of the paste itself.

Given the strong likelihood that the composer made these cuts, an important question is why he felt them necessary. Significantly, they are far from random abbreviations. As we have already seen, four of them appear to relate to last-minute changes, reflected also in the autograph score and the two librettos, which stemmed from difficulties caused by the late casting of Dorotea Bussani as Despina.

## *An Early Cut not 'Agreed'*

A further cut in the Act I finale seems to have been under consideration at an early stage, but did not in the end form part of the 'agreed' text and was thus not transmitted. Remarkably, this would have resulted in the complete loss of

Despina's scene as doctor. The limited palaeographical evidence in **V1** is inconclusive, but the relationship between this cut and the much shorter 'agreed' cut in the Act I finale (bars 461–75) provides food for thought. The 'agreed' cut is the only one of its type to result in the loss of a short passage of text from the opera. The lines are: 'In poch'ore, lo vedrete, / Per virtù del magnetismo / Finirà quell parossismo, / Torneranno al primo umor' ('Very soon now, by virtue of magnetic power, this seizure will end, and they will return to their original mood'). This is the only further reference in Act I to Despina's magnetic cure, and its removal would obviously have been necessary had the original scene itself been abandoned. Mozart was quite capable of suggesting drastic action if he felt that an acting performance in rehearsal was below an acceptable standard. The fact that at some point action was taken to seal this large cut in **V1** shows that it was not just a passing idea, yet it was evidently unsealed very quickly and the charade remained an integral part of the Act I finale.

The possible impact of the hypothetical casting problems on this decision are worth considering. If Villeneuve was cast briefly as the maid during the phase with lovers uncrossed, she could have rejected the idea of taking a burlesque role such as the doctor or else have been deemed totally unsuited to it, while in recompense perhaps excelling in the verbal flightiness of Despina.

## Wind Scores

The wind scores copied on extra sheets in **V1** are fully discussed in the *NMA: KB*, and so it will be sufficient here to summarise the main issues.[19] The *NMA* derives its text from the scores bound in with **V1** which, as both Edge and the editors agree, date from the early nineteenth century.[20] A slightly different version of these scores is extant in many copies, the earliest of which **L** includes them under the rubric: 'gli stromenti da fiato per l'opera: La Scuola degli Amanti'. The use of the original title here is a further indication of early provenance. Their main interest lies in the fact that they present a different text in the Act II finale in two places, and on balance these readings, shown in Table 26, must be regarded as having a stronger claim than those in **V1**.

Why should a mere five bars of the second flute part in the middle of this lengthy finale exist in two different versions? The explanation (or at least the context) is more interesting than might at first sight appear likely. In the short section from bars 356–71, a 'thousand terrifying thoughts' flit through the minds of the two sisters who are resigned to the imminent arrival back from the war of their original lovers. There are several indications that this section came under some scrutiny. In the autograph there is no new tempo indication here, implying that the previous 'Allegro' is still in force. In **V1**, however, this section is marked 'Andante'. Moreover, a large ink bar total at the end of the

TABLE 26  Alternative readings in the wind scores in the Act II finale

| Item | Alternative reading |
|------|---------------------|
| Misericordia | The second flute part is different for five bars from the second half of bar 366: minim A, semibreves A–B♭; crotchets (with rests) B♭–A–G–G–D. |
| Fortunato | The second flute has a tie between bars 581–2.<br>The bassoon upbeat to bar 614 is slurred in.<br>The first flute and the first clarinet have a whole-bar slur in bars 640–2.<br>From bar 647 the rhythm dotted-crotchet / quaver is not slurred.<br>Oboes appear to be included in bars 632–5. |

Act II finale in this source runs from this bar, apparently marking it out as the start of a significant subsection.[21] There is insufficient information to determine what happened here, and we can only speculate. One obvious factor is that this short section has the clear dramatic function of prolonging the time between the departure of the disguised Albanians and their return as the real officers. Was this section then a late addition to the score to allow time for the removal of the disguises? Some change of plan might account for the differences in the second flute part. A very similar argument can be made in relation to the numerous minor differences of wind articulation in the section 'Fortunato'. Here there is firm evidence that a cut was made from bar 596 to bar 631 and then restored fairly quickly.

There is one further fact of considerable significance in establishing a chronology of the wind scores: the flute parts for 'Bella vita militar' and the clarinet parts for 'Di scrivermi' were, for a period at least, unknown in some branches of Transmission Line B stemming from **V2**. In **S**, for example, there is no sign of them or of any instruction indicating their existence. In the *Mädchentreue* score **V3**, which also stems from **V2**, these wind lines are clearly later additions. Moreover, the sporadic absence of some of the Act I wind parts in other sources suggests that this problem was by no means confined to Transmission Line B. There were, for example, originally no clarinet parts for 'Di scrivermi' or flute parts for 'Bella vita militar' in **K**. The parts associated with this score were marked 'tacet' for these pieces, although their lines were later added in. In **D1**, however, a score with the Italian text sold by the same Prague retailer, they are there.

# Early Manuscript Scores and Parts

THERE IS little doubt that **V1** was involved centrally in the process of transmitting the text of *Così fan tutte*. A few copies seem to derive directly from **V2**, which contained not only all the 'agreed' cuts but also the further revisions which Mozart made at a slightly later date, but **V1** was clearly the main reference score to which copyists turned when they received a commission for a manuscript replica. Its relationship to other early copies must now be taken into consideration. Copies of the opera that date from before around 1815, the era of *Die Zauberprobe*, are listed in Table 27.[1]

I have made an attempt to put the sources in approximate chronological order, although this is far from easy to determine, not least because many of them are composite scores, the component parts of which date from very different periods. Before the publication of a full score in 1810, the only way to obtain performance materials was to purchase a manuscript copy. Those that survive today range in character from unified scores compiled at the same time and place, to miscellaneous assemblages from many different periods. Although there were early Italian language productions in Prague, Dresden and Leipzig, German translations predominate markedly throughout the 1790s and beyond, and it was not until well into the nineteenth century that the opera was once again given regularly in its original language. Yet notwithstanding the prevalence of productions in German, the dissemination of scores with the Italian text remained central to the transmission of the opera. When a new German language staging was agreed, the first requirement was evidently still for a score with Italian which would act as the local source text. It might generate a further copy with only the new German text or it might itself be annotated with the new text. The local source score might remain in use for a considerable period, with subsequent adaptations of the libretto being added in, as and when new productions were mounted. Some have three or four such added texts. Overall, the main period for the dissemination of manuscript scores was the two decades from 1790 until 1810. After the publication of the printed full score, the flow diminishes, whilst by no means ceasing altogether. Once an opera house had invested in performance materials, they often remained in use for a very long time.

Another important early source of *Così fan tutte* is the vocal score made by the keyboard player Kuchař, a significant figure in the early Czech reception

TABLE 27    Early manuscript copies deriving from **V1** or **V2** (†)

| MS | Library | Siglum | Shelfmark | Original text | Date |
|----|---------|--------|-----------|---------------|------|
| L | London, British Library | GB:Lbl | R.M.22.h.10–11 | Italian | c.1790–1 |
| T | London, British Library | GB:Lbl | Tyson 16–17 | Italian | c.1790–1 |
| C2 | Copenhagen, Det Kongelige Bibliotek | DK:Kk | KBS/MA C I, 280, Acc. Nr. Mu 7502.0337 | Italian | c.1790–1 |
| K | Karlsruhe, Badische Landesbibliothek | D:KA | Mus.Ms.1389a-d | German | c.1791 |
| D1 | Dresden, Sächsische Landesbibliothek | D:Dl | Mus 3972-F-518 | Italian | c.1791 |
| Lo | Lobkowicz Roudnice Library, Nelahozeves Castle | CZ:Nlobkowicz | X.De.10 k.588 | Italian | c.1791–5 |
| C1† | Copenhagen, Det Kongelige Bibliotek | DK:Kk | KBS/MA Weyses Samling, Acc. Nr. Mu 7502.0336 | Italian | c.1791–5 |
| Be1 | Berlin, Staatsbibliothek zu Berlin, Preußischer Kulturbesitz | D:Bsb | Mus ms 15 153 | German | c.1792 ? |
| H | Hamburg, Staats- und Universitätsbibliothek Carl von Ossietzky | D:Hs | ND VII 250 | Italian | c.1793 ? |
| F1 | Frankfurt, Stadt- und Universitätsbibliothek | D:F | Mus ms 380 (1) | German | c.1795 |
| S† | Salzburg, Internationale Stiftung Mozarteum | A:Sm | Rara 588/14 (M.N.9b I & II) | Italian | 1790s |
| B | Brno, Moravské Zemské Museum | CZ:Bm | A17.031 | Italian | late 1790s |
| D2 | Dresden, Sächsische Landesbibliothek | D:Dl | Mus 3972-F-99 | Italian | late 1790s |
| Be2 | Berlin, Staatsbibliothek zu Berlin, Preußischer Kulturbesitz | D:Bsb | Mus ms 15 153/1 | Italian | late 1790s |
| V3† | Vienna, Österreichische Nationalbibliothek | A:Wn | O.A.328 | German | various |
| V4† | Vienna, Österreichische Nationalbibliothek | A:Wn | Mus. Hs. 39.321 | German | c.1805 |
| Fl† | Florence, Biblioteca del Conservatorio di Musica 'Luigi Cherubini' | I:Fc | F.P.T.260 | Italian | c.1805–10 |
| F2† | Frankfurt, Stadt- und Universitätsbibliothek | D:F | Mus ms 380 (2) | German | c.1815 |
| Ca† | Cambridge, MA, Harvard University, Eda Kuhn Loeb Music Library, Merritt Room | US:CAe | Mus 745.1.661.9 | Italian | unclear |

of Mozart's operas. He was an experienced arranger, having done versions of both *Figaro* and *Don Giovanni*.[2] His arrangement of *Così fan tutte* follows the Vienna score **V1** exactly, making all the 'agreed' cuts, but there is no sign of any of the features of Domenico Guardasoni's 1791 Prague version. This suggests that Kuchař made the arrangement from a Viennese score as part of his normal portfolio of commercial activities, rather than in direct connection with the current Prague production. His arrangement does not include any of the *secco* recitatives, and he incorporated only the solo accompanied recitatives – that is, those that do not involve any other singer.

## Evidence of Chronology

Two categories of evidence have proved especially useful in establishing the lines of transmission of *Così fan tutte*: the analysis of page- and line-breaks, and errors and variants. Some comments on these now follow. In a brief discussion of some early manuscripts of the opera, Tyson reported that the page and line-breaks in his personally owned early copy (**T**) were virtually identical to those in **V1**.[3] Recently, the summary results of such comparisons have been incorporated into *NMA: KB*. I undertook a systematic survey of this feature in all the early copies of the opera that I examined. A small selection of the results is presented in Appendix 5. Although it is time-consuming to collate this kind of detail, the results amply reward the effort involved, as it quickly becomes apparent that page-break analysis is a particularly useful tool with which to evaluate the relationships between late-eighteenth-century manuscripts.

The underlying premise of page-break analysis is that it was the practice of copyists to replicate the physical layout of their source text unless there was a compelling reason not to do so. This procedure had one very useful practical advantage: it provided a fail-safe mechanism for the early detection of errors such as missed or wrongly duplicated bars. The practice was evidently widespread, because the preservation of the layout of the original often persists through several copying stages. But individual movements copied for the commercial market do not seem to adhere to the system. The page- and line-breaks in an early Viennese score of 'Fra gli amplessi' which was copied before the month of August 1792 when corrections in it were dated, bears no relationship at all to the central tradition.[4]

There are a few common exceptions to this concept of complete fidelity. Some copyists adopted the habit of ironing out the distribution of half bars. The copyist of **F1** almost invariably changed a pair of lines divided 3.5//3.5 to either 4//3 or 3//4. It is also apparent that the iron discipline with which this system was implemented tended to break down in the final few pages of a piece as its end came into view. With only a handful of bars left to copy on two or three remaining sides, copyists took whatever space they needed. And although it happens with surprising infrequency, the occasional transposition of bars on two sides of an opening (such as 5//6 to 6//5) was also not felt to violate the integrity of the system.

Once all the results of page-break analysis are placed in a table, certain features immediately catch the eye. At one end of the spectrum there is notable regularity: almost all copies of 'E voi ridete' have the same layout, which is perhaps not so surprising considering its almost mono-rhythmic character. In marked contrast are very short pieces like 'Tutti accusan le donne' which rarely appear the same twice. As a general rule, the shorter the piece, the less likely it is to adhere to the system. The editors of the *NMA* are correct to point out that there is also a significant correlation between the occurrence of page-break variants and places in **V1** where there are cuts.[5] Different copyists reacted in different ways when they encountered material crossed out in red crayon or obliterated by a pasted slip. A typical case is the page containing the wind repeat of the trills in the 'magnetic' music of the Act I finale, which was inserted into **V1** on an additional leaf. Some scribes coped with this by distributing the extra music over several pages, others by cramming in an unusually large number of bars on one page. In all cases, however, the objective was to resume the normal relationship with the physical layout of the original as soon as possible.

Once all these essentially routine differences have been accounted for, there remains a small core of more significant variants which contain valuable information on the character of **V1** and indirectly on the final stages of the compositional process itself. In particular, they enable us to determine the extent to which **V1** itself is a fully unified source, one in which all the component parts were produced at the same time and for the same purpose. Like other opera scores of this period, the Vienna Court Theatre score was the work of several copyists, but because all the individual movements in the score are of very similar date (other than a few later additions), the usual palaeographical tools such as watermarks, staff-ruling and handwriting are insufficient to determine its coherence in the sense that is meant here. When taken in conjunction with features of textual transmission, however, page-break analysis provides a useful level of discrimination. It has already been established that the additional wind scores bound in **V1** date from the *Mädchentreue* era, and Edge suggests that 'Tutti accusan le donne' with its preceding recitative is of similar date, although this is not mentioned in *NMA: KB*.[6] Page-break analysis suggests the possibility that alternative versions, available alongside (or instead of) the extant materials eventually bound in **V1**, played some role in the process of transmission in the following cases: the overture; both of Despina's arias; and 'Secondate'. Fiordiligi's 'Per pietà' should also be considered here, although in this case it is not the page-break analysis that suggests the existence of another copy.

1 **Overture** The considerable variation in the layout of the overture is due mainly to the three cuts entered into **V1**, yet the divergence goes beyond this, and a group of scores ends with a different sequence. This small constellation of sources also has one very distinctive textual feature. In **V1** and in the majority of copies the overture ends *piano*, thereby providing a dramatically dynamic connection with what follows. The *fortissimo* ending in *NMA* (which follows the autograph) characterises it as a separate piece. Three copies (**L, F1, H**) end *fortissimo* and as all three share the same page breaks for the last eight pages, the strong likelihood is that there was a common source copy of the overture.

2 **'In uomini'** Analysis of the page-break discrepancies in Despina's arias has the potential to shed some light on the compositional process itself. In the case of her Act I aria, the most significant divergence comes at the start of the piece. (See Appendix 5.) The early copy **T** derives from what is now in **V1**, and, indeed, this was the piece cited by Tyson himself to demonstrate the relationship. The other very early copy **L** differs in its opening layout with pages 3–4 divided 6//5 rather than 7//4. It is surely no coincidence that in the autograph itself at the same location – the start of bar 18 – there is a clear copying break in the particella. This of itself affords us no insights into the reasons for the changes that were being made or even what they were, yet it does direct the spotlight to a precise location with notable clarity. At the very least, it raises the question as to whether a version laid out as in **L** at the start of this movement, was for a time in **V1** before its replacement with what is there now. A very relevant consideration here is that the recitative leading into 'In uomini' in **V1** (earlier in the gathering) contains some of the most significant textual variants in the whole opera – the officers are reported as having left from Venice, for example – and thus it certainly cannot have been copied directly from what is now in the autograph.

3 **'Una donna'** The pattern of transmission in Despina's Act II aria is similar: **T** replicates the layout of **V1** as it now stands; on the other hand, **L** presents a different scheme of page breaks (for the first eleven pages) deriving from another copy, one which apparently bore the erroneous instruction 'fagotti' on its opening brace. (See Appendix 5.) This was replicated in some other copies, and a few years later **F1** even provided a second bassoon part. The gathering structure of 'Una donna' in **V1** consists of seven nested bifolia from which one page (12) was cut. The missing page is preceded by two pages with a markedly larger number of bars per side (8//7) than the prevailing average, presumably because the copyist

wished to make up the space quickly. To fit in the extra bars, he had to extend by hand the staves on the first of these pages, and scratch out a few bar-lines in the first violin part on the second page, as these had originally been written with too much space. He was therefore adapting as he went along, responding to some disturbance in his source text, rather than revising this passage after completing the whole movement. The conjoined leaf of the cut page contains (or would have contained) the start of the aria. While it is far from clear what happened here, it is at least possible that L, with its even spread of page breaks represents the layout of an earlier source text. The reason for this disturbance is almost certainly that a cut was being proposed which was then abandoned. Other early copies differ as to how the page breaks around pages 8–12 should go, a typically varied response to this kind of difficulty.

4 **'Secondate'** The first two folios of the Act II duet for the men in **V1** are at the end of a gathering. The remainder of the piece is copied on a gathering of four nested bifolia, from which page 2 was cut, leaving page 7 as a single sheet. The cut leaf (the fifth of the movement) would have begun with bars 23–4 followed in all probability by a continuation different from the thirteen bars now in **V1**. This passage (bars 25–37) exists only in this source, and it must have been crossed out in red crayon very soon after having been written, as it appears in no other manuscript. The copyist seems to have been unclear about the materials from which he was working. He appears to have thought that his first continuation (on the cut page) was wrong, yet his second continuation (with the extra bars) too turned out to be incorrect – a mistake that was identified before any further transmission of the piece. Ink colours show what the original particella was in **V1** but provide no further clue: the first clarinet (bars 1–37, including the bars later deleted); Ferrando and Guglielmo (bars 38–71); the chorus (bars 72–82); and then back to the first clarinet (bars 83–4). The last two bars of the clarinet part were later scratched out and overwritten with the flute parts, confirming that this pair of instruments was a later addition. L and many other copies show a version of 'Secondate' with evenly paced page breaks. T and a few other copies use the version now in **V1**, and as usual they rationalise the cut in various ways. It therefore seems certain that the extra bars were a mistake on the part of the copyist, and further confirmation is to be seen in the fact that the ink bar total for 'Secondate' omits them.

5 **'Per pietà'** One other piece that may not have been associated with the original collection of **V1** materials is Fiordiligi's Act II rondò, even though there are no hints of this in the page-break analysis. Together with its preceding *accompagnato*, it is copied on two regular gatherings of four nested bifolia. There are several unusual features in the **V1** copy. The character name given at the head of

the *accompagnato* was apparently about to begin with a capital 'L'. This was then erased, but the name that replaced it ('Fiordilici') was still wrong, though later corrected. The aria itself is attributed to 'Fiordili', an uncommon way of abbreviating this name. Some of these unusual features are replicated in **L** and **T**, but this does not prove that the **V1** copy was their exemplar, since it too could have been copied from this alternative source. Another small clue to the possibility of an additional early copy of 'Per pietà' lies in a corruption found in the three notes for second horn in bar 24. This is correct in **V1** but wrong in several other copies, although usually corrected later.

Overall, these examples of divergent traditions of page breaks provide a steady accumulation of evidence that second copies of some movements from *Così fan tutte* existed, and that there was some interplay between them and the pile of scores that were eventually bound as **V1**. One obvious candidate is the second early Viennese copy **V2** produced for practical use in the theatre, but other early copies cannot be excluded. This small but significant element of shuffling shows how important it is to recognise that the order imposed on materials at the time of their nineteenth-century binding may not have been the original one.

Other useful evidence to emerge from page-break analysis can be succinctly summarised. It provides a very clear overview of the versions of the opera for which materials are extant. Not surprisingly, the main divergences from the central line of transmission occurred when scores were being provided for new German productions. In each case there is a decisive departure from the central tradition. Of considerable value too is the way that page-break analysis assists with the appraisal of individual scores, allowing us in several cases to identify differing ancestries for component parts. Finally, page-break analysis sheds much light on the chronology of later cuts.

Patterns in the transmission and correction of textual errors provide another powerful tool for the chronological analysis of early sources. It is interesting to see how infrequently Mozart himself contributed to the circulation of an error. In the autograph the first bassoon note on beat three of bar 50 of 'Come scoglio' is unclear. An imprecise bassoon note in bar 29 of 'Per pietà' similarly initiated an error that proved quite persistent. And Mozart did not write the top note of the ascending theme in the first violin line at the start of 'Non siate ritrosi' clearly enough. Copyists, however, were in general less accurate. From the point of view of the scholar attempting to establish lines of transmission, it is fortunate that **V1** contains a number of significant copying errors, much more serious than erroneous accidentals or misreadings of single notes. These errors also appeared in **V2**, which demonstrates that the two scores were not both copied independently from the autograph. I compiled specimen lists of errors in three categories: uncorrected, corrected, and correct. If an error is corrected, it means that the passage was first copied wrongly and only later rectified. For the purposes of establishing the line of transmission, the uncorrected and corrected categories amount to the same thing: in both cases the mistake was as yet unidentified in the source text. The overall pattern of transmission sees the gradual correction of errors in the reference copy **V1** as we would expect, while, quite naturally, the practical copy **V2** (as shown by scores deriving from it) largely ignores them: the dissemination of the opera was not its intended function.

## Lines of Transmission

The main relationships between the sources can be represented by two lines of transmission. Such a scheme, however, inevitably over-simplifies the picture because some of the early copies are not unified sources. A critical question is: which of the two initial Viennese copies **V1** and **V2** came first? Having assessed all the evidence, I have come to the tentative conclusion that the latter probably pre-dates the former, even if only by minutes. It is entirely possible that the two copies were produced in tandem by relays of scribes. As we have already seen, some shuffling between the two piles of manuscripts of individual movements took place early on, and there was at least one further instance of a switch of material in 1804. To reiterate what we have already established, the 'agreed' cuts would first have been entered into **V2** during rehearsals, very probably by Mozart himself, and then these changes would have been noted by an assistant in the reference score **V1**, although not immediately made permanent. In marked contrast, the changes required by the composer's subsequent revision of the opera were entered by him in **V2**, but a decision was taken by some unknown person not to include them formally in the final version of **V1**.

Transmission Line A, given in Fig. 13, represents commercial copies produced directly or indirectly from **V1**. Prague was a highly significant secondary centre of distribution through the shop of Anton Grams.

Transmission Line B, on the other hand, comes directly from **V2**, and copies made from it are thus of particular significance. Until the Eda Kuhn Loeb Library in Harvard University placed a reproduction of its score **Ca** on-line, the parameters of the revised version were rather obscure, but once this resource had been made available, it was immediately apparent that, whatever its own date may be, it must reflect the state of **V2**. Guardasoni's Prague version was also based on **V2**, almost certainly because he or his copyists gained access to this source while it was still in Mozart's possession, a fact of no small historical significance. This version survives in the Bohemian score **C1**, which matches the 1791 Prague libretto quite well, although two of the musical cuts made in

FIG. 13   Transmission line A

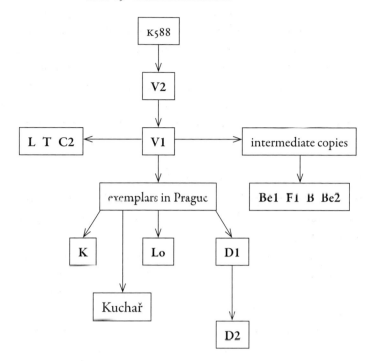

V2 and reproduced in **Ca** and **S** were countermanded. It must be admitted that the relationship between this branch and the Prague branch (if indeed they are two branches) remains somewhat elusive. Back on firmer ground, the score **V2** was used as a basis for Treitschke's 1804 revival of the opera as a *Singspiel*, which demonstrates the important further point that the Court Theatre regained possession of this score from Mozart or his surviving relatives. Transmission Line B is illustrated in Fig. 14.

All this makes it abundantly clear that Transmission Line B will provide the main evidence for Mozart's subsequent involvement with his last *opera buffa*, following the end of its first production run in Vienna in the summer of 1790.

One other aspect of the relationship between **V1** and **V2** concerns the title of the opera. In **V1** *Così fan tutte* was a late addition to the original title-page, which at first contained only what was to become the alternative title, *La scuola degli amanti*. It seems more than probable that Mozart's chosen title was not added to **V2** so quickly, and then perhaps only as the *ossia* title. The fact that *La scuola degli amanti* appears as the sole or the primary title in some scores in Transmission Line B may thus be a historical accident rather than a deliberate choice. This might also explain why the extra wind parts were so often supplied under the heading *La scuola degli amanti*.

FIG. 14  Transmission line B

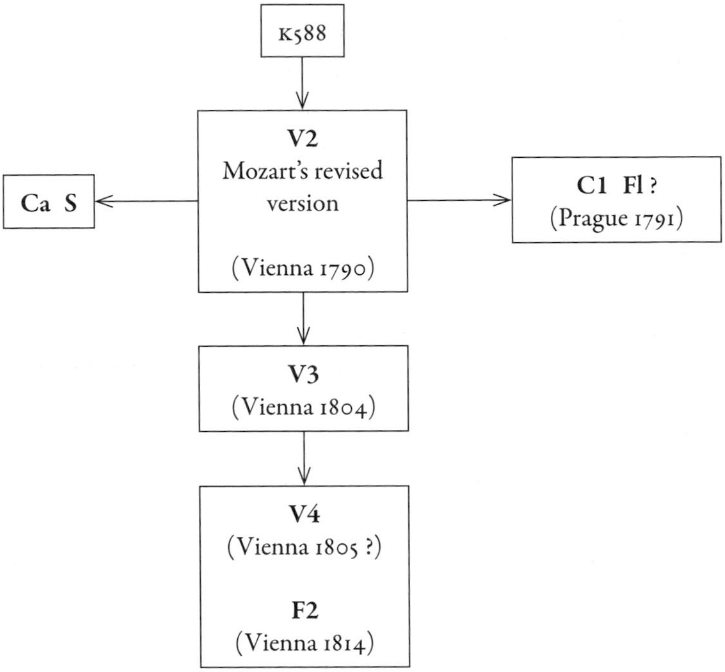

```
                    ┌──────────┐
                    │   K588   │
                    └──────────┘
                         │
                         ▼
┌──────────┐    ┌──────────────────┐    ┌──────────────┐
│          │    │        V2        │    │              │
│  Ca  S   │◄───│ Mozart's revised │───►│   C1  Fl ?   │
│          │    │     version      │    │ (Prague 1791)│
└──────────┘    │                  │    └──────────────┘
                │  (Vienna 1790)   │
                └──────────────────┘
                         │
                         ▼
                 ┌──────────────┐
                 │      V3      │
                 │ (Vienna 1804)│
                 └──────────────┘
                         │
                         ▼
                 ┌────────────────┐
                 │      V4        │
                 │ (Vienna 1805 ?)│
                 │                │
                 │      F2        │
                 │ (Vienna 1814)  │
                 └────────────────┘
```

## Early Viennese Copies

A few Viennese scores of *Così fan tutte* appear to have been copied directly from **V1** at a very early stage, and the extent to which they incorporate the 'agreed' cuts, therefore provides useful evidence as to when these changes were formalised – that is to say, not just identified but fully implemented. The Viennese score **L** in the British Library is very likely one of the earliest extant copies.[7] It could date from 1791 or even 1790. Edge provided a brief account of its likely provenance in his thesis: 'It seems to be at least partly in the hands of copyists who are known to have worked for Sukowaty, including at least one (Sukowaty 6) found in the original performing score of *Così fan tutte* [**V1**]. Thus this score may be from Sukowaty's shop, and the watermarks suggest that it may be quite early.'[8] This score includes the 'agreed' cuts to ensembles, arias and recitatives.

Another Viennese score in the British Library **T** could again date from as early as 1790–1.[9] In any event it must pre-date 1795 when the house number mentioned on its title-page changed. Edge comments: 'The score appears to have been copied by at least three copyists, none of whom appears in O.A.146 [**V1**]: these include Viennese Mozart-Copyist 4b ... and the copyist I have tentatively identified ... as Jacob Klein.'[10] This score makes the 'agreed' cuts to ensembles and arias, except for the introduction to 'Bella vita militar', but it gives the full uncut text of the recitatives. This would suggest that the 'agreed' recitative cuts were formalised slightly later than the others.

A third early Viennese copy **C2** could also date from 1790–1.[11] Like **T** it does not make the 'agreed' recitative cuts, and it too includes the orchestral introduction to 'Bella vita militar', adding further weight to the suggestion that there was a short delay in fully implementing these elements. The score (or scores) was (or were) dismembered and reconstituted for a nineteenth-century Danish production which must amount to one of the most radical reshapings of the opera ever to have been attempted. The revised order was: Act I: Overture, 7, 21, 5, 26, 5, 19, 25, Finale II (sections), 10, Finale I (sections), (Danish piece), 17, 3, 22, 8, Finale I (sections): Act II: 28, 23, 29, 24, 11, (Danish piece), 15, 27, (Danish piece), 1, 20, 14, 6, Finale II (sections). Before this cataclysm, however, the score seems not to have been used much.

There are in addition many early Viennese copies of individual arias and choruses, but I have not examined these as part of this study. An interesting and little studied aspect of the early transmission of Mozart's comic operas is the copying of finales for use in aristocratic entertainments. On 7 March 1802 the Empress Marie Therese joined in a performance of the Act I finale. She wrote in her diary: 'Das Finale vom 1$^{ten}$ Act d$^{ro}$ gesungen von mir, Marchesi, Weinmüller, Wallaschek, Ratmayer und Korner.'[12] The Lobkowicz family also ordered a copy of the Act I finale, no doubt for a similar entertainment. In this case the manuscript copy can be linked to an entry in an account book. According to Libin, who is studying the Lobkowicz accounts, a payment to Wenzel Sukowaty for a score and parts of the Act I finale was approved on 4 April 1799.[13] The extant score at Nelahozeves is headed: 'Cosi fan tutte / osia / La scuola degli amanti / Finale primo / Ah che tutta in un momento. / Del Sig$^r$ Wolf: Ama: Mozart'. Edge noted a partly illegible annotation with the name Lobkowicz on the verso of the last leaf containing the Act I finale in **V1**, which is surely related to this copying request.[14] The purchase of these materials rather suggests that the family did not yet have the full opera in their collection. The Lobkowicz Act I finale score was thus very probably copied from **V1**, but, as was usual in the case of commissions for single movements, no attempt was made to match the page breaks. Also at Nelahozeves Castle is a set of instrumental parts and vocal rolebooks for this finale, doubtless copied at the same time. A remarkable feature of these books is that they contain the full text of the finale, even the 'agreed' cut, a very rare eighteenth-century instance of the inclusion (if only by accident) of these bars. The mistake was quickly rectified.

# Mozart's Revised Vienna Version

IT HAS TO BE presumed that the second copy of *Così fan tutte* which contained Mozart's revised version **V2** is lost, but we have already encountered many signs of its existence. The likely contents of this all-important source can best be reconstructed from the score **Ca** in Harvard, which stems from a branch of Transmission Line B. For Act I at least, the very closely related score **S** provides additional confirmation, while Treitschke's decision to use it as the basis for his 1804 translation *Mädchentreue* confirms the essential integrity of this revision as a 'version' of the opera. Unusually for an early copy of a Mozart opera, there are indications that **Ca** was at one time owned by an English speaker.[1] Ferrando's Act I aria was restored (or perhaps repositioned) with the comment 'Un aura amorosa comes next'. The score is, however, unconnected to the 1811 London première which was based on a very different version. The copyists hands do not show features of the Viennese system, yet the Harvard manuscript is of considerable significance, since it incorporates all the new cuts and revisions that define Mozart's revised Vienna version. These are listed in Table 28.

The score **Ca** also provides a fascinating glimpse into how **V2** must have looked before the 'agreed' recitative cuts were sealed. It is quite clear that at this early stage these cuts were identified in some way, but in a manner that was wide open to misinterpretation. The original copyist who started the branch of transmission from which **Ca** derives, notably failed to understand some of these indications. The mistakes are listed in Table 29.

A fascinating page in **Ca** is the start of the recitative 'Ah non partite'. The first intervention from one of the sisters ('E che pretendereste') is clearly attributed

TABLE 28  Cuts and revisions in Mozart's revised Vienna version

|  | *Item* | *Cut* |
|---|---|---|
| Act I | Finale | bars 515–86 |
| Act II | Una donna | bars 67–79 |
|  | Finale | the canon and its transition, bars 173–207 (an autograph replacement is extant) |
|  |  | bars 545–58 |
|  |  | bars 596–631 |

TABLE 29  Misunderstandings of the 'agreed' recitative cuts in **Ca**

| Recitative | Comment |
| --- | --- |
| Oh la saria | The cut is identified in the full musical text but without the red crayon revisions which in **V1** smooth the new join. |
| Andate là | At the start of the cut, the copyist erroneously includes one bar ('Per Bacco ci faresti') which properly belongs at the start of the continuation after the cut, but he then proceeded to join it incorrectly to the cut material, using the word 'faceste'. The harmony is wrong. At the end of the material that should have been cut, the phrase 'Per Bacco ci faresti' appears again, this time in the right place, but now with wrong harmony. The indications in **V2** were thus comprehensively misunderstood. |
| Sorella, cosa dici? | The red crayon revisions needed to link the passages either side of the cut are made, but the cut material is not in fact then cut. The musical joins do not work. |

to Fiordiligi, and thus Dorabella does not sing anything. (It will be recalled that Mozart first gave this phrase to Fiordiligi in the autograph and then changed the part label to Dorabella.) If Fiordiligi had once been the only sister present, that would certainly explain the use of the singular 'ragazza' with which Don Alfonso refers to her.

A score of Act I in Salzburg **S** is very closely related to **Ca** and it therefore provides valuable confirmation of the identity of this version.[2] The only change required to Act I in Mozart's revised version is made rather crudely. The cut was first copied out, but then the relevant pages were excised and the few remaining bars crossed out. This might suggest some ambiguity in the instruction mandating the cut.

Page-break analysis confirms that the layout of **Ca** is virtually identical to that of **S** throughout. The pressmark of the latter indicates that it came from the Mozart family *Nachlass*, and, unlike **Ca**, all three of its copyists show strong signs of having been trained in the Viennese system. I was unable to make any sense of the watermarks, all of which appear to be letters, as the paper is relatively opaque and they invariably appear tight up against the central binding. In order to further the comparison between these two scores, it is, of course, possible to look for errors common to both. One such is in 'Vorrei dir', in which the second viola part in **Ca** in bars 3–4 was copied wrongly. In **S** the same error was made and then corrected.

A striking point of resemblance between **S** and **Ca** is the unclear manner in which the 'agreed' recitative cuts were initially made. In fact **S** makes different mistakes. In the recitative 'Che silenzio', for example, the agreed cut is made but with significant errors: Despina's clef is missing before her exclamation

'Ih!', and Don Alfonso's name is missing from the start of his phrase 'Prendi ed ascolta', which follows the cut. On the other hand, in the case of the second 'agreed' recitative cut, the source leading to **S** got it right, whereas that leading to **Ca** misconstrued it. The relatively ambiguous state of 'Ah non partite' in **V2** is reflected in **S** in the striking absence of any part labels at all after the first three phrases. One final feature of real interest in **S** is the presence of the incorrect cue ('e tradimento') at the start of 'Come scoglio'. As we have already seen, that leaves open the possibility that this position might even have been under active consideration during the compositional process itself.

### Signs of Mozart's Revised Version in the Autograph

The most significant element of Mozart's revised version, the replacement passage for the Act II finale canon, is, of course, extant in his own hand.[3] The location of the big Act I finale cut is also marked in the autograph. In the Allegro (bar 515) there is a red crayon XX-sharp sign at the start of the first-violin triplet quavers, and an equivalent sign at the start of the repeat of this section (bar 586). A similar XX-sharp sign in ink (forward slanting where the red crayon sign goes backwards) appears in bar 515 between the second violin and viola lines. There is also a '+' sign above the staff in bar 524, again in ink, although there is no mark at the equivalent place (bar 595). A further 'x' in ink appears above the staff at bar 557. Again there is no mark at the equivalent place (bar 628). The implication of these indications is that, having decided upon this cut, Mozart (or someone else) was uncertain as to where best to begin it. The pair of red crayon XX-sharp signs indicates the location finally chosen. It cannot be ruled out that the ink XX is in Mozart's hand.[4]

### Mozart's Changes to the Act II Finale in the Court Theatre Score

One of the genuinely satisfying aspects of a prolonged engagement with the minutiae of sources is the way that seemingly unrelated and insignificant details can suddenly come together in a finding of importance. It was a full ten years after I had first studied **V1** that light finally dawned: the explanation for its current state, in which Mozart's hand is clearly identifiable in connection with the changes made in the Act II finale but much less certainly anywhere else, is that the Act II finale from the transition after the canon onwards is in fact the **V2** copy. The man responsible for merging this concluding section with the rest of the existing (still unbound) **V1** copy of the opera was very likely Treitschke, since he used this version in his 1804 revival. Once this essential point had been grasped, then many seemingly obscure palaeographical facts suddenly acquired meaning. The exceptional turbulence in **V1** around the end of the canon is simply because this was the juncture of the join. Hitherto inexplicable features of the small number series and the bar totals in **V1** suddenly made sense. The small number series appear throughout Act II in **V1**, except for a few cases in which the autograph itself was used, but they cease at the canon. The reason is now clear: **V1** was the reference score used to generate performance materials, and so it had these number series; **V2** was not used for this purpose, and it therefore lacked them. Even clearer is the message of the bar totals. The Act II finale in **V1** contains totals for both versions. The presence of the canon is necessary for the original sequence of brown ink totals to add up; a later black sequence, on the other hand, must include the thirteen-bar replacement section. The various sequences of bar totals convey a significant message: the text of the Act II finale in **V2** as first copied was exactly as in **V1**, but it was then edited by Mozart to produce the revised version.

Of the two cuts that the composer himself undoubtedly entered into **V2** in the Act II finale (and which thus survive in O.A.146) the more significant is that of the celebrated canon. Copies of both the original and the replacement section are in **V1**. Tyson suggested that at one time the autograph of the replacement was itself in this source and that when it was recognised for what it was, a copy was substituted.[5] The end of the canon and the transition into the E major section is one of the most complex moments in the opera from the point of view of the palaeographical evidence in **V1**, and it deserves to be considered in detail. All the relevant pages have been reproduced in modern studies.[6]

In the autograph itself, Mozart polished the four-bar transition leading from the Ab canon to the new section in E major. What had been a rather routine passage of four bars of chugging crotchets in the bass line was revised, the last two bars becoming semibreves, better encapsulating the flowing character of the transition. The copyist wrote out this version with the semibreves in the bass line. In a hand identified as Mozart's by the editors of the *NMA*, a red crayon amendment was then made to the first violin part, so that it would double the flowing quavers of the first oboe in bars 3–4 of the transition. Not noted in the *NMA*, however, is the fact that there was also a semibreve B in bar 2 of the transition, hidden by the imperfectly lifted pasted slip that was once stuck over this bar. This note can be seen clearly in outline and it should be added to the *ossia* in bar 205 of the *NMA*, so that the first violin doubles the oboe. This change necessitated a small revision to the start of the new section. The first note of the first violin now needed to be G♯ rather than E.

In a major change of plan, Mozart decided to compose a substitute for the canon. Not only is this shorter and simpler in style, but the transition to the new section is more abrupt, two staccato chords in a single bar replacing the four-bar passage. The new link required some further revisions to the start of the E major section. Mozart again did this himself. In the first violin part, he restored the original note E by thickening its note-head, and for clarity added the letter 'e' above. The first note of the second violin and viola parts also had to be revised, and the redundant crotchets in the flute, oboe and bassoon deleted and the rests amended accordingly. He also added 'All°' at the top, necessary because the four-bar transition, now to be lost, had itself marked the start of the faster section.

Up to this point, the sequence of events seems clear enough, as does Mozart's involvement, but matters now take a rather complicated turn with the transition from the canon being involved in several separate decisions to seal by stitching a number of pages. The palaeographical evidence is very complex indeed and need not be considered here, but to summarise, it seems probable that the canon and the following transition were sealed up when Mozart decided to compose the replacement section. When, at an early stage, it was decided to restore the canon, the process was reversed. To compound the confusion, it was probably sealed up yet again when in 1804 Treitschke decided to use Mozart's revised version.

The second cut in the Act II finale with which Mozart's hand is clearly associated is from bar 545 to bar 559. The location of its start is indicated by an NB sign and a large vertical + above the staff and a large X below it, both in blackish ink. One bar before the end of the cut, there is a large + which was crossed out neatly (perhaps by Mozart) with five lines. Two large Xs, above and below the staff were inserted one bar later, together with hand direction signs, both slightly cropped. Mozart's hand is clearly evident in the corrections necessary to tidy up this join. In bar 559 he added an '8$^{tava}$' sign in the viola line (the one three bars earlier now being lost) and a crotchet for the two oboes with rests. He deleted with a series of short lines Don Alfonso's two bars (the last two bars of the cut passage) and the two beats after this, and substituted the final syllable '-rò', a crotchet and rests. He crossed out with a single long line Ferrando's text and replaced it with 'te lo credo gioia'. (Obviously this was to apply to Guglielmo's line as well.) On the verso the single crotchet which ended this phrase was replaced with a dotted-quaver / semiquaver / crotchet figure for the new final word 'bella' in both Ferrando's and Guglielmo's lines.

When the original was restored, Mozart's corrections were not themselves deleted, but a single red crayon ascending stem reinstated the final crotchet. Both Tyson and the *NMA* editors accepted that these changes were done by Mozart, and it is surely no coincidence that these bars (545–58) and the following statement of this material (bars 559–74) exist in a rare sketch, the survival of which perhaps points to its origin in a period apart from the main composition of the opera.[7]

The third cut in this revised version of the Act II finale runs from bar 596 to bar 631. Given the clear evidence of the composer's involvement in the other two cuts, it is reasonable to look for signs of it here as well. In order to make the cut, the first four bars were crossed out in red crayon, and the next four folios were stitched up together. The instruction 'vi-' marks the start of the cut, '-de' the end. Later, when the cut was restored, the syllable 'vi-' at the foot of the page was turned into 'gilt'. After the cut, the join was tidied up. Lightly indicated in red crayon were the first violin crotchet E and the second violin crotchet C and their remaining rests, also the viola notes and rests. Someone confirmed by writing over the red crayon in ink in the violin parts, and the viola notes, but leaving the viola rests as they were.[8] With such tiny fragments of writing, a firm identification of the hand is unlikely to be possible.

The clear message of the palaeographic evidence of the Act II finale in **V1** (actually the section of it that comes from **V2**) is that Mozart himself made two and perhaps all three cuts, but that they were then restored. Of the two other cuts required in the composer's revised version, the removal and then the replacement of a passage in 'Una donna' left traces in **V1** which are most evident in page-break analysis. There is physical evidence of the Act I finale cut. A bluish paper slip pasted over the first bar of the cut passage (515–86), the last bar of a recto, was not the original slip as it contains no stitching holes and the paste patch marks on the page underneath do not appear on it. Eight folios in total were stitched together. There was an attempt to begin the cut one bar earlier. The spot was marked with a very big blackish X later scratched out (another appears also one bar before the end of the cut passage). By locating the cut one bar later, it was possible to make its end coincide with the last bar of a recto, thereby simplifying the task of putting this revision into practice. In character this is a very large cut of repeated material. There were therefore numerous places where the cut signs could have been placed with identical musical results.

## *Evidence of Mozart's Revised Version in Other Early Scores*

Further clues about the relationship between the two Court Theatre scores are to be found in two of the earliest Viennese copies of the opera **T** and **L**, which represent different states of the Act II finale in the transition after the canon. Both were copied long before Treitschke's involvement with the opera. It is striking that **L** appears entirely unaware of Mozart's changes (or more particularly their consequences), while **T** is seriously confused by them. Either **L** was copied from a source in which Mozart's changes were not included, or else its copyist understood the need to avoid alterations (made to institute the revised version but then rescinded) rather better than his contemporary. The copyist of **T** retained the B in the second violin and the G♯ in the viola in bar 208, which are required to follow on from the end of the canon replacement, even though he in fact copied the canon. Similarly, while **L** includes the wind crotchets in bar 208 that end the transition from the canon, **T** has a semibreve rest in each of these parts, an obvious misunderstanding of this join. [9] This pattern persists and indeed is even clearer in connection with Mozart's second change to the Act II finale, the cut of bars 545–59. Again there are unambiguous signs that the copyist of **T**, even though not himself making the cut, was confused by changes required to smooth the joins. Thus the 8$^{ve}$ sign in the viola part in bar 559 is unnecessarily retained. Even more strikingly, the notes added by Mozart to the parts of Ferrando and Guglielmo at the start of bar 561 to cope with the new text, were at first entered in **T** but then scraped out. Again **L** presents the correct text in an untroubled fashion. What all this demonstrates is that at least one early source in Transmission Line A reflects a state of the text *after* the removal of Mozart's additions. Who authorised this is entirely unclear.

## *The 1804 Vienna Revival*

Although well beyond the chronological limits of this study, a brief comment on Treitschke's use of Mozart's revised version of *Così fan tutte* for his 1804 Vienna revival of the opera as *Mädchentreue* is necessary, as it was this decision that led to the reappearance and quite possibly the ultimate survival of the autograph replacement for the canon. The complex of *Mädchentreue* scores presents an incredibly tangled knot to untie, but the basic facts are clear enough. Treitschke based his *Singspiel* on a score containing Mozart's revised version **V2**, as shown by his adoption of the composer's changes. As Tyson pointed out, we can date his discovery of the canon replacement, because he appended a note of it to the autograph: 'Eine Abkürzung zu Cosi fann tutte, um dass Larghetto im 2n Finale zu ersparen, von Mozarts eigener Handschrift, für die kais: Hoftheater. / Sie ist in keine anderen Hände gekommen. / gefunden am 29 August 1804 / Fr. Treitschke.'[10] In the excitement of his discovery, Treitschke came to the conclusion that the simplified version was what Mozart wanted, and he accordingly made sure that it was incorporated in *Mädchentreue*. It is significant that he described this revision as having been done 'for' the Hoftheater – one small piece of evidence to suggest that Mozart's revision was specifically for Vienna. In the course of preparing performance materials for his new version, Treitschke seems to have merged the score of most of the Act II finale containing Mozart's revisions (**V2**) with the existing Court Theatre score (**V1**). However, although at some point he clearly used **V1** as a reference, marking it up with the numerous cuts required to produce *Mädchentreue*, the new score **V3** appears to have been copied from the text of **V2**, as a result of which it perpetuates quite a few of the serious uncorrected inaccuracies that characterise scores in Transmission Line B.

# Early Italian Language Performances

I T was to be several generations before *Così fan tutte* was given again in Italian in Vienna following the conclusion of the first run on Saturday 7 August in 1790. That the opera continued to receive performances in its original language at all was largely as a result of its promotion by Domenico Guardasoni, whose association with Mozart went back to the première of *Don Giovanni* in Prague in 1787. After that success, he took full control of the company from the impresario Bondini, and he was responsible for further Italian language performances of the opera in both Prague and Leipzig. A possible commission for a new opera was discussed with the composer during his visit to Prague in the spring of 1789. A Guardasoni production of *Così fan tutte* in Prague was thus always likely, and the opera was eventually staged by him some time during 1791. His company also presented the opera in Leipzig in subsequent years, but the other contemporary Italian language production, staged in Dresden in 1791, seems to have been a different version.

## Domenico Guardasoni's 1791 Prague Production

It has been generally accepted that Mozart had no involvement with any staging of *Così* outside Vienna. In the nineteenth century, it was claimed that he provided material for a Munich performance, but this theory has long since been abandoned.[1] Yet in the case of Guardasoni's 1791 Prague performances, we must not discount too quickly the possibility that the composer might have been involved in some way. Guardasoni returned to Prague on 10 June 1791 in order to prepare for the staging of *La clemenza di Tito*.[2] Following Salieri's rejection of this commission, it was offered to Mozart, who arrived in Prague on 28 August. His renewed collaboration with Guardasoni provides an obvious context for the decision to stage a Prague production of *Così*, but the lack of information about the exact date of the première hampers discussion. With new major projects to complete, Mozart would have had little time to devote to a revival of his earlier opera, yet he could have offered his views on what Guardasoni was planning in something as simple as a ten-minute conversation. The sources certainly suggest that the impresario either consulted the composer or else was given access to materials in his possession.

The Prague libretto of 1791 is clearly a source of major importance in the reception history of *Così* during the composer's lifetime. Its title-page runs:

COSI FAN TUTTE / O SIA / LA SCUOLA / DEGLI AMANTI. /
DRAMMA GIOCOSO / IN DUE ATTI / DA RAPPRESENTARSI
/ NEL TEATRO NAZIONALE DI PRAGA / SOTTO L'IMPRESA,
E DIREZIONE / DI DOMENICO GUARDASONI / L'ANNO 1791.
PRAGA / Imprimato nella Stamparia Elsenwanger[3]

A clue to its date appears on the verso of the title-page, on which Da Ponte is still accredited with his court position in Vienna: 'La Poesia è dell'Abbate DA PONTE. / Poeta del Teatro Imperiale'. The Prague libretto clearly used the 1790 Vienna book as its exemplar, adopting a very similar layout and typeface, and even reproducing some of its idiosyncrasies such as the misalignment of the word 'Alfonsetto' (p. 7), but it omitted the text of all five of the 'agreed' recitative cuts. In his discussion of the libretto for the 1786 Prague version of *Figaro*, Tyson reached exactly the same conclusion about the relationship between the Prague and the Vienna books: 'The compositor of the Prague libretto had a somewhat altered copy of the Vienna libretto in front of him when he set the work; for the layout of the lines, the hyphenation of certain words, and even one or two spelling mistakes or similar peculiarities serve to indicate that the text supplied to the Prague compositor was not basically a manuscript, but an amended copy of the Viennese printed text.' [4]

The text of the Vienna exemplar of *Così* was given a very careful reading prior to its adaptation as the basis for the Prague text. The corrections are listed in Appendix 6. The reviser was meticulous in his approach. Redundant text in the 1790 libretto was deleted and substantial discrepancies with the autograph nearly all eliminated. The only significant inconsistencies allowed to stand (or not noticed) were the erroneous attribution of the aside '(non otterà nientissimo)' to Guglielmo in the recitative 'Oh che bella giornata' and the failure to add in the missing lines in 'Donne mie'.[5] Again there is an exact parallel with the way in which the 1786 Prague libretto for *Figaro* was prepared. Tyson wrote: 'It is important to observe that some of the passages in which the Prague libretto differs from the Vienna one do not represent special 'Prague changes'; they are merely changes to bring the text into line with the version that Mozart had set to music in the first place, and that had now been transferred to Prague.'[6] A few changes to the stage directions in the Prague libretto of *Così* are of interest, as these too stem from the process of revision. The instruction 'parte' was added after two arias where it is needed but missing in the Vienna libretto. The sharp eye of the reviser spotted that whereas Ferrando and Guglielmo depart in travelling costume ('da viaggio'), they return in full military dress. He altered a stage instruction so that they could return clothed as they had left, a visually sharper representation of the point. In the Act II finale, where the variety of joy was in dispute, Da Ponte has 'giolito', the autograph 'gaudio' – there seems to be an example of humour, possibly even Mozartean humour: why not have 'giubilo' instead!

An obvious question, then, is who supplied Guardasoni with this carefully annotated libretto? No one would have been in a better position to identify speedily those places where the score and libretto needed to be aligned than the composer himself, and, given his contacts with him in the late summer of 1791, it is entirely plausible that he assisted his colleague by correcting a copy of the Vienna book. Indeed, he may already have had such a document in his possession. At the same time, there are difficulties with the theory that an assistant working independently made the corrections. Such a person, checking the 1790 libretto against a copy of the score purchased in Vienna, would no doubt have quickly spotted the mistakes in Da Ponte's imperfectly revised book, but he would also have encountered a range of additional discrepancies, the origins of which lay not in any disagreement between the autograph and the libretto but in the process of copying **V1** from the autograph. Without detailed inside information, he would not have been able to distinguish these from libretto-autograph variants, and yet it is clear that he systematically made this distinction, ignoring the **V1** peculiarities.[7] Most of these were trivial in character, but in a few cases such as the retention of 'Venezia' as the port of departure in the source score, the reviser still did not make the change. He knew that the libretto was right. He either had access to the autograph or the composer, or else he was in contact with someone who was very well informed about the necessary changes.

The discovery of a score associated with the 1791 Prague libretto allows us to progress further in reconstructing what Guardasoni's company probably performed. Despite its current location in Copenhagen, **C1** is a Bohemian score.[8] It is written on what is almost certainly Bohemian paper, watermarked with a large letter B and surmounted by a crown, with the exception of a few interpolations on paper (probably north Italian) which has a watermark of three crescents with the letters AFH or GFA.[9] The gathering structure of this source is unusual. Act I is written on a series of conventional gatherings (1–26) of which two (17/1 and 18/1) are on the non-Bohemian paper. In addition, the hand in these two gatherings is quite distinct, strongly resembling (though not actually identical with) the hand designated by Edge as Viennese Mozart Copyist 1. The gathering structure of Act II consists of two sequences: 1/2 to 17/2 is a complete series in which 11/2 is on the 'foreign' paper. Interleaved with this sequence rather randomly is a second series in which there are quite a few missing numbers: 4/2 to 21/2. The best explanation that I can come up with is that there were two copyists (or teams of copyists) working in tandem. Was there perhaps an urgent requirement for two copies of the score? The insertions in the hand that resembles Viennese Mozart Copyist 1 include 'Come scoglio', 'Non siate ritrosi' and 'È amore'. This copyist perhaps had his own supply of paper, and it cannot be ruled out that these were later replications of gatherings that had become lost or damaged. Another feature of interest is that the page-break analysis of 'Come scoglio' suggests the strong probability that some connection exists with the other score in Copenhagen (**C2**), an early Viennese copy. Of course, this link was not necessarily a direct one, and it probably has nothing to do the current location of these two scores. If speed was a factor in the production of **C1**, its consequence was that the Italian text is extremely corrupt. In the Act II finale, for example, Fiordiligi is to marry 'Semprompto'. Virtually all the changes incorporated in the Prague libretto are present, excluding the added or changed stage directions. There is only one significant difference: the fifth 'agreed' recitative cut is not made. This is interesting as it points to the possibility of a deliberate restitution of this passage in Prague.

A small number of very minor changes to the musical text were made in order to ensure that the score matched the Prague libretto. These are listed and briefly discussed in Appendix 7. The amount of material involved in these musical changes is far too tiny to allow any firm musical attributions to the composer, and there is, of course, no direct palaeographical evidence. Nonetheless, the possibility that Mozart quickly annotated the score that Guardasoni was intending to use, certainly cannot be ignored. What these small changes demonstrate is that **C1** constitutes an edited version of the musical text which incorporates, but also goes slightly beyond, the changes made in the Prague libretto. While it is not possible to prove that Mozart was involved, the sense of the composer's proximity seems fairly strong. In any event, a discerning eye was responsible for the changes made both to the libretto and the musical text of the 1791 Prague version.

In the light of all this, it is of interest to see whether **C1** repeats or retracts significant variants in the verbal text that arose during the copying of **V1**: in other words, to what extent were the remaining mismatches between the Prague libretto and the Vienna-derived score a cause for concern? The picture is mixed. Some obvious errors were spotted and changed but others remained undetected or else were allowed to stand: it is often hard to know which is the case. The correct port of departure was inserted, but the serious misreading in **V1** in the same recitative ('d'infedeltà' instead of 'di fedeltà') remained. Fiordiligi still speaks of you ('voi') rather than us ('noi') in 'Come scoglio', but 'morrò' in 'Fra gli amplessi' was replaced by 'verrò'. Not surprisingly, there is no sign at all of any concerted attempt to change unimportant details such as spelling variants, elisions and punctuation marks.

Much the most important feature of Guardasoni's Prague version as revealed by **C1** is that it was based on Mozart's revised Vienna version. The score contains most of the cuts made in **V2**, but it restores the material lost in 'Una donna' and at the end of the Act II finale. The process of ongoing revision was easily capable of coping with repeated changes of mind on the part of the composer or anyone else.

Another score that may contain the Prague version is **Fl**. I have not seen this manuscript. After a brief examination, Edge concluded that it is a Viennese copy dating from the first decade of the nineteenth century. From the account in *NMA:KB*, it appears to be linked to the Prague branch of Transmission Line B, as it includes the two changes made by Mozart to the Act II finale and the big Act I finale cut, but not the cuts in 'Una donna' and at the end of the Act II finale.[10] There is insufficient detail in this description, however, to tell whether the Italian text of the recitatives is that of the 1791 Prague version. If it is a Viennese score, however, then it probably postdates 1804 when Mozart's revised version became the basis for *Mädchentreue*.

An interesting source relating directly to the Prague version is a vocal role-book to be found in the Lobkowicz collection in Nelahozeves Castle. This important manuscript is in two parts. Act I is headed: 'La / Scuola degli Amanti / osia / Così fan tutte / Atto Primo / Guilelmo Sig$^{re}$, [followed by the name 'Bassi' added later in red crayon]. Act II is headed: La / scuola degli Amanti / Atto II$^{do}$ / Guilelmo / Basso'. As was usually the case with materials deriving from **V2**, the inversion of the titles was not corrected. The role-book contains all the material the singer of this role had to learn, although interestingly the big Act II aria 'Donne mie' is missing. (This is doubtless accidental, although it is worth noting that in **K** (a Prague score) this aria was reassigned to Don Alfonso at quite an early stage.) In the recitatives, only verbal cues are given, so that until the first rehearsal with other members of the cast, the singer would have had no idea of what (musically) preceded all his entries. Its musical text matches the Bohemian score in Copenhagen **C1** which contains the Prague version. There are at least six hands, all of which display features of the Viennese system. The fact that 'Bassi' is the only performer's name inserted into this role-book, reinforces the feeling that it was copied specifically in connection with Guardasoni's production. Luigi Bassi was a long-serving and popular member of this opera company, and he was indeed cast as Guglielmo. His later connections with the Lobkowicz family provide ample explanation for the current location of this role book at Nelahozeves.

It seems likely that Guardasoni approached Mozart personally to obtain the necessary scores and parts for his proposed Prague production and that he was given access to **V2**, which may then have been further amended in consultation with the composer. What he clearly did not do was to purchase materials commercially available in Prague itself. Scores of this kind usually give the standard Vienna version of **V1** with the 'agreed' cuts, whether Italian full scores like **D1**, German *Singspiel* versions like **K**, or the numerous copies of Kuchař's keyboard arrangement.

## A Mystery Italian Production

This account of Mozart's subsequent involvement with *Così fan tutte* will conclude with evidence of another Italian language version recorded in **V1** that remains wholly baffling. The reason for considering this hypothetical version is that although the main evidence for it comes from as late as 1811, it could date from Mozart's lifetime. When all the revisions in **V1** and **V2** associated with the performances in 1790 have been accounted for, as well as the numerous interventions relating to Treitschke's *Mädchentreue* of 1804 (and later *Singspiel* versions), there remains one final layer of changes in O.A.146 that defines an unidentified Italian version. Yet there is no documentary evidence of such a production in Vienna, even by 1811. This layer of revisions was entered in a distinctively dull-looking red crayon, different in appearance from the rich brick-red colour (thought to be early) and the orange-tinged colour (thought to be late) seen elsewhere in this source. Multiple thick vertical lines sometimes indicate the start of cuts made for this version. The changes are listed in Appendix 8. Some of the revisions, notably the removal of Guglielmo's mistimed interventions in the recitatives 'Come tutto congiura / L'abito di Ferrando', appear to represent the results of an informed reading of the opera. Another obvious feature is the continuing editorial intervention in the part of Despina, a process begun by Mozart in 1790. It is also striking that the cuts made to 'Mi par che stamattina' and 'Signora Dorabella' remove the only two occasions in Act I when the sisters refer by name to their real lovers, an action that would have been necessary if any re-pairing was being contemplated. This cannot be excluded as a motive, because in the most eye-catching change of all, Fiordiligi loses her aria 'Per pietà' and acquires as a replacement Dorabella's 'È amore'. None of these revisions appears to have been formalised or accepted as 'agreed', and they do not therefore appear in subsequent Viennese copies deriving from this score.

There is unequivocal evidence to support the view that these changes constitute a distinct revision. It comes in a surprising source: the libretto of the version given at the London première of the opera at the King's Theatre in 1811. The reception of Mozart's operas in early nineteenth-century London has been the focus of studies by Raeburn, Senici and Cowgill, but these have concentrated on issues of reception rather than the ancestry of the score.[11] Although the immediate origins of the London version of *Così* remain a complete mystery, one component that went into the melting pot at an earlier stage of its development is clearly identifiable as this set of revisions in **V1**. Most of the cuts and changes seen in this layer match exactly what is in the London libretto, while the remainder, very similar in essence, have minor adjustments at the start or end.

The ultimate source of the text of the London version was the first Dresden libretto of 1791, which introduced savage cuts, reducing the opera in length by about a third. It also includes some substitute recitative passages added by the arranger where significant plot-related action would otherwise have been lost: for example, a short recitative 'Alla bella Despina' replaces the sestetto 'Alla bella Despinetta'. How the Dresden version came into contact with the Vienna revisions is unknown, but certainly there must have been at least one intermediate source, because the **V1** changes do not appear in either of the 1791 Dresden librettos or their associated scores (**D1** and **D2**).

Yet another ingredient of the London cocktail is harder to trace, but seems to represent developments in Germany during the 1790s. An undated Donaueschigen libretto from this period reflects these revisions in spirit at least, if not always in substance. They include: (1) a change in the characters singing 'Prenderò quel brunettino' – in Donaueschigen the duet was performed *in situ* but by Dorabella and Despina, whereas in London, much more radically, it became a duet between Guglielmo and Fiordiligi immediately prior to the Act II finale; (2) the transfer of Guglielmo's Act II aria to Don Alfonso and the insertion of a replacement – 'Voi che sapete' in London; and (3) a duet for Don Alfonso and Despina after 'Tutti accusan le donne' – 'La ci darem la mano' in Donaueschigen, the afore-mentioned duet between the serious couple in London. The entry of these ideas into the melting pot of the London version suggests that there was more than one intermediate version. Its probable ancestry is shown in Fig. 15.

In its general aspect, this London version represents a second phase of *Così* reception. The earliest translations and adaptations usually reflect a single authorial voice embodying reactions to perceived shortcomings in the plot. As time passed and certainly by the early nineteenth century, even that limited sense of coherence began to diminish and hotchpotch versions gained favour, seemingly almost random confluences of ideas and materials from widely differing sources. Such arrangements still performed a useful function: they brought a good selection of Mozart's operatic music before a public increasingly desirous of hearing it; and they continued to offer vehicles for star singers who, through the continuing practice of aria substitution, could make of the score virtually whatever they wanted.

FIG. 15  The ancestry of the 'London' Version

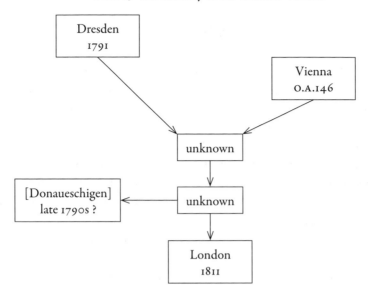

In the light of all this, it is impossible to say whether any of the remaining changes made to the libretto of 1811 relate directly to the King's Theatre production or stem from an earlier intermediate source. Perhaps the star singer who introduced it (Teresa Bertinotti) encountered this version earlier in her career and then travelled with it to London, as one of her favoured pieces. But when the **V1** layer of revisions was done and for what purpose remains obscure. A connection with Mozart seems fairly unlikely, but one cannot be ruled out altogether.

# Conclusion

IT WILL BE useful at the end of this investigation to summarise the main phases of change that Mozart's last *opera buffa* went through during his lifetime and to which he may have contributed. These are shown in Table 30.

During its composer's lifetime, *Così* thus consisted of at least four distinct (if far from dissimilar) versions, any one of which could easily be reconstructed in a modern performance. The version in the *NMA* comes closest to representing the composer's initial conception, before he came up against the realities of theatrical life during the rehearsal period. A version which made the 'agreed' cuts would very likely match what was performed on 26 January 1790 and was thereafter accepted as the 'standard' text. Mozart's revised Vienna version seems to have had further abbreviation as its main goal, although there were several significant artistic rethinks. And finally there is the Prague version, staged by Guardasoni either during the composer's visit to the city in 1791 or else shortly thereafter. This was based on Mozart's revised Vienna version, information about which might well have been provided by the composer himself.

The most significant of the revised versions is that represented by **V2** and is attributable to Mozart himself, yet its exact date remains frustratingly elusive. The evidence of paper types is inconclusive. Both the canon replacement and a sketch (of unclear purpose) for the bars removed later in the finale (545–58) are written on type 91 paper, on which Mozart completed the finales of the string quartets K589 and K590 some time in the spring or summer of 1790 after finishing work on *Così*. These dates are consistent with the idea that Mozart's revisions to the opera were made some time during the Vienna production run rather than in 1791. In the absence of any other firm evidence, we should take seriously Treitschke's comment that the canon replacement was an abbreviation done 'for' the Court Theatre.

Despite the very real uncertainty over whether these changes were all made in Vienna, or whether some of them were introduced specifically for Guardasoni in the summer of 1791, it remains entirely appropriate to identify the Prague version as a distinct conception. Indeed, it is abundantly clear that *Così fan tutte* came into being along the same culturally fruitful Vienna–Prague axis as its immediate predecessor. In the light of all this, the lack of precise information about the date of Guardasoni's Prague première remains an important lacuna in the early historical record of this opera.

When in 1804 Treitschke revived the opera in a German translation entitled *Mädchentreue*, he gained access to **V2**, which he then integrated into his own

TABLE 30   Changes to *Così fan tutte* during Mozart's lifetime

| Category of change | Position | Comments |
|---|---|---|
| 'agreed' aria & ensemble cuts | Overture: (81–8, 149–56, 194–201)<br><br>Un'aura amorosa: (50–7, 63–6)<br><br>Act I finale: (461–75)<br><br>Ah lo veggio: (57–91) | There is every indication that these cuts were an integral part of the compositional process itself. They were invariably incorporated in both lines of transmission. |
| additional 'agreed' ensemble cut | Bella vita militar: (1–24) | This also achieved the status of an 'agreed' cut but perhaps slightly later than the others. There seem to have been several changes of mind about whether this orchestral introduction was needed, and it appears in two early Viennese scores **T** and **C2**, which stem from **V1**. |
| 'agreed' recitative cuts | Che silenzio: from 'Ti vo fare del ben' (28) restarting at 'Prendi ed ascolta' (38)<br><br>[Oh la saria]: from 'È buon' (35) restarting at 'Ite' (57)<br><br>Andate là: from 'Che diavolo' (20) restarting at 'per Bacco ci fa' (46)<br><br>Sorella cosa dici?: from 'è mal che basta' (15) restarting at 'sorella mia' (30)<br><br>Ora vedo: from 'Ora vedo' (1) restarting at 'Sciagurate!' (15) | The five 'agreed' recitative cuts were made at an early stage and quickly became part of the accepted text of the opera. There are indications that they were not immediately formalised in **V1** and that the full recitative texts were transmitted for a short while, as seen in early copies such as **T** and **C2**. These cuts were indicated in **V2**, but in this source they were not thoroughly integrated into the text, the result being some confusion in sources such as **Ca** and **S**, which are aware of the cuts but which do not integrate them correctly. By the time that the Prague branch of Transmission Line B was established, these cuts were properly integrated. |
| Mozart's revised version | Act I finale: (515–86)<br><br>Una donna: (67–79)<br><br>Act II finale: (173–203) (replaced by a new section)<br><br>Act II finale: (545–58)<br><br>Act II finale: (596–631) | Mozart's revision of *Così fan tutte* is represented by **V2**, only the last part of which survives today, as it replaced the Act II finale after the canon in O.A.146. It remains uncertain whether this revision was undertaken: before the première; or during the first performance run; or in connection with Guardasoni's plan to stage the opera in Prague. It is also unclear whether these changes were made sporadically or as part of a concerted effort to revise. This layer of changes does not appear in Transmission Line A. |
| Guardasoni's Prague version | Una donna: (67–79) (replacement of cut)<br><br>Act II finale: (596–631) (replacement of cut) | This stemmed from **V2** and therefore included all the 'agreed cuts' (with the possible exception of the one at the start of the recitative 'Ora vedo') as well as the changes made by Mozart in his revision. However, the confusion surrounding the 'agreed' recitative cuts in **V2** was sorted out, two of the cuts made during Mozart's revision were revoked, and some very small musical changes were made in response to minor problems in the libretto. |

*Singspiel* version. The basis of this choice could certainly have been information passed down orally from the period of the première, but even without such guidance, he made the logical decision to use the score with what he probably assumed were Mozart's last thoughts.

We can therefore claim three things about the **V2** version: (1) that Mozart himself was responsible for it; (2) that if he was consulted over Guardasoni's Prague production, he might have indicated his preference for it; (3) that Treitschke, the man responsible for the first major revival in Vienna, also chose it, possibly basing the decision on received knowledge. This amounts to a pedigree of some weight, yet it is equally undeniable that the reference copy **V1**, responsible for the dissemination of the opera throughout Europe, did not incorporate the changes needed for this version, which, therefore, remained very much a minority reading of the work. Who was responsible for this decision and upon what authority they acted remain unclear.

The underlying premise of this investigation into the early sources of *Così fan tutte* has been my belief that the value of a detailed study of these materials has increased rather than diminished in the light of our changing concept of what the 'text' of a Mozart opera really is. The fundamental shift in our perception of this issue has been succinctly expressed by Senici:

> Stefan Kunze's assertion that 'the idea of different but equally authentic versions [of a Mozart opera] seems intolerable' gives voice to what until very recently was a general belief, and a direct consequence of the fact that Mozart's operas have been retrospectively conceived as 'texts' in the strong sense of the word. At the root of this conception is the myth of the composer as *the* author of opera – a nineteenth-century invention. It is easily understandable, then, why operatic and especially Mozartian scholarship has devoted great attention to what is under the composer's control, while everything that comes after (or, for that matter, before) is ignored as 'non-authentic'. If 'the idea of different but equally authentic versions' seems intolerable, all the more so will be the 'non-authentic' ones, shameful distortions that disrupt the unity of the work as its author – the composer – conceived it.[1]

The object under the lens of the operatic scholar was and is a living, evolving art-work, and the tools of textual scholarship, once used to fix a single, static 'text', can now be deployed in pursuit of a moving target. We must learn to set aside our stills cameras and acquire the techniques of cinematography. It follows that where once a study such as this one would probably have sought to delineate an even more 'authentic' text to replace an earlier attempt, now its emphasis must be on tracking the continuing development of the work. To be sure, what the composer as author actually wrote or did not write remain matters of great interest, but representing this information as an ongoing process, limited neither by an undue emphasis on the initial moments of creation nor by the inevitably arbitrary circumstances of the first formal public hearing, will in the end provide a much better record of the original reality.

# The First Phase of Copying

| Item | Opening brace | Score |
| --- | --- | --- |
| La mia Dorabella | violins, viola, Ferrando, Don Alfonso, Guglielmo, bass, clefs, key signatures, time signature **C** | Ferrando, Don Alfonso, Guglielmo, bass, fragments of the first violin |
| È la fede delle femine | violins, viola, Ferrando, Don Alfonso, Guglielmo, bass, clefs, key signatures, time signature **C** (not **₵**) | Ferrando, Don Alfonso, Guglielmo, bass, fragments of the first violin |
| Una bella serenata | Ferrando, Don Alfonso, Guglielmo, bass, clefs and time signatures (including those for violins), Allegro | Ferrando, Don Alfonso, Guglielmo, bass, fragments of the first violin |
| Al fato | violins, viola, Ferrando, Guglielmo, bass, clefs, key signatures, time signatures | Ferrando, Guglielmo, bass, fragments of the first violin, some dynamics in the bass |
| Alla bella Despinetta (first section up to 3/4) | violins, viola, Dorabella, Fiordiligi, Despina, Ferrando, Guglielmo, Don Alfonso, bass, clefs, time signatures | Dorabella, Fiordiligi, Despina, Ferrando, Guglielmo, Don Alfonso, bass, fragments of the first and second violins |

# Hypothetical Recitative Sequences

| Item | Recitative sequence |
|---|---|
| **Act I** | |
| Sequence 1   Fuor la spada<br><br>Scioccherie di poeti! | This sequence was copied in a light brown ink with a warm tinge. It contrasts with the black looking ink of the opening ensembles. The use of the spelling 'Guillelmo' probably implies that these recitatives were composed early, although the retention of this spelling might merely reflect the fact that this early section of the libretto was not subject to any other revision. In any case, there was no particular reason to delay copying them, because they link ensembles. (Recitatives leading into arias were not usually done before the key of the aria had been established.) |
| Sequence 2   Mi par che stamattina<br><br>Stelle! per carità<br><br>Non pianger<br><br>La commedia è graziosa | This sequence was copied in a medium brown ink. It represents the feigned 'call-to-war' and the preparations for the men's departure, and it terminates abruptly with the chorus, which was almost certainly a later addition. Although written on the earlier of the two main paper types, these recitatives have several characteristics of material otherwise written on the later paper type. As Tyson noted, the spelling 'Guilelmo' is used in the recitative 'Mi par che stamattina', and Fiordiligi's line is placed above that of Dorabella, when the two women sing a short passage together. These recitatives were thus apparently written on a few remaining sheets of the first consignment of paper to be used. |
| Non v'è più tempo | This comes across as an isolated recitative, at least in terms of its appearance. It was copied in a similar brown ink, but with a newly sharpened nib, giving it a very fine character. There is much evidence that the plot sequence involving the military chorus and its repetition (which fall either side of 'Non v'è più tempo'), was inserted here quite late on in the compositional process, and it seems very likely that, despite its use of another left-over sheet of the earlier paper type, this recitative was not copied until |

| | Item | Recitative sequence |
|---|---|---|
| | | after 'Di scrivermi' (which also starts with the earlier paper type) had been composed. |
| | Dove son?<br><br>Non son cattivo comico<br><br>Che vita maledetta (up to bar 6, beat 3) | Also difficult to place in any obvious sequence are these recitatives. They are copied in medium brown ink, similar to the above. There appears to be no break in ink colour at the point at which the accompagnato passage 'Nel mare solca' evolves out of the simple recitative 'Non son cattivo comico'. The break in ink colour shortly after the start of 'Che vita maledetta', however, is striking. |
| Sequence 3 | Che vita maledetta (after bar 6, beat 3)<br><br>Signora Dorabella<br><br>Che silenzio<br><br>Che sussurro (up to bar 7) | This sequence is copied in a light brown ink with a distinctive yellow-gold tinge. It begins after the word 'noi'; the semicolon (after 'noi'), the quaver rest and everything that follows is in this ink. This place in the recitative is also marked with a '+' sign, a copying instruction of some sort. This ink was also used to copy the accompagnato 'Ah scostati', to add in the second violin part and the slurs in the first violin part on the opening side of 'Smanie implacabili' and also to do the start of 'In uomini', including the whole of the first side (fol. 71) except for the tempo designation 'Allegretto', the flute part, and bars 9–10 of the strings. On the verso, a further seven bars (and one crotchet) are copied in this ink in the voice and bass. Thereafter a new ink takes over. The identification of this copying sequence illuminates many aspects of this much revised section of the opera, which saw the cutting of Despina's cavatina, its replacement by a recitative, and the incorporation of her later aria 'In uomini' with its unorthodox beginning. It is likely that the copying of this continuity sequence started when the arias for Dorabella and Despina were finally put in place. The redundant 'dopo' indication for Despina's 'lost' cavatina (indicating a different original order) appears at the start of the recitative 'Che vita maledetta', but apparently only six and a bit bars were at first copied, after the decision to get rid of the cavatina had been made. It is reasonable to assume that Mozart had to wait for Da Ponte to come up with new text. |

*continues overleaf...*

| Item | Recitative sequence |
|---|---|
| Che sussurro (from bar 7) | There is a dramatic interruption to the ink colours at Dorabella's words 'Oh ciel!' in the recitative 'Che sussurro', when a darker ink makes its appearance, albeit one which gradually lightens. As we shall see, this copying break, together with the sequence of errors at the start of 'Ah non partite!' suggests that Mozart did not yet know whether Dorabella or Fiordiligi was to interject 'Oh ciel!' |
| Sequence 4 Ah non partite!  Si può sapere | This sequence was copied in mid-brown chocolate coloured ink. |
| Oh la saria | This recitative was copied in dark looking ink which fades (often in the note-stems) to a brown. The appearance of the words 'Atto primo' in red crayon (the only time such an identification is made for a recitative) could indicate that he was recopying a recitative composed for another location. (One possibility might be before the garden scene in Act II.) Other textual features in the libretto hint at a change of location for this recitative. |
| **Act II** | |
| Sequence 1 Andate là  Sorella, cosa dici?  Ah correte al giardino  Il tutto deponete  Oh che bella giornata | The sequence that includes the first part of Act II up to the start of the seduction scenes, was copied in a dark brown ink, fairly consistent in character, but which fades to a medium brown. The *segue* indications all appear to be written in this ink. |
| Sequence 2 Amico, abbiamo vinto!  Bravo: questa è costanza  Ora vedo | There are relatively few recitatives in this part of the opera. The ink colour is similar to the first sequence in Act II, but the much finer tip to the quill concentrates the dark colour. It is possible that the particellas of the two accompagnatos 'Il mio ritratto' and 'In qual fiero' were done during this sequence. |
| Sequence 3 Come tutto congiura  L'abito di Ferrando | These are in the hand of a copyist. |
| Sequence 4 Vittoria, padroncini! | The ink is brown, but significantly lighter than before. |

# APPENDIX 3

## *The Bifoliation Numbers of Act II*

| *Item* | *Modern foliation (pencil)* | *Original bifoliation: the long sequence* | *Original bifoliation: shorter sequences* |
|---|---|---|---|
| Andate là | 175 | 1 | |
| | 176 | | |
| Una donna | 177 | | 1 (light brown) |
| | 178 | | |
| | 179 | | 2 |
| | 180 | | |
| | 181 | | 3 |
| | 182 | | |
| Sorella, cosa dici? | 183 | 2 | |
| Prenderò | 184 | 3 | |
| | 185 | | |
| | 186 | 4 | |
| | 187 | | |
| | 188 | 5 | |
| | 189 (blank) | | |
| Ah correte | 190 (verso blank) | 6 | |
| [Secondate] | missing | | |
| Il tutto deponete | 191 | 7 | |
| La mano a me date | 192 | | 1 (light brown) |
| | 193 | | |
| | 194 | | 2 |
| | 195 | | |
| | 196 | | 3 |
| | 197 | | |
| | 198 | | 4 |
| | 199 (blank) | | |
| Oh che bella | 200 | 8 | |
| | 201 (verso blank) | | |
| Il core vi dono | 202 | 9 | |
| | 203 | | |
| | 204 | 10 | |
| | 205 | | |
| | 206 | 11 | |
| | 207 | | |
| | 208 | 12 | |

*continues overleaf...*

| Item | Modern foliation (pencil) | Original bifoliation: the long sequence | Original bifoliation: shorter sequences |
|---|---|---|---|
| Barbara! | 208v | | |
| | 209 | | |
| Ah lo veggio | 210 | | 1 (faint red crayon) |
| | 211 | | |
| | 212 | | 2 |
| | 213 | | |
| | 214 | | 3 |
| | 215 | | |
| | 216 | | 4 |
| | 217 | | |
| | 218 (verso blank) | | [5] |
| | 219 (blank) | | |
| [Ei parte] | missing | | |
| Per pietà | 220 | | 1 (brown) |
| | 221 | | |
| | 222 | | 2 |
| | 223 | | |
| | 224 | | 3 |
| | 225 | | |
| | 226 | | 4 |
| | 227 | | |
| | 228 (verso blank) | | [5] |
| Amico, abbiamo | 229 | 13 | |
| Il mio ritratto | 230 | | |
| | 231 | 14 | |
| | 232 (verso blank) | | |
| Donne mie | 233 | | 1 (brown) |
| | 234 | | |
| | 235 | | 2 |
| | 236 | | |
| | 237 | | 3 |
| | 238 | | |
| | 239 | | 4 |
| | 240 | | |
| | 241 (verso blank) | | [5] |
| In qual fiero | 242 | 15 | |
| | 243 (verso blank) | | |
| Tradito | 244 | | 1 (faint red crayon) |
| | 245 | | |
| | 246 | | 2 |
| | 247 (verso blank) | | |
| Bravo: questa | 248 | 16 | |
| Ora vedo | 248v | | |
| | 249 | | |

| Item | Modern foliation (pencil) | Original bifoliation: the long sequence | Original bifoliation: shorter sequences |
|---|---|---|---|
| È amore | 250 | | 1 (brown) |
| | 251 | | |
| | 252 | | 2 |
| | 253 | | |
| | 254 | | 3 (overwritten?) |
| | 255 | | |
| | 256 | | 4 |
| | 257 (blank) | | |
| Come tutto | 258 (copyist) | | |
| | 259 | | |
| | 260 (verso blank) | | |
| | 261 (blank) | | |
| Fra gli amplessi | 262 | | 1 (brown) |
| | 263 | | 2 (light brown) |
| | 264 | | 2 (brown) (→ 3) |
| | 265 | | |
| | 266 | | 3 (different brown) |
| | 267 | | |
| | 268 | | 4 |
| | 269 | | |
| | 270 | | 5 |
| | 271 (blank) | | |
| Ah poveretto me [Tutti accusan] | | 18 | |
| Vittoria | 272 (verso blank) | 19 | |
| Finale | separate sequence | 1–20 | |

# The Two Sisters Problem

THE IDEA that Fiordiligi and Dorabella were left stranded in the wrong characters in the first part of Act I (up to Scene V) as a result of a change of plan during the compositional process is what I describe as the Two Sisters Problem. A significant number of translators of *Così* seem to have been aware this difficulty and tried to do something about it, which suggests that the problem was to some extent 'common knowledge'. Various remedies were tried out:

| | Da Ponte 1790 | Mozart 1790 | Prague 1791 | Dresden 1791 | Mihule 1791 | Bretzner 1794 | Treitschke 1805 |
|---|---|---|---|---|---|---|---|
| Who begins the duet 'Ah guarda sorella'? | F | F | F | F | F | D | D |
| Who sings / speaks the first words in Scene III 'Non son essi'? | F | D | D | D | F | F | F |
| Who sings / speaks the outburst beginning 'Cos'è'? | F | D | F | F | F | D | D |
| Who begins the individual phrases in 'Sento oddio'? | D | D | D | D | D | F | F |

*Key:* F = Fiordiligi; D = Dorabella

Mozart's own solution to the problem caused by the change of plan was only a partial one. He switched text between the two sisters part way through the recitative 'Mi par che stamattina'. The autograph starts with the text as given in the libretto, and the result is that Fiordiligi correctly names her lover as Guglielmo, although arguably the two sisters remain for the moment in the 'wrong' characters. At the start of Scene III, however, Mozart switched the libretto text between the two sisters, so that they are now in the 'right' characters. The 1791 Prague and Dresden versions (C1 and D1) both compromise by switching only the text of the first two phrases of Scene III between the two sisters, leaving the following dialogue as in the original libretto. In view of Mozart's contact with Guardasoni in the summer of 1791, it cannot be ruled out that this was his suggestion. Of the major *Singspiel* versions, Mihule remains faithful to Da Ponte, but a radical solution was attempted by Bretzner in *Weibertreue*. He had the idea of reversing the text sung by the two sisters in the whole of the first part of the opera, including the duet 'Ah guarda sorella'. Thus it is Julchen (i.e. Dorabella) who begins 'Sieh Schwester'. But there was a large flaw in the execution of this idea. Bretzner forgot that if he merely switched text between the two sisters, the wrong names would be bandied about. The effect is chaotic and it is hard to believe that this series of obvious gaffes could have survived rehearsal, let alone performance. The trouble begins in the recitative 'Mi par che stamattina'. Having heard Fernando eulogise his 'Julchen' at the start of the opera, the audience might well have been stunned to hear this sister then refer to 'my Guglielmo' ('mein Wilhelm'). At the start of Scene III, the two sisters still do not know who their lovers are: Julie asks about Wilhelm again, while Charlotte cannot even get the name of her wrong lover right. It should be Fernando not Ferdinand. Perhaps to counteract the impersonal character of much of Da Ponte's representation of the 'real' couples, Bretzner makes a particular point of having the two sisters refer by name to their (real) lovers, a rare occurrence in the original text. As the names are still wrong in 'Stelle! per carità', the effect is hardly as intended: Charlotte asks: 'Ist mein Ferdinand todt?' Julie: 'Lebt Wilhelm nicht mehr?' Finally, in 'Non piangere' Julie manages to get the name of her lover almost correct: it is still Ferdinand rather than Fernando. After the first hearing of the chorus in Scene V, both women are spot on with the names of their lovers, although in 'Signora Dorabella' Julie lapses one last time into calling her lover Ferdinand. Bretzner made one further change in his attempt to restore the right characters to the sisters. In the quintet 'Sento oddio', he reversed the sisters for the two short pairs of single lines beginning with Dorabella's 'Ah, no, no non partirai'.

Authors of versions of the opera stemming from *Weibertreue* realised that Bretzner's 'corrections' would not do, and they amended them in various ways. This seems to have happened quite quickly. In the earliest published keyboard score by Siegfried Schmiedt, issued by Breitkopf in *c*.1795, all these changes were reversed. In the Hamburg *Weibertreue* of 1796 and in *Die Wette*, the sisters revert to the order of the autograph at the start of 'Ah guarda sorella', with Charlotte (Fiordiligi) beginning 'Sieh Schwester'. As these versions include only the 'Gesänge' from the opera, it is not clear what happens in the spoken text, but in the quintet (where it does not matter much either way) the reversed order of the sisters was allowed to stand. On the other hand, the 1797 Weimar libretto reverses the changes both in the duet and the quintet.

The solution adopted by Treitschke in his 1805 libretto of *Mädchentreue* was to leave the two sisters in the order that Bretzner had them both in the duet and the quintet, but to correct the names (other than the persistent Fernando / Ferdinand ambiguity) in the spoken dialogue. Making sense of the musical sources, however, is a nightmare, a phenomenon sent to test the sanity of any scholar.

Not only is it necessary to cope with multiple cast changes between different productions, it is also vital, in the early part of the opera at least, to take into account the two real difficulties that faced Treitschke and his copyists as they prepared for *Mädchentreue* using pre-existing scores. The first problem was that shortly after the publication of Bretzner's libretto, an alternative version gained currency in which Mihule texts were substituted for the first three ensembles, complete with the wrong names for the sisters. Once this was spotted, it was easy enough to replace the names. The fact that the duet for the two sisters in the *Mädchentreue* scores **V3** and **V4** also uses the Mihule name Dorchen, suggests that the first response was to assume that the names as given in the first three ensembles were right. Only when the alternative names were encountered throughout the rest of the opera, was the decision taken to amend the opening ensembles. A trickier problem altogether was that by switching the names of the sisters in some elements in the first part of the opera, Bretzner produced irreconcilable conflicts. Treitschke and his assistants would soon have noticed these difficulties. For example, the name of the woman eulogised by Ferrando at the start of the opera (the Dorabella character) would, as a direct result of the interventions by Bretzner, have been the sister who began the duet (the Fiordiligi character in Mozart's original). It is interesting to see that none of these changes had been agreed by the time that the fair copy *Mädchentreue* score **V4** had been started. Both **V3** and **V4** therefore contain the same sequence of name changes. However, only **V4** embodies the realisation that the solution that was being attempted was unworkable, as it would result in uncrossed pairings for the seduction scenes. This could simply have been an accident, but it cannot be ruled out entirely that it was a deliberate attempt to recast the opera. In any event, wiser councils soon prevailed, and in **V4** the sisters' names were switched back. Thereafter, the sequence of name changes for later Viennese productions is relatively straightforward, as follows:

| Autograph (1790) | | | Mädchentreue (1805) | Die Zauberprobe (1814) | |
|---|---|---|---|---|---|
| | V3 | | V3 | V3 | V3 |
| | V4 | | V4 | | |
| | V4 | | V4 | | |
| Fiordiligi | Isabelle | Julie | Charlotte | Laura | Isabella |
| Dorabella | Dorchen | Charlotte | Julie | Isabella | Rosaura |

The extraordinary number of changes to the names of the two sisters demonstrates starkly the extent to which the reception of this opera in early nineteenth-century Viennese theatres was dominated by the Two Sisters Problem.

After the departure scene in Act I, the sisters' names are un-amended in **V4**, which confirms that the Two Sisters Problem was the source of all this confusion, rather than a simple decision to switch the names throughout the opera. There was certainly a consensus that the problem of the two sisters disappears by the time of the recitative 'Non v'è più tempo', from which point Fiordiligi and Dorabella had always been in the correct character, yet that did not stop the author of *Mädchenrache* (Breslau, 1806) from extending his solution a little, so that it is Julchen (Dorabella) who begins 'Di scrivermi'.

The earliest layer of **V3** represents the well-established version of *Weibertreue* in which the first three trios made use of Mihule's text but without correcting the names of the sisters to bring them into line with Bretzner's new cast. (I owe this significant point to the generosity of Claudia Zenck, who sent me a copy of her article '"Ach wir alle sind von Flandern". Frühe deutsche Übersetzungen von *Così fan tutte*', in *Österreichische Oper oder Oper in Österreich?*, ed. Herbert Schneider (Hildesheim, 2005). Where this score came from is unclear, although a performance of Bretzner's version under the interesting title *Die zwei Tanten aus Mailand* is recorded in Vienna in 1802.

The only other place in the opera that might conceivably have been affected by Mozart's decision to switch the character of the two sisters is at the start of Act II. The first two recitatives are light-hearted in tone, and (in the first one at least) it is as yet unclear that Dorabella will surrender first and then try to persuade her sister to follow suit. Even at the start of 'Sorella, cosa dici?', it seems to be Fiordiligi who is taking the lead in proposing a little flirtation. The failure to make a clear distinction between the characters of the two sisters here led eventually to further misunderstandings, especially in the duet where they express their preferences. Bretzner, by now no longer concerned by the Two Sisters Problem, followed the original libretto in the dialogue leading up to the duet: Julchen: 'Der Schwarzkopf wär mir am liebsten.' Charlotte: 'Hm! Der Blondin ist auch nicht übel.' Treitschke, however, apparently under the impression that the character reversal in the first part of Act I still needed to be enforced, switches the choices, with Julie going for 'Der Blauaugige' and Charlotte 'Der Schwarzkopf'. In view of the prevailing confusion, the opening couplets of the duet itself were sensibly reworked so that there is no mention of hair colour at all. The materials in **V3** appear to show that both alternatives were current. In one violin part from the *Mädchentreue* era, there is a cue leading into the duet, not attributed to a character: 'Der Blauaugige ist auch nicht übel'. This uses the *Mädchentreue* term for the blue-eyed boy, but apparently reverts to the choices made in Bretzner's translation.

Most early solutions to the Two Sisters Problem focused on the first part of Act I, where the difficulty had originated, but a much more radical solution was possible. This appears in a German translation that accompanies the first full score, published by Breitkopf & Härtel in 1810. This borrows the *Weiber-treue* texts for the ensembles and arias, and incorporates them into a full translation of the recitatives. The fact that in this German translation the first duet is started by Julchen (Dorabella), might well have puzzled anyone comparing it with the accompanying full score, where it is Lottchen (Fiordiligi) who begins. The libretto translation thus starts to put into effect Bretzner's 'solution'. At first, the translator dealt carefully with the names of the men, replacing the reference to Guglielmo in the recitative 'Mi par che stamattina' with the unspecific 'mein Geliebter'. A major surprise follows at the start of Scene VI, as Lottchen (Fiordiligi) takes over Dorabella's words: 'Dove son?' Thereafter it quickly becomes apparent that this particular reviser has switched the two women throughout the rest of the opera, and before long Fiordiligi embarks upon 'Smanie implacabili'. The effect of this drastic action is not only to reverse the characters of the two women entirely, but also to oblige the officers to serenade their own women (much as suggested in the hypothesis of the lovers uncrossed). Almost immediately, however, there is a mistake. In the recitative 'Signora Dorabella' the names of the two officers are not switched. Thus Julchen: 'Ach! Wenn ich meinen Guglielmo verlöre, so glaube ich, dass ich stürbe.' Lottchen: 'Ach! Wenn ich meinen Ferrando verlöre, so glaube ich, dass ich mich lebendig begrübe.' The plot continues effectively enough for a time. When it comes to choosing the men, it is Lottchen (Fiordiligi) who selects 'der Schwarzkopf'. The stage directions at the start of Act II, Scene V are altered appropriately: Guglielmo & Lottchen 'am Arm'; Ferrando & Julchen 'ohne sich den Arm zu geben'. But after this the plot falls apart completely, as no attempt is made to revise the scenes in which the men react to the news of their betrayal. Here the names are totally wrong. Ferrando reports of Julie (his own lover and now the target of his own seduction) that she has remained as true as a dove to her 'Guglielmo'. It is rather surprising that so flawed a version should have been accorded the prestige of appearing alongside the first published full score, although in this context it functions merely as a preliminary translation. The musical score itself is largely faithful to the original text, together with the 'agreed' recitative, aria and ensemble cuts transmitted in **V1**.

A possible explanation for this bizarre turn of events is that some hack, ignorant of the complexities of the issue, noted the discrepancy in the early part of the opera and then unthinkingly corrected (wrongly) all subsequent occurrences of the sisters' names. The second explanation is that it was a rather more reasoned and indeed imaginative response to a problem that had long defied a final resolution. Rather than attempt to solve the insoluble problem of the sisters in the first part of Act I, why not escape from the difficulty by rearranging the rest of the opera? Needless to say, such an action was never going to produce a coherent drama. Yet if there remained even vestigial knowledge of how this issue had evolved during the opera's genesis, the new plan could have been seen as a logical response: if this was how the problem had arisen in the first place, perhaps the best solution was to backtrack and try and reconstitute a might-have-been 'School for [uncrossed] lovers'.

If the German translation accompanying the Breitkopf & Härtel full score of 1810 represents the Two Sisters Problem as an open chasm bisecting Act I, then collectively the twenty or so early manuscript scores and their associated sets of parts reflect the issue as something of a subterranean fault-line: the symptoms, often no more than the slightest of tremors, are manifest, the underlying causes usually invisible. Examples include librettos in which one or more character names are spelt one way up to this point in the opera, and then another way thereafter. Performance materials quite often seem to have a different ancestry, either side of this dividing line. The widespread agreement that some response was necessary to the Two Sisters Problem in itself demonstrates some aware-ness of the creative decision that led to these perceived difficulties. Although no commentator referred directly to this problem in public, it is nonetheless not at all unlikely that the view that there was some fundamental problem with the libretto had its origins in this issue. Niemetschek provided the classic formula-tion: Mozart had been obliged by circumstances to waste his heavenly melodics on a dreadfully botched libretto. In effect, this single statement set the para-meters for the critical reception of *Così fan tutte* – the mismatch between music and text – that have persisted to the present day.

# Page- and Line-break Analysis

/ = line break     // = page break

| Item | Source | Page- and line-breaks | Total bars |
|------|--------|------------------------|------------|
| La mia Dorabella | V1 | 3//4//4//4//4//4//4//4//4//4//4//4//4//4//4//2 | 61 |
| | L | | |
| | T | | |
| | D1 | | |
| | C1 | | |
| | F1 | | |
| | H | | |
| | D2 | | |
| | Be1 | | |
| | Ca | 3//3//3//3//3//3//3//3//3//3//3//3//3//3//3//3//3//4//4//2 | |
| | K | 3//4//4//3.5//3.5//3.5//3.5//3.5//3.5//3.5//3.5//3.5//3.5//4//4//3.5 | |
| | B | 3//4//4//4//4//4//4//3//3//3//3//3//3//3//3//3//3//4 | |
| | S | 3//4//3//3//2.5//2.5//3//3//3//3//3//3//3//3//3//3//4//4//3//2 | |
| | Be2 | 5//5//6//5//5.5//4.5//5//5//5//5//5//5 | |
| | V3 F2 | 3//4//3//3//3//3//3//3.5//3.5//3//3//3//3//3//3//3//3//3//2 | |
| | V4 | as V3 but pages 8 & 9 are 3//4 | |
| Ah guarda sorella | V1 L | 4//5//5//5//5//5//5//4//4//5//5//5//5//5//5//5//5//5//6//5//6//6// 5//5//6//5//5//5//5//5//5//5//3 | 154 |
| | T | | |
| | C2 | | |
| | D1 | | |
| | C1 | | |
| | K | | |
| | H | | |
| | D2 | | |
| | Be1 | | |
| | F1 | ends 4//4 | |
| | B | 4//4//4//4//4//4//4//4//4//4//4//4//4//4//4//4//4//5//5//5// 5//5//5//5//5//5//5//5//5//5//5//4//4//4//3 | |
| | Ca S | 4//5//5//5//5//5//5//4//4//5//5//5//5//5//5//5//5//5//5//5//5// 5//5//5//5//5//5//4//5//5//5//5//3 | |
| | Be2 | 7//8//8//7//8//6//8//8//7//9//9//8//8//9//9//10//11//8//6 | |
| | V3 F2 | 3//5//5//5//5//5//5//4//4//4//4//5//4//4//4//5//5//5//5//5// 5//5//5//5//4//5//5//4//4//4//4//4//4//2 | |
| | V4 | 3//4//4//4//4//4//4//4//4//4//3//4//4//3//4//4//4//4//4//4// 4//4//4//4//4//4//4//5//4//4//4//4//4//4//4//4//4//4 | |

| Item | Source | Page- and line-breaks | Total bars |
|------|--------|----------------------|------------|
| Vorrei dir | V1<br>L<br>T<br>C2<br>D1<br>C1<br>H<br>D2<br>Be2 | 4/5//5/5//5/5//5/4 | 38 |
| | K | 3/4.5//4.5/5//4/4//4/4//5 | |
| | Ca<br>F1<br>B<br>S<br>Be1 | 3/4//4/4//4/4//4/4//4/3 | |
| In uomini | V1<br>T<br>C1<br>Ca<br>S | upbeat + 4//7//7//4//5//4//5//5//5//4//5//5//4//5//4//4//5//<br>5//5 | 92 |
| | L | upbeat + 4//7//6//5//5//4//5//5//5//4//5//5//4//5//4//4//4//<br>4//4//3 | |
| | F1 | ends 7 | |
| | H | starts upbeat + 4//6//5//4//4//4 | |
| | D1<br>D2 | ends 4//5//5//5 | |
| | K | upbeat + 4//7//6//4//4.5//4//3.5//4.5//4.5//4//3.5//4//4.5//4//<br>3.5//4.5//3.5//4.5//4//3.5//4//2.5 | |
| | B | upbeat + 3//5//5//4//4//4//4//4//4//4//4//4//4//4//4//<br>4//4//4//4//3//4//4 | |
| | Be1 | upbeat + 3//6//4//4//4//4//4//4//4//4//4//3//3//4//4//3//3//<br>4//3//4//3//3//3//3//4 | |
| | Be2 | upbeat + 8//8//6//6//5//6//7//5//8//5//7//7//7//7 | |

*continues overleaf...*

| Item | Source | Page- and line-breaks | Total bars |
|------|--------|------------------------|------------|
| E voi ridete? | V1 | 4//5//5//5//5//5//5//5//6//5//5//6 | 61 |
| | L | | |
| | T | | |
| | D1 | | |
| | Lo | | |
| | C1 | | |
| | Ca | | |
| | K | | |
| | F1 | | |
| | B | | |
| | H | | |
| | D2 | | |
| | S | | |
| | V3 | | |
| | F2 | | |
| | Be1 | 4//5//5//4//4//4//5//5//4//4//4//4//4//5//4 | |
| | Be2 | 8//7//6//7//7//7//6//5//6//2 | |
| Un'aura amorosa | V1 | missing | 68 |
| | L | 4//6//5//5//5//5//5//6//5//3 (bars 50–57 are cut) 1//4//1 | |
| | C2 | (bars 63–66 are cut) 4//5//4 | |
| | D1 | | |
| | Lo | | |
| | C1 | | |
| | Ca | | |
| | F1 | | |
| | B | | |
| | D2 | | |
| | S | | |
| | T | ends 5//4//4 | |
| | H | pages 8 & 9 are 5//6 | |
| | K | 4//5//5//6//5//5//5//5//5//4// (bars 50–57 are cut) 5// bars 63–67 are cut) 5//5//4 | |
| | Be1 | 4//5//5//5//5//4//4//4//5//4//4//4//5//4//4//2 | |
| | Be2 | 6//7//8//7//7//7//7//7//8//4 | |

| Item | Source | Page- and line-breaks | Total bars |
|---|---|---|---|
| Una donna | V1 T | 3//4//5//5//5//5//5//4//4//8//7//5//5//5//4//4//5//5//4//4//3 | 99 |
| | C2 | pages 9–12 run: 4//6//7//7 | |
| | C1 | pages 9–11 run: 5//6//8 | |
| | D1 Lo B D2 Be1 | pages 8–12 run: 5//5//6//6//6 | |
| | L F1 H | 4//5//5//5//5//5//5//5//6//5//5//5//5//5//5//4//4//5//5//4//4//3 | 86 |
| | Ca | 3//4//5//5//5//5//5//4//5//5//5//5//5//4//5//5//5//4//4//3 (bars 67–79 are cut) | 86 |
| | K | 3//4//4//4//4//5//4//4//4//4//5//5//4//4//4//4//4//4// 5//5//4//4//3 | |
| | Be2 | 5//5//5//5//6//6//5//6//7//6//6//5//5//6//9//7//5 | |
| | V3 | 2.5//3//3//3//3.5//3.5//3.5//3.5//3.5//3.5//3//3.5//4//4//4//4//3// 3//3.5//3.5//3//3//3//4//4//4//3//3//3//1 | 99 |
| | V4 F2 | 2.5//3//3//3//3.5//3.5//3.5//3.5//3.5//3.5//3//3.5//4//4//4//4//3// 3//3.5//3 5//4//4//3//3// 3//1 ends 4 | 86 |
| Secondate | V1 | 5//7//5//5//2 (cut of bars 25–37) 4//6//6//6//6//6//5//5//3 | 71 [84] |
| | T | pages 4–5 run: 4//3 (extra bars omitted) | |
| | C2 | pages 4–8 run: 4//4//5//5//5 (extra bars omitted) | 71 |
| | C1 | pages 4–6 run: 4//4//5 (extra bars omitted) | |
| | L D1 Lo F1 B H D2 Be1 | 4//5//5//5//5//5//5//6//6//6//6//5//5//3 (extra bars omitted) | 71 |
| | Ca | 5//7//5//6//6//5//5//5//5//6//4//4//5//3 (extra bars omitted) | |
| | K | 4//5//5//5//5//5//5//5//5//5//4//5//5//3 (extra bars omitted) | |
| | Be2 | 10//11//10//7//8//9//10//6 (extra bars omitted) | |
| | V3 | 3//4//4//4//3//4//4//4//4//5//5//4//5//5//4//5//4 (extra bars omitted) | |
| | F2 | ends 4//5//5//4 | |

| Item | Source | | Page- and line-breaks | Total bars |
|---|---|---|---|---|
| Per pietà | V1 | | half bar + 3//5//4//4//4//5//4//4//4//5//5//5//5//5//5//5//5// | 127 |
| | L | | 5//5//5//5//5//5//5//4//4//4//4//3 | |
| | T | | | |
| | C2 | | | |
| | D1 | | | |
| | Lo | | | |
| | C1 | | | |
| | Ca | | | |
| | B | | | |
| | F1 | | | |
| | H D2 | | | |
| | K | | half bar + 2//4//4//3//4//4//4//4//4//4//4//5//5//5//5//4//4//5// | |
| | | | 5//4//4//5//5//5//4//5//5//4//4//4//4//4 | |
| | Be1 | | half bar + 2//4//4//3//4//3//5//4//4//4//5//5//5//5//5//5//5// | |
| | | | 5//5//5//5//5//5//5//5//4//4//4//3 | |
| | Be2 | | half bar + 4//5//4//4//4//7//6//7//6//8//7//7//7//7//8//7// | |
| | | | 7//8//7//7 | |
| | V3 | | half bar + 2//3.5//3.5//3//3//3//3//3//3//3//3//4//4//3//4//4// | |
| | | | 4//3//3//4//4//3//4//4//4//4//4//4//4//3//3//3//3//3//4//4// | |
| | | | 3 (many cuts of later date) | |
| Tutti accusan le donne | V1 | | 3//3//3.5//3.5//3//3//4//3 | 26 |
| | L | | | |
| | T | | | |
| | D1 | | | |
| | C1 | | | |
| | F1 | | | |
| | Ca | | 3/3//4/3//3/3//4//3 | |
| | K | | 3/3//3.5/3.5//3/3//3.5//3.5 | |
| | B | | 5/4.5//3.5/3//3/4//3 | |
| | Lo | | | |
| | H | | 3/3//3.5/3.5//3/3//4/3 | |
| | D2 | | 3/3//3.5/3.5//2.5/2.5//3/3//2 | |
| | Be1 | | 3/3//3.5/3.5//3/3//7 | |
| | Be2 | | 4//4/4//4/5//5 | |
| | V3 | | 3/4//3/3//3/3//4/3 | |
| | F2 | | 3//3//3//3//3//2//3//2//4//3 | |

# APPENDIX 6

# Corrections to Guardasoni's *1791 Prague Libretto*

| Item | Character | Vienna 1790 | Prague 1791 | Comments |
|---|---|---|---|---|
| **Act I** | | | | |
| Mi par che stamattina | Fiordiligi | Non son essi ... | | This is the first recorded response to the Two Sisters Problem. After |
| | Dorabella | | Non son essi ... | this switch of these two lines at the start of Scene III, the text |
| | Dorabella | Ben venga ... | | reverts to the Vienna version. As Mozart had been responsible |
| | Fiordiligi | | Ben venga ... | for the problem in the first place, it certainly cannot be ruled out that he drew Guardasoni's attention to it and even that this new solution was his idea. |
| Che vita maledetta | Despina | Per bacco vo assaggiarla: cospettaccio | Per bacco vo assaggiarla: | The word 'cospettaccio' was not set by Mozart, an omission that was possible because it turned an eleven-syllable line into a seven-syllable line. |
| Che silenzio | | | text of the agreed recitative cut removed | |
| Che silenzio | Despina | (Per me questa mi preme.) | omitted | This line was not originally set by Mozart. He later added seven small notes in his autograph (without the words) but these did not find their way into **V1**, which, however, has the text added as an insert. |
| Alla bella Despinetta | Fiordiligi Dorabella | Di dispetto e di furor | Di dispetto e di terror | The word 'terror' appears in the autograph. |
| Non siate ritrosi | | | two stanzas omitted | These were in the Vienna libretto but not set by Mozart. A further line ('Siam due cari matti') was also left out in the Prague libretto by accident. |
| Oh la saria da ridere | | | text of the agreed recitative cut removed | |
| Oh la saria da ridere | Don Alfonso | Ma intanto queste pazze? | Ma intanto quelle pazze? | The Prague libretto follows the autograph. |

*continues overleaf...*

| Item | Character | Vienna 1790 | Prague 1791 | Comments |
|---|---|---|---|---|
| Oh la saria da ridere | Despina | Le povere buffone ... lagnarsi | Le povere buffone ... lagnarsi | It is interesting to note in the light of the other revisions made to this recitative, that Da Ponte's 'buffone' and 'lagnarsi' were not changed to Mozart's 'padrone' and 'sognarsi'. |
| Finale | Despina | Bonae puellae | Bones puelles | The Prague libretto incorporates Mozart's bogus Latin. |
| Finale | Despina | Bebberla, o in piu | O vero in piu | Mozart has 'ovvero in piu'. |
| Act II | | | | |
| Andate là | | | text of the agreed recitative cut removed | |
| Andate là | Despina | (amiche siamo in porto) | omitted | This aside was not set by Mozart. |
| Una donna | Despina | Quel che il cor più brama e loda | Dove il diavolo ha la coda | The Prague libretto reverts to the line set by Mozart which was in the draft Vienna libretto. |
| Sorella, cosa dici? | | | text of the agreed recitative cut removed | |
| Ei parte | Fiordiligi | Guilelmo, anima mia! ... | omitted | The six lines at the end of this recitative not set by Mozart were cut in the Prague libretto. |
| Per pietà | | | (par.) | This stage direction is not in the Vienna libretto. |
| Donne mie | Guglielmo | Vi do marche d'amistà | Vi do segno d'amistà | Mozart was inconsistent in the autograph, writing 'segno' once and then 'marche' twice. |
| Donne mie | | | parte | This stage direction is not in the Vienna libretto. |
| Ora vedo | | | text of the agreed recitative cut removed | |
| Ora vedo | | Dorabella, Despina, e poi Fiordiligi | Dorabella, Despina, e Fiordiligi | The stage direction is revised to take account of the fifth 'agreed' recitative cut. Fiordiligi is present from the start. |
| Come tutto congiura | | ... che passano | ... alla porta | This recitative does not survive in Mozart's autograph. |
| L'abito di Ferrando | | ... dalla camera etc | ... dalla porta etc | This recitative does not survive in Mozart's autograph. |
| Fra gli amplessi | Fiordiligi | Tra gli amplessi | Fra gli amplessi | The spelling follows the autograph. |

| Item | Character | Vienna 1790 | Prague 1791 | Comments |
|------|-----------|-------------|-------------|----------|
| Ah poveretto me | | ironicamente | ironicamente | The stage direction is still misplaced in the Prague libretto. |
| Finale | | Una scena più piacevole | La più bella comediola | The Prague libretto follows the autograph. |
| Finale | | isso fatto | isso fato | The Prague libretto retains 'isso fatto' despite the autograph reading 'ipso fatto'. |
| Finale | | ... con mantelli e cappelli militari etc | ... da viaggio | When Guglielmo and Ferrando return, they are not in military costume but 'da viaggio' as they had left. |
| Finale | Ferrando Guglielmo | Pieni il cor di contento, e di giolito | Pieni il cor di contento, e di giubilo | Mozart has: Pieni il cor di contento, e di gaudio. |

# Small Musical Changes (and Non-changes) in C1

| | |
|---|---|
| Signora Dorabella | In the libretto an odd six-syllable line appears: 'Dite cosa è stato?' Mozart, evidently aware of the problem, set it with an equally unusual eight-syllable line as 'Ditemi che cosa è stato?' This difficulty was not resolved in the libretto, but **C1** gives a solution: 'Dite che cosa è stato?' The line now has the correct seven syllables, but the musical text was not altered to accommodate the improvement. |
| Signora Dorabella | Although 'Napoli' correctly replaces 'Venezia' as the port of departure for the men, the musical accentuation was not amended. The rhythm appropriate for 'Venezia' (and Mozart's penultimate choice 'Trieste') is incorrect when applied to 'Napoli'. Needless to say, the composer would have changed this if he had become aware of it. |
| Amico abbiamo vinto | In his libretto Da Ponte has Guglielmo, rejoicing in Ferrando's news of the steadfastness of Fiordiligi, embrace his brother officer with the words 'O mio fedele messagier Mercurio' (eleven syllables). Mozart, however, set a snappier version 'O mio fido Mercurio' (seven syllables). For the Prague production, however, the decision was taken to revert to the longer line in the libretto for which a musical revision in the score was needed. |
| Ah poveretto me | In the first version of Da Ponte's libretto, Ferrando refers back caustically to the words ('v'han delle differenze in ogni cosa') with which the self-satisfied Guglielmo had proclaimed his superiority in 'Bravo! questa è costanza!' But the next line ('un poco di più merto') is missing, either by accident, or because it had not yet been decided to extend this ironical recall. In the revised version of the 1790 libretto, this line was inserted, but then the word 'amico' was accidentally omitted from the following phrase 'Ah cessa amico, cessa di tormentarmi'. In **C1** the word was restored with three extra semiquavers (G G A) leading into bar 22. (That the whole issue of the recall was under consideration at this period is also clear in the 1791 Dresden libretto, in which the entire passage is pointedly omitted.) |

# *A Layer of Revisions in* **V1**
# *for an Unknown Italian Production*

| Item | Changes | London 1811 |
|------|---------|-------------|
| **Act I** | | |
| Mi par che otamattina | A cut removes most of this recitative. The whole of the first page and the second page up to Dorabella's 'Ma che diavol' are deleted with heavy red crayon crossing out. The new start is marked with a vertical line with two London tube / semibreve signs above and below. | This cut is made. |
| Stelle! per carità | There is a neat red crayon crossing out with an xxxx of Fiordiligi's opening words. Don Alfonso begins the recitative with 'Convien'. | This cut is made. |
| Signora Dorabella | A red crayon '+' marks the start of this cut at Fiordiligi's 'Signora'. The intervening leaves are crossed out in red crayon. The next side is crossed out with a single X, the third by further red crayon Xs. The new join is worked out in red crayon. There is a vertical red crayon line, a red crayon part label 'Desp' and a C clef on the lowest line to identify the restart at Despina's words 'Pensate a divertirvi'. Red crayon noteheads indicate how the join is to be made. The first bass minim in bar 45 is changed to an F, and Despina's first three quavers become C. This cut removes the passage in which Fiordiligi and Dorabella refer by name to their lovers. Edge does not rule out the possibility that the red crayon recomposition is in Mozart's hand. (Edge, 'Copyists', 1942.) That seems unlikely, however, as the clef is not Mozart's usual shape. (A further small cut later in this recitative, subsequently countermanded, is probably unrelated.) | This cut is made. |
| Che silenzio | Despina's lines 'Hanno una buona borsa / i vostri concorrenti?' (presumably also including the aside 'Per me questa mi preme') are crossed out in red crayon with short diagonal lines ascending to the left. | The cut is made, but it begins three lines earlier (from after Despina's 'questa proposizione') and ends three lines later, where the text resumes with 'E dove son?' |

*continues overleaf...*

| Item | Changes | London 1811 |
|------|---------|-------------|
| **Act II** | | |
| Andate là | There is a lengthy red crayon cut from Dorabella's 'Cioè?' to Fiordiligi's 'No, no: son troppo audaci'. A red crayon line and a red crayon '+' mark the start, with a series of neat red crayon xxxx. Two noteheads were revised in red crayon to make the new join, Despina's 'far' (C♯ changed to D), her 'da' changed to D, and her 'do'-[nne] changed to E. There are large red crayon X marks on intervening pages (except for those sealed in the earlier cut). A pencil 'vi' and 'de' mark the cut. Some of the red crayon crossing out runs directly across pages sealed in the earlier 'agreed' cut. | This cut is even larger. It starts at Fiordiligi's 'Cosa pretenderesti?' and runs through to Despina's 'E chi dice'. |
| Oh che bella giornata | A cut runs from Dorabella's 'un core', marked with a vertical line and crossed out in thick red crayon, to her 'l'accetto'. A pencil 'vi-' '-de' marks this cut. A semibreve E in the bass had to be changed to a minim. | The cut begins four lines later. |
| Barbara! perché fuggi? | In bar 19 there is a red crayon sign like a semiquaver without its notehead below the staff and an NB sign in red crayon above at Fiordiligi's 'Partiti!', indicating a cut. The place is also marked with a pencil x. Red crayon crossing out starts after the E♭ forte chords, and continues (faintly) overleaf until the end of the accompagnato. There is a similar sign (facing the other way) at the start of 'Ei parte' and also a pencil x. Apparently this cut would have linked Fiordiligi's demand 'Partiti!' ('Leave!') directly with her 'Ei parte' ('He's left'). | This cut is made. |
| Ei parte | There is a cut in red crayon from 'Ah no' (bar 2) to 'io ardo' (bar 18). A thick red crayon line marks the end of the cut. | This cut is made. |
| Ei parte | This accompanied recitative is followed by the instruction 'Siegue Amor un ladroncello No. 28' written in red crayon. The red crayon *segue* to Dorabella's aria is remarkable, as it would require a character switch for Fiordiligi, yet her name replaced that of Dorabella's at the start of 'È amore'. | This is the sequence in the London libretto. |
| Come tutto congiura | There is a red crayon cut starting after Fiordiligi's 'e non si ceda' and ending before her 'in casa mia'. A thick red crayon line marks the start. Some rewriting was necessary. The semibreve A in the bass was changed at the start of the cut to a minim. At the end of the cut a minim F replaces the minim G in the bass, and Fiordiligi's 'in casa mia' becomes three semiquavers C and two quavers A. This removes Guglielmo's off-stage observation. | The cut ends one line earlier with Fiordiligi's 'piano'. |
| L'abito di Ferrando | There is a short red crayon cut perhaps beginning with Fiordiligi's 'io vi detesto' and ending after Guglielmo's 'simile a questo'. It appears to be countermanded with a red crayon 'bleibt' above. This cut removes Guglielmo's line, which should not perhaps have been there in the first place. | The cut begins three lines earlier after Fiordiligi's 'gli sposi nostri'. |

# Notes

## Preface

1 Alan Tyson, *Mozart: Studies of the Autograph Scores* (Cambridge, MA, 1987).
2 Ian Woodfield, 'Mozart's Compositional Methods: Writing for his Singers', in *The Cambridge Companion to Mozart*, ed. Simon P. Keefe (Cambridge, 2003), pp. 35–47.

## Introduction

1 John Rosselli, *The Life of Mozart* (Cambridge, 1988), pp. 2–3.
2 Bruce Alan Brown and John Rice, 'Salieri's *Così fan tutte*', *COJ* 8 (1996), p. 17.
3 Bruce Alan Brown, *W. A. Mozart: Così fan tutte*, Cambridge Opera Handbooks (Cambridge, 1995), p. 11; Brown and Rice, 'Salieri's *Così*', pp. 17–43.
4 Rosemary Hughes (ed.), *Vincent and Mary Novello, A Mozart Pilgrimage: Being the Travel Diaries of Vincent & Mary Novello in the Year 1829* (London, 1955), p. 127.
5 Dorothea Link, *The National Court Theatre in Mozart's Vienna: Sources and Documents, 1783–1792* (Oxford, 1998), p. 18.
6 John Rice, *Antonio Salieri and Viennese Opera* (Chicago, 1998), pp. 498–500.
7 The reference is to 'geschmacklosen, holpernden und unzusammenhängenden operntext'. Ibid., p. 497.
8 'Nicht, eine einzige Note mehr zu einem *da Pontischen Text zu* schreiben'. Ibid., p. 497.
9 'Ich ging also zu Guardassoni – welcher es auf künftigen Herbst fast richtig machte mir für die Oper 200# und 50# Reisegeld zu geben.' *Briefe*, iv, p. 80.
10 The suggestion that this was an early reference to *La clemenza di Tito* (performed in Prague by Guardasoni in 1791) has been refuted in Sergio Durante, 'The Chronology of Mozart's *La clemenza di Tito* Reconsidered', *M&L* 80 (1999), pp. 560–94.
11 Maynard Solomon, *Mozart: A Life* (London, 1995), pp. 437–54.
12 Brown, *Così*, p. 9.
13 Lorenzo Da Ponte, *Memorie*, ed. Cesare Pagnini (Milan, 1960), p. 174.
14 Ibid., p. 179.
15 Brown and Rice, 'Salieri's *Così*', p. 18.
16 *Briefe*, iv, p. 28.
17 Ibid., p. 92.
18 'In ein paar Monathen muss mein Schicksal in der *geringsten Sache* auch entschieden sein'. Ibid., p. 92.
19 Neal Zaslaw, 'Waiting for Figaro', in *Wolfgang Amadè Mozart: Essays on his Life and Music*, ed. Stanley Sadie (Oxford, 1996), pp. 413–35.

20 Dexter Edge, 'Mozart's Viennese Copyists' (PhD diss, University of Southern California, 2001), p. 1436.

21 'Künftigen Monat bekomme ich von der Direction (nach ietziger Einrichtung) 200 Ducaten für meine Oper.' *Briefe*, iv, p. 100.

22 'Donnerstag aber lade ich Sie (aber nur Sie allein) um 10 Uhr Vormittag zu mir ein, zu einer kleinen Oper=probe; – nur Sie und *Haydn* lade ich dazu. – Mündlich werde ich Ihnen Cabalen von Salieri erzählen, die aber alle schon zu Wasser geworden sind. Adjeu'. Ibid., p. 100.

23 Dexter Edge, 'Mozart's Fee for *Così fan tutte*', *Journal of the Royal Musical Association*, 116 (1991), p. 215.

24 'Unruhen, Kabalen u. dgl', Brown, *Così*, p. 23.

25 'Costei dimenticò tutte le beneficenze e cortesie della mia amicizia perchè non l'ho fatta entrare nell'*Ape musicale*'. Brown and Rice, 'Salieri's *Così*', pp. 36–7; Otto Michtner, 'Der Fall Abbé da Ponte', *Mitteilungen des Österreichischen Staatsarchivs* 19 (1966), pp. 170–209.

26 'N.B. muss eine jede Stimme besonders ausgeschrieben werden'. I am most grateful to Professor Neal Zaslaw for bringing this reference to my attention in *Die Presse* (14 February 1956).

27 'Morgen ist die erste Instrumental-Probe im Theater – Haydn wird mit mir hingehen.' *Briefe*, iv, p. 102.

28 *NMA: Verzeichnüss.*

29 'Ich bin hier um meine Opera zu dirigiren.' *Briefe*, iv, p. 110.

30 *NMA: Dokumente*, p. 318.

31 'Von der Musik ist, glaub ich, alles gesagt, dass sie von Mozart ist.' Ibid., p. 319.

## Chapter 1: The Autograph

1 Wolfgang Plath, 'Mozartiana in Fulda und Frankfurt', *MJ* (1968–70), pp. 333–86.

2 Daniel Heartz, 'When Mozart Revises: The Case of Guglielmo in *Così fan tutte*', in *Wolfgang Amadè Mozart: Essays on his Life and Music*, ed. Stanley Sadie (Oxford, 1996), p. 359.

3 *NMA: Così*, p. xxxix; Tyson, *Studies*, pp. 201–3.

4 *NMA: Così*, pp. 634–5.

5 *NMA: Così*, pp. 636–7; Tyson, *Studies*, p. 193; Richard Kramer, review of *NMA: Skizzen*, *Notes* 57 (September 2002), pp. 188–93.

6 Roland Tenschert, 'Fragment eines Klarinetten Quintetts von W. A. Mozart', *ZfM* 13 (1930–1), pp. 218–22.

7 Alan Tyson, 'A Feature of the Structure of Mozart's Autograph Scores', in *Festschrift Wolfgang Rehm zum 60. Geburtstag am 3 September 1989*, ed. Dietrich Berke and Harald Heckmann (Kassel, 1989) pp. 95–105; Edge, 'Copyists', p. 390.

8 Tyson, *Studies*, pp. 177–221.

9 Edge, 'Copyists', p. 383.

10 Ibid., pp. 412–38.

11  Tyson, *Studies*, p. 17.

12  Edge, 'Copyists', p. 405. For a further critique of Tyson's methodology, see Sergio Durante, 'The Chronology of Mozart's *La clemenza di Tito* Reconsidered', *M&L* 80 (1999), pp. 560–94.

13  Tyson, *Studies*, pp. 216–21.

14  Edge, 'Copyists', p. 435.

15  Karl-Heinz Köhler, 'Mozarts Kompositionsweise – Beobachtung am Figaro-Autograph', *MJ* 30 (1967), pp. 31–45.

16  Edge, 'Copyists', pp. 175–92.

17  Ibid., p. 183.

18  Ibid., p. 180.

19  Ibid., p. 179.

20  Ibid., p. 189.

21  Ibid., p. 177.

22  Daniel Leeson, 'The Gran Partita's Mystery Measure', *MJ* (1991), pp. 220–5.

23  John Arthur, 'Some Chronological Problems in Mozart: the Contribution of Ink-Studies', in *Wolfgang Amadè Mozart: Essays on his Life and Music*, ed. Stanley Sadie (Oxford, 1996), pp. 35–52.

24  Christoph Wolff, 'The Challenge of Blank Paper: Mozart the Composer', in *On Mozart*, ed. James Morris (Cambridge, 1994), pp. 113–29.

25  Dexter Edge, 'Attributing Mozart (i): Three Accompanied Recitatives', *COJ* 13 (2001), pp. 209.

26  Ibid., pp. 210–11.

27  Köhler, 'Mozarts Kompositionsweise', pp. 37–8.

28  Tyson, *Studies*, pp. 36–47.

29  Ibid., p. 45.

30  The editors of *NMA: Così*, p. x, argue for a date in the autumn.

31  Tyson, *Studies*, pp. 182–6.

32  Ibid., p. 184.

33  Ibid., p. 185.

34  The suggestion that Ferrando's apparent recall of 'A voi s'inchina' at the climax of the Act II finale was in fact a non-recall, relies upon the fact that the sestetto is copied on the earlier of the two main paper types. Caryl Clark, 'Recall and Reflexivity in *Così fan tutte*', in *Wolfgang Amadè Mozart: Essays on his Life and Music*, ed. Stanley Sadie (Oxford, 1996), pp. 339–54. However, it is possible that although an appropriate consignment of the earlier paper type was allocated to this ensemble at the start, the actual copying of the middle and final sections of the movement was done later.

35  *NMA: Così*, p .xxxiv.

36  *NMA: KB*, p. 97.

37  Daniel Heartz, '"Attaca subito": Lessons from the Autograph Score of *Idomeneo*, Acts I and II', in *Festschrift Wolfgang Rehm zum 60. Geburtstag*, ed. Dietrich Berke and Harald Heckmann (Kassel, 1989) pp. 83–92.

38  Edge, 'Attributing Mozart (i)', pp. 227–8.

39  Tyson, *Studies*, p. 187.

40  Ibid., pp. 217–21.

41  *NMA: Così*, p. xxi.

42  Brown, *Così*, p. 111.

43  *NMA: Così*, p. xxii.

44  Brown, *Così*, p. 111.

45  Heartz, 'Attaca subito', p. 83.

45  Ibid., p. 86.

## Chapter 2: Singers and their Arias

1  *Letters*, p. 497.

2  Ibid, pp. 551–3.

3  Daniel Heartz, 'Raaff's Last Aria: a Mozartian Idyll in the Spirit of Hasse', *MQ* 60 (1974), p. 533.

4  Brown and Rice, 'Salieri's *Così*', p. 29.

5  Woodfield, 'Mozart's Compositional Methods', pp. 35–47.

6  *NMA: KB*, p. 171.

7  Julian Rushton, 'Buffo Roles in Mozart's Vienna: Tessitura and Tonality as Signs of Characterisation', in *Opera Buffa in Mozart's Vienna*, ed. Mary Hunter and James Webster (Cambridge, 1997), p. 423.

8  *NMA: KB*, pp. 124–5.

9  Ferrarese did not have a voice with a very high register, and effectively a high A was her 'practical limit for sustained upper singing'. Patricia Lewy Gidwitz, 'Mozart's Fiordiligi: Adriana Ferrarese del Bene', *COJ* 8 (1996), p. 202. Gidwitz also cites evidence to suggest that it was occasionally necessary to transpose her arias downwards. For the high B♭ in 'Come scoglio', Mozart took the precaution of writing in an alternative note an octave lower, although later the singer cannot easily avoid the high C at the climax in the dominant. In 'Per pietà', he perhaps held off from extending the range up to high B, until he had consulted with the singer. At the other end of her range, Ferrarese had a powerful voice, a characteristic exploited by Mozart and others with plunging downwards leaps.

10  *Letters*, p. 678.

11  Edmund Goehring, 'Despina, Cupid and the Pastoral Mode of *Così fan tutte*', *COJ* 7 (1995), pp. 107–33.

12  Ibid., p. 120.

## Chapter 3: Refining the Musical Text

1 The 'recall', a precise repeat of material first heard elsewhere, and the 'reference', a more allusive technique, may usefully be distinguished. Clark, 'Recall and Reflexivity in *Così fan tutte*', p. 343.

2 *NMA: Così*, p. xxii.

3 Ibid., p. xxiv.

4 *Letters*, p. 704.

5 Tyson, *Studies*, p. 347.

6 *NMA: Così*, p. 349.

7 Brown thought it 'odd' that the men's plea to the friendly zephyrs should be made in front of the women, but perhaps the thinking was that the two sisters would be further tempted to depart from the paths of rectitude by this beguiling serenade. Brown, *Così*, p. 43.

8 *NMA: Così*, pp. xxiv–xxv.

9 Edge, 'Copyists', p. 1932.

10 *Letters*, p. 769.

11 *NMA: Così*, p. xxi.

12 Heartz, 'Raaff's Last Aria', pp. 528–9.

13 Daniel Leeson and Robert Levin, 'Mozart's Deliberate Use of Incorrect Key Signatures for Clarinets', *MJ* (1998), pp. 139–52. The authors develop an observation made by Marius Flothius.

14 *NMA: Così*, p. xiii.

15 Hans Keller, 'Mozart's Wrong Key-Signature', *Tempo* 98 (1972), pp. 21–7.

16 *NMA: Così*, pp. 634–5.

17 Ian Woodfield, 'Reflections on Mozart's "Non so più cosa son, cosa faccio"', *Eighteenth Century Music* 3 (2006), pp. 133–9.

18 Heartz, 'Attaca subito', pp. 83–92.

19 Woodfield , 'Reflections', p. 137.

20 Heartz, 'Attacca subito', p. 85.

21 Mary Hunter, *The Culture of Opera Buffa in Mozart's Vienna : A Poetics of Entertainment* (Princeton, 1999), pp. 285–96.

22 On Mozart's sketches, see Ulrich Konrad, *Mozarts Schaffenweise: Studien zu den Werkautographen, Skizzen und Entwürfen* (Göttingen, 1992). There is a facsimile of this page and an edition in *NMA: Così*, pp. 634–6.

## Chapter 4: Casting the Roles

1 Rice, *Antonio Salieri*, p. 503.

2 Edge, 'Copyists', p. 1546.

3 Daniel Heartz, *Mozart's Operas* (Berkeley, 1990), p. 293.

4 Heartz, 'When Mozart Revises', p. 360.

5  He was familiar in this guise, having played the philosopher in Salieri's *La grotta di Trofonio*. Rice, *Antonio Salieri*, p. 369.

6  Rushton, 'Buffo Roles in Mozart's Vienna', p. 423.

7  Heartz, *Mozart's Operas*, p. 243.

8  Rushton, 'Buffo Roles in Mozart's Vienna', pp. 423–4.

9  The libretto too contains signs of this: blank space at the end of the piece; and the absence of the usual continuity syllable at the foot of the previous page.

10  Tyson, *Studies*, p. 194.

11  *NMA: Così*, p. xxvi.

12  Brown, *Così*, p. 80.

13  Ibid., p. 5.

14  Heartz, 'When Mozart Revises', p. 360.

15  Ibid., p. 360.

16  One other factor to be considered is the possibility that the Act I finale was originally going to start in G major, and that the opening D major duet was added at a later stage.

17  Heartz, 'Attacca subito', p. 84.

18  Heartz, 'When Mozart Revises', p. 357.

19  The stylistic parallels are close enough for this piece to be identified as a 'conspicuous parody'. Bruce Alan Brown, 'Beaumarchais, Paisiello and the Genesis of *Così fan tutte*', in *Wolfgang Amadè Mozart: Essays on his Life and Music*, ed. Stanley Sadie (Oxford, 1996), pp. 315–19.

20  Link, *The National Court Theatre*, pp. 484–5.

21  Zinzendorf was consistently cool about Bussani. In a performance of Salieri's *La scuola de' gelosi* on 22 April 1783, Vanucci [*sic*] was 'tres bon', Bussani 'moins'. In *Il barbiere* on 13 August 1783, Benucci 'joue a merveille', Bussani 'n'est pas mal'. In *La grotta di Trofonio* on 12 October 1785 Bussani 'fit mediocrement son rôle'. Link, *The National Court Theatre*, pp. 204, 210, 255.

22  Andrew Steptoe, *The Mozart–Da Ponte Operas* (Oxford, 1988), p. 108.

23  Edge notes that in one of the original parts for the Vienna *Figaro*, 'Voi che sapete' is marked 'La S: Vilneuf'. From this he suggests the possibility that Villeneuve replaced Dorotea Bussani in this role some time during the 1789–1791 Vienna revival of the opera. Edge, 'Copyists', p. 1509.

24  A sign of the late reorganisation of the libretto at this point is that at the end of the recitative replacing the cavatina ('Che vita maladetta') is a blank space for four further lines. Usually the printer ran the text on without a break, but perhaps he did not want to reset everything that followed. This might also explain why the first line of the next scene in which the maid offers the two sisters a beverage ('Madame, ecco la vostra collazione') appears wrongly at the end of the maid's first scene. A further sign of this reorganisation is the failure of the libretto at the start of Scene IX to use what would be the normal indicator for a female character already on stage 'La sudetta' (the aforesaid) as in the autograph.

25 'In uomini is best seen not as Despina's *Weltanschauung* but as a formal refutation of Dorabella's aria.' Goehring, 'Despina, Cupid and the Pastoral Mode', p. 115.

26 *NMA: KB*, p. 37.

27 Again, a clear sign of the late incorporation of this piece into the libretto is the blank space after it.

28 Dorothea Link, '"Così fan tutte": Dorabella and Amore', *MJ* (1991), pp. 888–94.

29 Brown, *Così*, p. 49.

30 Goehring, 'Despina, Cupid and the Pastoral Mode', pp. 125–9.

31 Brown, *Così*, p. 22.

32 Da Ponte was scathing indeed about Dorotea: 'An Italian diva who, though a ridiculous person of little merit, had by dint of facial contortions, clown's tricks, and perhaps by means more theatrical still, built up a great following among cooks, barbers, lackeys.' Steptoe, *The Mozart–Da Ponte Operas*, p. 150. Other reviews suggest that this was a prejudiced view. An Italian report of her performance in the première of Salieri's *La cifra* in Vienna, shortly before *Così fan tutte* was first given, was very complimentary: 'Sig. Bussani, who showed herself in this opera, as in many others, worthy of unanimous applause.' Rice, *Antonio Salieri*, p. 441.

## Chapter 5: Lovers Crossed or Uncrossed?

1 Jessica Waldoff and James Webster, 'Operatic Plotting in *Le Nozze di Figaro*', in *Wolfgang Amadè Mozart: Essays on his Life and Music*, ed. Stanley Sadie (Oxford, 1996), p. 258.

2 Ibid., pp. 257–8.

3 Ibid., p. 257.

4 On the sources of the libretto, see: Ernst Gombrich, '*Così fan tutte* (Procris included)', *Journal of the Warburg and Courtauld Institutes* 17 (1954), pp. 372–4; Kurt Kramer, 'Da Ponte's *Così fan tutte*', *Nachrichten der Akademie der Wissenschaften in Göttingen* (Göttingen, 1973), pp. 1–27; Andrew Steptoe, 'The Sources of *Così fan tutte*: a Reappraisal', *M&L* 62 (1981), pp. 281–94. The fullest treatment of the Ariostan antecedents of *Così* is given in Brown, *Così*, pp. 60–70, in which ideas suggested by Elizabeth Dunstan in an unpublished essay are acknowledged.

5 Heartz, *Mozart's Operas*, p. 231; Brown, *Così*, p. 73.

6 'In dem Jahre 1789 im Monat December schrieb Mozart das italienische komische Singspiel, *Così fan tutte*, oder die Schule der Liebenden; man wundert sich allgemein, wie der große Geist sich herablassen konnte, an ein so elendes Machwerk von Text seine himmlisch süßen Melodien zu verschwenden.' Franz Xaver Niemetschek, *Lebensbeschreibung des K. K. Kapellmeisters Wolfgang Amadeus Mozart, aus Originalquellen* (Prague, 1808), p. 43.

7 Brown, *Così*, p. 108.

8 Joseph Kerman, *Opera as Drama* (New York, 1956), pp. 92–3.

9 Mary Hunter, 'Some Representations of *Opera Seria* in *Opera Buffa*', *COJ* 3 (1991), pp. 89–108.

10  James Webster, 'The Analysis of Mozart's Arias', in *Mozart Studies*, ed. Cliff Eisen (Oxford, 1991), p. 110.

11  Julian Rushton, '*Così fan tutte*: Mozart's Serious Opera', *Studies in Music from the University of Western Ontario* 14 (1993), p. 75.

12  Archiv 437 829–2 AH3 (1993), pp. 12–15.

13  Kerman, *Opera as Drama*, p. 98.

14  Heartz, *Mozart's Operas*, p. 242.

15  Brown, *Così*, p. 41.

16  Konrad Küster, *Mozart: A Musical Biography* (Oxford, 1996), pp. 331–45.

17  Heartz, *Mozart's Operas*, p. 250.

18  Steptoe, *The Mozart–Da Ponte Operas*, p. 136; Rice, *Antonio Salieri*, p. 366.

19  Tyson, *Studies*, pp. 122–4.

20  Heartz, *Mozart's Operas*, p. 174.

21  Kerman, *Opera as Drama*, pp. 95–6.

22  Clark, 'Recall and Reflexivity in *Così fan tutte*', pp. 339–40.

23  Archiv 437 829–2 AH3 (1993), pp. 12–15.

24  Don Neville, 'The Rondò in Mozart's Late Operas', *MJ* (1994), pp. 154–5.

25  A feature of **V1** that is indicative of the late completion of the sestetto is that in the third section the copyist first wrote out the score using an incomplete particella. Short fragments of wind writing (matching those in the particella stage of the autograph) are clearly visible.

26  Heartz, *Mozart's Operas*, p. 244.

27  Tyson, *Studies*, p. 117.

28  Tenschert, 'Fragment eines Klarinetten Quintetts von W. A. Mozart', pp. 218–22.

29  Tyson, *Studies*, p. 349.

30  Hunter, 'Some Representations', p. 106.

31  Webster, 'The Analysis of Mozart's Arias', p. 112.

32  Edmund Goehring, *Three Modes of Perception in Mozart* (Cambridge, 2004), p. 142.

33  Tyson, *Studies*, p. 339.

34  Brown, *Così*, pp. 121–2.

35  Steptoe, *The Mozart–Da Ponte Operas*, pp. 231–2.

36  Brown, *Così*, p. 46.

37  Charles Ford, *Così? Sexual Politics in Mozart's Operas* (Manchester, 1991), p. 131.

38  Steptoe, *The Mozart–Da Ponte Operas*, p. 236.

39  Kerman, *Opera as Drama*, pp. 96–7.

40  Steptoe, *The Mozart–Da Ponte Operas*, p. 236.

41  *NMA: KB*, p. 136.

42  Ibid., p. 136.

43  Richard Stiefl, 'Mozart's Seductions', *Current Musicology* 36 (1983), pp. 151–66.

44 Brown, *Così*, p. 46; Heartz, *Mozart's Operas*, p. 237.

45 A sign of the late changes here is that this stage direction lacks its usual line of blank space above and below.

46 Clark, 'Recall and Reflexivity in *Così fan tutte*', pp. 339–54.

47 Tyson, *Studies*, p. 192.

48 Steptoe, *The Mozart–Da Ponte Operas*, p. 128.

49 Dorothea Link, 'The Viennese Operatic Canon and Mozart's *Così fan tutte*', *Mitteilungen der internationalen Stiftung Mozarteum* 38 (1990), p. 121.

50 *NMA: Così*, p. xxviii.

51 Clark, 'Recall and Reflexivity in *Così fan tutte*', p. 349.

52 Hunter, *The Culture of Opera Buffa in Mozart's Vienna*, p. 295.

53 Edward Dent, *Mozart's Operas*, 2nd edn (London, 1947), p. 206.

54 Steptoe, *The Mozart–Da Ponte Operas*, p. 129.

55 Heartz, *Mozart's Operas*, p. 250.

56 Ford, *Così? Sexual Politics*, p. 133.

57 Heartz, *Mozart's Operas*, p. 242.

58 Kerman, *Opera as Drama*, p. 92.

## *Chapter 6: The Vienna Court Theatre Score*

1 Tyson, *Studies*, pp. 177–221, 290–327.

2 Edge, 'Copyists', pp. 1294–1974.

3 Ibid., pp. 1922–61.

4 Ibid., p. 1924.

5 Ibid., pp. 1930–6.

6 Ibid., pp. 1938–9.

7 Ibid., pp. 1940–8.

8 Edge, 'Attributing Mozart (i)', pp. 209–10.

9 *NMA: KB*, pp. 66–7.

10 H. C. Robbins Landon, 'A Commentary on the Score', in *Così fan tutte: Wolfgang Amadeus Mozart*, ed. Nicholas John, English National Opera Guide (London, 1983), p. 29.

11 *NMA: KB*, p. 101.

12 Edge, 'Copyists', p. 1949.

13 Tyson, *Studies*, p. 210; *NMA: KB*, p. 35.

14 Tyson, *Studies*, p. 208.

15 *NMA: KB*, p. 35.

16 *Letters*, pp. 692–4.

17 Ibid., pp. 694–9.

18 Edge, 'Copyists', pp. 1952–6.

19 *NMA: KB*, pp. 88–9, 103–9, 150–60.

20  In *NMA:KB*, p. 34, the copyist is compared with the scribe who wrote Nos. 2, 15, 24, 26 and 29 in **V3**. As Nos. 2 and 15 do not appear in either the Vienna or Berlin *Mädchentreue* books, it is therefore possible that these copies date from still later, as suggested in Edge, 'Copyists', p. 1936.

21  *NMA: Così*, p. xxvii; *NMA:KB*, p. 147.

## Chapter 7: Early Manuscript Scores and Parts

1  Scores are turning up all the time, and it is impossible to see them all. At the time of writing, I have examined the following in person, in most cases on at least two occasions: **B, Be1, Be2, F1, F2, K, L, Lo, S, T, V1, V3** and **V4**. I have studied microfilms of **C1, C2, D1**, and **D2** and a microfiche of **H**. An excellent on-line reproduction of **Ca** has recently been published. Of the sets of parts, I have seen those associated with **Be1, Be2, F1, F2, K, Lo** and **V3**. There are some details of the parts archived with **D1** and **H** in RISM, and the score and parts of **Fl** are briefly described in *NMA: KB*, p. 48.

2  David Buch, 'Eighteenth-Century Manuscript Scores of Mozart's Comic Italian Operas in Prague's Conservatory of Music, and National Library' (forthcoming).

3  Tyson, *Studies*, p. 205.

4  Edge, 'Copyists', p. 1412. The inscription in this score (A: Wn, s.m.5216) referring to the process of correction runs: 'Ho corretto nel Mese d'Agosto 1792'.

5  *NMA: KB*, p. 46.

6  Edge, 'Copyists', p. 1924; *NMA: KB*, p. 40.

7  The title-page runs: 'Cosi fan Tutte / o sia / La Scuola degli Amanti / Dramma giocoso / in due Atti / Atto 1^mo / La Musica è Del Sig^r: Wolf: Ama: Mozart'; Act II: 'Atto Secondo [added later above] Cosi fan Tutte / osia / La Scuola degli Amanti [added later below] del Sig^r Wolfg: Mozart.'

8  Edge, 'Copyists', p. 1961.

9  The title-page runs: 'Cosi fan tutte / osia / La / Scuola degli amanti / Drama giocoso / in due atti / Rappresentata nel Teatro di Corte a Vienna L'Anno 1790. / La Musica, è del Sig^re Wolfgango Mozart / Si vende in Vienna presso Wencislau Sukowaty Editore di Musica e Copista dell' Imperial Teatro / nella Piazza di S^t Pietro N° 554 in Terzo Piano.' Act II: 'La / Scuola degli Amanti.'

10  Edge, 'Copyists', p. 1926; *NMA: KB*, p. 46.

11  The title-page runs: 'Cosi fan tutte / osia / La / Scuola degli amanti / Dramma giocoso / in due atti / Rappresentato nel Teatro di Corte a Vienna L'Anno 1790 / La Musica è del Sig^re Wolfgango Mozart.'

12  John Rice, *Empress Marie Therese and Music at the Viennese Court, 1792–1807* (Cambridge, 2003), p. 294.

13  I am very grateful to Kathryn Libin for sending me information on the Lobkowicz *Così* materials in an email (14 September 2005).

14  Edge, 'Copyists', p. 1924. A few details of a Lobkowicz performance are given by Jaroslav Macek, 'Franz Joseph Maximilian Lobkowitz, Musikfreund und Wirkungsgeschichte Beethovens', in *Beethoven und Böhmen*, ed. Sieghard

Brandenburg and Martella Gutiérrez-Denhoff (Bonn, 1988), pp. 147–80. The ensemble for this production came from Prague and was put together by Franz Strobach. The six soloists were Madame Wenzel, Katharine Ettrich, Aloisia Natter, Dr Johann Theobald Held, Anton Ramisch, and Franz Strobach himself.

## Chapter 8: Mozart's Revised Vienna Version

1   The title-page runs: 'La Scuola degli Amanti / ossia / Cosi fan tutte / Dramma gioccoso in Due Atti / Del Sig$^{re}$ Wolfango [sic] Amadeo Mozart.'

2   The title-page runs: 'La / Scuola degli amanti / osia / Cosi fan tutte / Dramma giocoso / in due Atti / La Musica è del Sig$^r$ Wolfgango Mozart.'

3   Tyson, *Studies*, pp. 201–3.

4   *NMA: KB*, p. 102.

5   Tyson, *Studies*, p. 208.

6   Ibid., pp. 201–3, 207, 209, 211, 213–15; *NMA: Così*, pp. xxxvi, xxxix–xli.

7   Tyson, on balance, concluded that this sketch postdates the completion of the opera. *Studies*, p. 192.

8   Mozart's hand is not recognised here in *NMA: KB*, p. 64.

9   The degree of confusion facing copyists at this juncture is demonstrated by the fact that the opposite error appears in some scores in Transmission Line D, in which the one-bar transition is followed (redundantly) by the crotchet in the three wind parts in bar 208.

10  Tyson, *Studies*, p. 348.

## Chapter 9: Early Italian Language Performances

1   *Staatsbibliothek Preussischer Kulturbesitz: Kataloge der Musikabteilung*: Erste Reihe: Band 6: *Wolfgang Amadeus Mozart: Autographe und Abschriften*, ed. Hans-Günther Klein (Kassel, 1982), Mus. ms. 15 153/30.

2   Durante, 'The Chronology of Mozart's *La clemenza di Tito* Reconsidered', pp. 560–94.

3   D:Bsb, Signatur Mus. Tm 1121–2: Rara; D:Mbs, Signatur: L.eleg.m.1021°.

4   Alan Tyson, 'The 1786 Prague Version of Mozart's *Le Nozze di Figaro*', *M&L* 69 (1988), p. 322.

5   The attribution of the aside to the correct character provides a good example of how carefully such seemingly minor points were considered. Shortly after Ferrando and Fiordiligi have moved away in the recitative 'Oh che bella giornata!', Guglielmo starts to woo Dorabella in earnest. Her response, cast as an aside, is: 'he'll get nothing at all from this' ('Non otterà nientissimo'). These words are attributed to Guglielmo in Da Ponte's libretto, but Mozart quite reasonably thought this was a mistake, and transferred the remark to Dorabella. The reviser of the Dresden libretto (unlike his counterpart in Prague) was aware of this and made the change. Yet it is far from clear what Da Ponte was intending, and a different but nonetheless plausible interpretation was added later to the Dresden score **D1**, in which the remark is attributed to Ferrando. He is still in the vicinity with

Fiordiligi (although in the process of leaving), and in this interpretation it is he who passes this comment on the efforts of his friend, fully confident that his lover will remain steadfast in the face of Guglielmo's intensifying attempts at seduction. Coming round full circle, it is even possible therefore that Da Ponte intended this remark to be made by Guglielmo after all, glancing over his shoulder to see what Ferrando was up to.

6  Tyson, 'The 1786 Prague Version', p. 322.

7  Two manuscript copies of Da Ponte's revised libretto survive in the library of the Vienna Gesellschaft der Musikfreunde: 2603² and 2603¹³, the latter coming from the estate of Köchel. These date from no earlier than the mid-1790s, as shown from a footnote pointing out that in printed keyboard scores one line of 'Una donna' is different: 'Anstatt dieses Verses steht in gedrückten Klavierauszüge: "Dove il diavolo ha la coda"'. Both these manuscripts stem from an intermediate source which in turn derives ultimately from Da Ponte's revised libretto. The manuscript 2603² has the word 'giubilo' in the Act II finale as in Guardasoni's Prague libretto, although there are no other features of this version. At some point this was crossed out and the correct word 'giolito' inserted.

8  The title-page runs: 'Cosi fan tutte / o sia / La Scuola degli Amanti / Atto Iᵐᵒ / Del Sigʳᵉ Mozart.'

9  I am very grateful to Anne Oerbaek Jensen for supplying me with details of the watermarks of this manuscript, also to David Buch for information that the title-page resembles other Prague scores of this period.

10  *NMA: KB*, p. 48.

11  Christopher Raeburn, 'Mozart's Operas in England', *Musical Times* 97 (Jan 1956), pp. 15–17; Emanuele Senici, '"Adapted to the Modern Stage": *La clemenza di Tito* in London', *COJ* 7 (1995), pp. 1–22; Rachel Cowgill, 'Mozart Productions and the Emergence of *Werktreue* at London's Italian Opera House, 1780–1830', in *Operatic Migrations: Transforming Works and Crossing Boundaries*, ed. R. Marvin and D. Thomas (Ashgate, 2006), pp. 145–86.

## Conclusion

1  Senici, 'Adapted to the Modern Stage', pp. 1–22.

# Bibliography

## Facsimile

*Così fan tutte, ossia, La scuola degli amanti, K.588. Facsimile of the Autograph Score, Staatsbibliothek zu Berlin-Preussischer Kulturbesitz, Biblioteka Jagiellonska Kraków (Mus. ms. autogr. W. A. Mozart 588), Stadt- und Universitätsbibliothek Frankfurt am Main (Mus. Hs 2350)*, with introductory essay by Norbert Miller; musicological introduction by John A. Rice. Mozart Operas in Facsimile 5 (Los Altos, CA, 2007)

## Neue Mozart Ausgabe

Serie II, Werkgruppe 5, Band 18: *Così fan tutte*, ed. Faye Ferguson and Wolfgang Rehm (Kassel, 1991)

Serie II, *Kritische Berichte*, Werkgruppe 5, Band 18: *Così fan tutte*, Henning Bey and Faye Ferguson (Kassel, 2003)

Serie X, Werkgruppe 30, Band 3: *Skizzen*, ed. Ulrich Konrad (Kassel, 1998)

Serie X, Werkgruppe 33, Band 1: *Mozarts Eigenhändiges Werkverzeichnis*, ed. Alan Tyson and Albi Rosenthal (Kassel, 1991)

Serie X, Werkgruppe 33, Band 2: *Wasserzeichen-Katalog*, Alan Tyson (Kassel, 1992)

Serie X, Werkgruppe 34: *Mozart: Die Dokumente seines Lebens*, Otto Deutsch (Kassel, 1961)

## Books and Articles

Anderson, Emily (ed.), *The Letters of Mozart & his Family*, 3rd edn (London, 1985)

Angermüller, Rudolph, 'Francesco Bussani – Mozarts erster Bartolo, Antonio und Alfonso und Dorotea Bussani Mozarts erster Cherubino und erste Despina', *Mozart Studien* 10 (2001), pp. 213–29

—— and Johanna Senigl, *Bibliographie der Mozart Libretti* (Internationale Stiftung Mozarteum Salzburg, 2000), pp. 215–40

Arthur, John, 'Some Chronological Problems in Mozart: the Contribution of Ink-Studies', in *Wolfgang Amadè Mozart: Essays on his Life and Music*, ed. Stanley Sadie (Oxford, 1996), pp. 35–52

Bauer, Wilhelm, Otto Deutsch and Joseph Eibl, *Mozart: Briefe und Aufzeichnungen: Gesamtausgabe* (Kassel, 1962–75)

Brown, Bruce Alan, *W. A. Mozart: Così fan tutte*, Cambridge Opera Handbooks (Cambridge, 1995)

—— 'Beaumarchais, Paisiello and the Genesis of *Così fan tutte*', in *Wolfgang Amadè Mozart: Essays on his Life and Music*, ed. Stanley Sadie (Oxford, 1996), pp. 312–38

—— and John Rice, 'Salieri's *Così fan tutte*', *COJ* 8 (1996), pp. 17–43

Buch, David, '*Così fan tutte, La scuola degli amanti* and *L'école des amants*', *Hudební věda* 38 (2001), pp. 313–20

——— 'Eighteenth-Century Manuscript Scores of Mozart's Comic Italian Operas in Prague's Conservatory of Music and National Library' (forthcoming)

Burnham, Scott, 'Mozart's *felix culpa*: *Così fan tutte* and the Irony of Beauty', *MQ* 78 (1994), pp. 77–98

Carter, Tim, 'Mozart, Da Ponte and the Ensemble', in *Wolfgang Amadè Mozart: Essays on his Life and Music*, ed. Stanley Sadie (Oxford, 1996), pp. 241–9

Clark, Caryl, 'Recall and Reflexivity in *Così fan tutte*', in *Wolfgang Amadè Mozart: Essays on his Life and Music*, ed. Stanley Sadie (Oxford, 1996), pp. 339–54

Cowgill, Rachel, 'Mozart Productions and the Emergence of *Werktreue* at London's Italian Opera House, 1780–1830', in *Operatic Migrations: Transforming Works and Crossing Boundaries*, ed. R. Marvin and D. Thomas (Ashgate, 2006), pp. 145–86

Csampi, Attila, and Dietmar Holland, *Wolfgang Amadeus Mozart, Così fan tutte: Texte, Materialen, Kommentare* (Hamburg, 1984)

Da Ponte, Lorenzo, *Memoirs of Lorenzo Da Ponte*, trans. Elizabeth Abbott (Toronto, 1929)

——— *Memorie*, ed. Cesare Pagnini (Milan, 1960)

Dent, Edward, *Mozart's Operas*, 2nd edn (London, 1947)

Deutsch, Otto, *Mozart: A Documentary Biography*, 2nd edn (London, 1966)

Diddion, Robert and Joachim Schulze, *Thematischer Katalog der Opernsammlung in der Stadt- und Universitätsbibliothek Frankfurt am Main*, Band 9: *Thematischer Katalog der Opernsammlung* (Frankfurt, 1990), pp. 171–6

Dietrich, Margret, 'Documentation zur Uraufführung', in *Così fan tutte: Beiträge zur Wirkungsgeschichte von Mozarts Oper*, ed. Susanne Vill (Bayreuth, 1978), pp. 24–53

Du Mont, Mary, *The Mozart–Da Ponte Operas: An Annotated Bibliography*, Music Reference Collection 81 (Westport, CT, 2000)

Durante, Sergio, 'The Chronology of Mozart's *La clemenza di Tito* Reconsidered', *M&L* 80 (1999), pp. 560–94

Edge, Dexter, 'Mozart's Fee for *Così fan tutte*', *Journal of the Royal Musical Association* 116 (1991), pp. 211–35

——— 'Mozart's Reception in Vienna, 1787–1791', in *Wolfgang Amadè Mozart: Essays on his Life and Music*, ed. Stanley Sadie (Oxford, 1996), pp. 66–120

——— 'Mozart's Viennese Copyists' (PhD diss, University of Southern California, 2001)

——— 'Attributing Mozart (i): Three Accompanied Recitatives', *COJ* 13 (2001), pp. 197–237

Eisen, Cliff, *New Mozart Documents: A Supplement to O. E. Deutsch's Documentary Biography* (London, 1991)

——— (ed.), *Mozart Studies* (Oxford, 1991)

——— (ed.), *Mozart Studies 2* (Oxford, 1997)

Farnsworth, Rodney, '*Così fan tutte* as Parody and Burlesque', *Opera Quarterly* 6 (1988–9), pp. 50–68

Finscher, Ludwig, 'Mozarts "musikalische Regie": eine musikdramatische Analyse', in *Così fan tutte: Beiträge zur Wirkungsgeschichte von Mozarts Oper*, ed. Susanne Vill (Bayreuth, 1978), pp. 9–23

Ford, Charles, *Così? Sexual Politics in Mozart's Operas* (Manchester, 1991)

Gallarati, Paolo, 'Music and Masks in Lorenzo Da Ponte's Mozartian Librettos', *COJ* 1 (1989), pp. 225–47

Gidwitz, Patricia Lewy, 'Mozart's Fiordiligi: Adriana Ferrarese del Bene', *COJ* 8 (1996), pp. 199–214

Goehring, Edmund , 'Despina, Cupid and the Pastoral Mode of *Così fan tutte*', *COJ* 7 (1995), pp. 107–33

—— *Three Modes of Perception in Mozart* (Cambridge, 2004)

Gombrich, Ernst, '*Così fan tutte* (Procris Included)', *Journal of the Warburg and Courtauld Institutes* 17 (1954), pp. 372–4

Halliwell, Ruth, *The Mozart Family: Four Lives in a Social Context* (Oxford, 1998)

Heartz, Daniel, 'Raaff's Last Aria: a Mozartian Idyll in the Spirit of Hasse', *MQ* 60 (1974), pp. 517–43

—— 'The Great Quartet in Mozart's Idomeneo', *Music Forum* 5 (1980), pp. 233–56

—— '"Attaca subito": Lessons from the Autograph Score of *Idomeneo*, Acts I and II', in *Festschrift Wolfgang Rehm zum 60. Geburtstag*, ed. Dietrich Berke and Harald Heckmann (Kassel, 1989), pp. 83–92

—— *Mozart's Operas* (Berkeley, 1990)

—— 'Mozart and Da Ponte', *MQ* 79 (1995), pp. 700–18

—— 'When Mozart Revises: The Case of Guglielmo in *Così fan tutte*', in *Wolfgang Amadè Mozart: Essays on his Life and Music*, ed. Stanley Sadie (Oxford, 1996), pp. 355–61

Hughes, Rosemary (ed.), *A Mozart Pilgrimage: Being the Travel Diaries of Vincent & Mary Novello in the Year 1829* (London, 1955)

Hunter, Mary, '*Così fan tutte* et les conventions musicales de son temps', *L'Avant-scène opéra* 131–2 [*Così fan tutte*] (1990), pp. 158–64

—— 'Some Representations of *Opera Seria* in *Opera Buffa*', *COJ* 3 (1991), pp. 89–108

—— *The Culture of Opera Buffa in Mozart's Vienna: A Poetics of Entertainment* (Princeton, 1999)

—— and James Webster (ed.), *Opera buffa in Mozart's Vienna* (Cambridge, 1997)

John, Nicholas (ed.), *Così fan tutte*, English National Opera Guide (London, 1983)

Keller, Hans, 'Mozart's Wrong Key-Signature', *Tempo* 98 (1972), pp. 21–7

Kerman, Joseph, *Opera as Drama*, 2nd edn (New York, 1988)

Kivy, Peter, *Osmin's Rage: Philosophical Reflections on Opera, Drama and Text* (Princeton, 1988)

Klein, Hans-Günther, *Staatsbibliothek Preussicher Kulturbesitz: Kataloge der Musikabteilung: Erste Reihe*, Band 6: *Wolfgang Amadeus Mozart: Autographe und Abschriften* (Kassel, 1982)

Köhler, Karl-Heinz, 'Mozarts Kompositionsweise – Beobachtung am Figaro-Autograph', *MJ* (1967), pp. 31–45

—— 'Mozarts Da Ponte-Vertonungen in den Inszenierungen Goethes auf der Weimarer Hofbühne im Jahrzehnt nach Mozarts Tod', *Mozart Studien* 6 (1996), pp. 205–20

Konrad, Ulrich, *Mozarts Schaffenweise: Studien zu den Werkautographen, Skizzen und Entwürfen* (Göttingen, 1992)

Kramer, Kurt, 'Da Ponte's *Così fan tutte*', *Nachrichten der Akademie der Wissenschaften in Göttingen* (Göttingen, 1973), pp. 1–27

Kunze, Stefan, *Mozarts Opern* (Stuttgart, 1984)

Küster, Konrad, *Mozart: A Musical Biography* (Oxford, 1996)

Leeson, Daniel, 'The Gran Partita's Mystery Measure', *MJ* (1991), pp. 220–5

—— and Robert Levin, 'Mozart's Deliberate Use of Incorrect Key Signatures for Clarinets', *MJ* (1998), pp. 139–52

Link, Dorothea, 'The Viennese Operatic Canon and Mozart's *Così fan tutte*', *Mitteilungen der internationalen Stiftung Mozarteum* 38 (1990), pp. 111–21

—— '*Così fan tutte*: Dorabella and Amore', *MJ* (1991), pp. 888–94

—— '*L'arbore di Diana*: A Model for *Così fan tutte*', in *Wolfgang Amadè Mozart: Essays on his Life and Music*, ed. Stanley Sadie (Oxford, 1996), pp. 362–76

—— 'Vienna's Private Theatrical and Musical Life, 1783–92, as Reported by Count Karl Zinzendorf', *Journal of the Royal Musical Association* 122 (1997), pp. 205–57

—— *The National Court Theatre in Mozart's Vienna: Sources and Documents, 1783–1792* (Oxford, 1998)

Macek, Jaroslav, 'Franz Joseph Maximilian Lobkowitz, Musikfreund und Wirkungsgeschichte Beethovens', in *Beethoven und Böhmen*, ed. Sieghard Brandenburg and Martella Gutiérrez-Denhoff (Bonn, 1988), pp. 147–80

Michtner, Otto, 'Der Fall Abbé da Ponte', *Mitteilungen des Österreichischen Staatsarchivs* 19 (1966), pp. 170–209

Neumann, Frederick, 'Improper Appoggiaturas in the *Neue Mozart Ausgabe*', *Journal of Musicology* 10 (1992), pp. 505–21

Neville, Don, 'The Rondò in Mozart's Late Operas', *MJ* (1994), pp. 141–55

Niemetschek, Franz Xaver, *Life of Mozart (Leben des K. K. Kapellmeisters Wolfgang Gottlieb Mozart, 1798)*, trans. Helen Mautner (London, 1956)

Noiray, Michel, 'Commentaire musicale et littéraire', *L'Avant-scène opéra* 131–2 [*Così fan tutte*] (1990), pp. 39–144

Plath, Wolfgang, 'Mozartiana in Fulda und Frankfurt', *MJ* (1968–70), pp. 333–86

Platoff, John, 'Tonal Organization in the *Opera Buffa* of Mozart's Time', in *Mozart Studies 2*, ed. Cliff Eisen (Oxford, 1997), pp. 139–74

Raeburn, Christopher, 'Mozart's Operas in England', *Musical Times* 97 (Jan 1956), pp. 15–17

Rehm, Wolfgang, 'Ideal and Reality: Aspects of the *Neue Mozart Ausgabe*', *Notes* (1991), pp. 11–19

Rice, John, *Antonio Salieri and Viennese Opera* (Chicago, 1998)

——*Empress Marie Therese and Music at the Viennese Court, 1792–1807* (Cambridge, 2003)

Rosselli, John, *The Life of Mozart* (Cambridge, 1988)

Rushton, Julian, *W. A Mozart: Idomeneo*, Cambridge Opera Handbooks (Cambridge, 1993)

——'*Così fan tutte*: Mozart's Serious Comic Opera', *Studies in Music from the University of Western Ontario* 14 (1993), pp. 49–78

——'Buffo roles in Mozart's Vienna: Tessitura and Tonality as Signs of Characterisation', in *Opera buffa in Mozart's Vienna*, ed. Mary Hunter and James Webster (Cambridge, 1997), pp. 406–25

Sadie, Stanley (ed.), *Wolfgang Amadè Mozart: Essays on his Life and Music* (Oxford, 1996)

Schötterer, Reinhold, 'Das Addio-Rezitativ in *Così fan tutte*: Da Pontes Text und Mozarts Musik', *Mozart Studien* 3 (1993), pp. 79–89

Schuler, Manfred, 'Eine Prager Singspielfassung von Mozarts *Così fan tutte* aus der Zeit des Komponisten', *MJ* (1991), pp. 895–901

Senici, Emanuele, '"Adapted to the modern stage": *La clemenza di Tito* in London', *COJ* 7 (1995), pp. 1–22

Solomon, Maynard, *Mozart: A Life* (London, 1995)

Spaethling, Robert, *Mozart's Letters, Mozart's Life* (London, 2000)

Steptoe, Andrew, 'The Sources of *Così fan tutte*: a Reappraisal', *M&L* 62 (1981), pp. 281–94

——'Mozart, Mesmer and *Così fan tutte*', *M&L*, 67 (1986), pp. 248–55

——*The Mozart–Da Ponte Operas* (Oxford, 1988)

——'Mozart's Personality and Creativity', in *Wolfgang Amadè Mozart: Essays on his Life and Music*, ed. Stanley Sadie (Oxford, 1996), pp. 21–34

Stiefl, Richard, 'Mozart's Seductions', *Current Musicology* 36 (1983), pp. 151–66

Tenschert, Roland, 'Fragment eines Klarinetten Quintetts von W. A. Mozart', *ZfM* 13 (1930–1), pp. 218–22

Till, Nicholas, *Mozart and the Enlightenment: Truth, Virtue and Beauty in Mozart's Operas* (London 1992)

Trowell, Brian, 'Mozart at the Time of "Così fan tutte"', in *Così fan tutte*, ed. Nicholas John (London, 1983), pp. 7–16

Tyson, Alan, *Mozart: Studies of the Autograph Scores* (Cambridge, MA, 1987)

——'The 1786 Prague Version of Mozart's *Le Nozze di Figaro*', *M&L* 69 (1988), pp. 321–33

——'A Feature of the Structure of Mozart's Autograph Scores', in *Festschrift Wolfgang Rehm zum 60. Geburtstag am 3 September 1989*, ed. Dietrich Berke and Harald Heckmann (Kassel, 1989), pp. 95–105

—— 'Proposed New Dates for Many Works and Fragments Written by Mozart from March 1781 to December 1791', in *Mozart Studies*, ed. Cliff Eisen (Oxford, 1991), pp. 213–26

Vill, Susanne (ed.), *Così fan tutte: Beiträge zur Wirkungsgeschichte von Mozarts Oper* (Bayreuth, 1978)

Waldoff, Jessica, *Recognition in Mozart's Operas* (Oxford, 2006)

—— and James Webster, 'Operatic Plotting in *Le Nozze di Figaro*', in *Wolfgang Amadè Mozart: Essays on his Life and Music*, ed. Stanley Sadie (Oxford, 1996), pp. 250–95

Warburton, Ernest, *The Librettos of Mozart's Operas* (New York, 1992)

Webster, James, 'Mozart's Operas and the Myth of Musical Unity', *COJ* 2 (1990), pp. 197–218

—— 'The Analysis of Mozart's Arias', in *Mozart Studies*, ed. Cliff Eisen (Oxford, 1991), pp. 101–99

Williams, Bernard, 'Passion and Cynicism: Remarks on *Così fan tutte*', *Musical Times* 114 (Apr 1973), pp. 361–4

Wolff, Christoph, 'The Challenge of Blank Paper: Mozart the Composer', in *On Mozart*, ed. James Morris (Cambridge, 1994), pp. 113–29

Woodfield, Ian, 'Mozart's Compositional Methods: Writing for his Singers', in *The Cambridge Companion to Mozart*, ed. Simon Keefe (Cambridge, 2003), pp. 35–47

—— 'Reflections on "Non so più cosa son, cosa faccio"', *Eighteenth-Century Music* 3 (2006), pp. 133–9

Zaslaw, Neal, 'Waiting for Figaro', in *Wolfgang Amadè Mozart: Essays on his Life and Music*, ed. Stanley Sadie (Oxford, 1996), pp. 413–35

Zenck, Claudia Maurer, *Mozarts 'Così fan tutte': dramma giocoso und deutsches Singspiel: Frühe Abschriften und frühe Aufführungen* (Schliengen, 2007)

# Index